PHILIP'S

STREET ATLAS
Oxford

www.philips-maps.co.uk

First published in 2007 by

Philip's, a division of
Octopus Publishing Group Ltd
www.octopusbooks.co.uk
2-4 Heron Quays, London E14 4JP
An Hachette Livre UK Company

First edition 2006
Second impression with revisions 2007

ISBN-10 0-540-08945-1
ISBN-13 978-0-540-08945-1

Photographic acknowledgements:
VII nagelestock.com / Alamy
VIII 360 / Alamy
X nagelestock.com / Alamy

Printed by Toppan, China

Contents

II **Key to map symbols**
III **Key to map pages**
IV **Route planning**
VI **Sights of Oxford**

2 **Street maps** at 4½ inches to 1 mile
58 **Street maps of Oxford city centre** at 7 inches to 1 mile

60 **Index**
73 **List of numbered locations**
74 **Oxford bus maps**

Key to map symbols

Roads

Motorway with junction number

Primary route – dual, single carriageway

A road – dual, single carriageway

B road – dual, single carriageway

Through-route – dual, single carriageway

Minor road – dual, single carriageway

Rural track, private road or narrow road in urban area

Path, bridleway, byway open to all traffic, road used as a public path

Road under construction

Pedestrianised area

Gate or obstruction to traffic restrictions may not apply at all times or to all vehicles

P P&R Parking, Park and Ride

Railways

Railway

Miniature railway

Metro station, private railway station

Emergency services

Ambulance station, coastguard station

Fire station, police station

H Hospital, Accident and Emergency entrance to hospital

General features

PO Place of worship, Post Office

Information centre (open all year)

Bus or coach station, shopping centre

Important buildings, schools, colleges, universities and hospitals

Woods, built-up area

Tumulus FORT Non-Roman antiquity, Roman antiquity

Leisure facilities

Camping site, caravan site

Golf course, picnic site

Boundaries

Postcode boundaries

County and unitary authority boundaries

Water features

River Ouse Tidal water, water name

Non-tidal water – lake, river, canal or stream

Lock, weir

Enlarged mapping only

Railway or bus station building

Place of interest

Parkland

Scales

Blue pages: 4½ inches to 1 mile 1:14 080

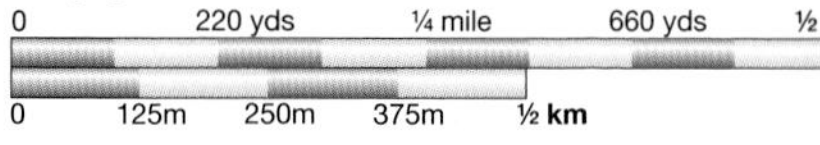

Red pages: 7 inches to 1 mile 1: 9051

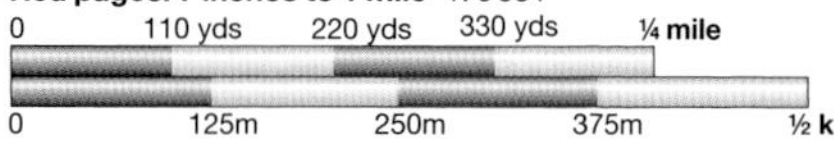

Adjoining page indicators The colour of the arrow and the band indicates the scale of the adjoining page (see above)

Abbreviations

Acad	Academy	Mkt	Market
Allot Gdns	Allotments	Meml	Memorial
Cemy	Cemetery	Mon	Monument
C Ctr	Civic Centre	Mus	Museum
CH	Club House	Obsy	Observatory
Coll	College	Pal	Royal Palace
Crem	Crematorium	PH	Public House
Ent	Enterprise	Recn Gd	Recreation Ground
Ex H	Exhibition Hall	Resr	Reservoir
Ind Est	Industrial Estate	Ret Pk	Retail Park
IRB Sta	Inshore Rescue Boat Station	Sch	School
		Sh Ctr	Shopping Centre
Inst	Institute	TH	Town Hall/House
Ct	Law Court	Trad Est	Trading Estate
L Ctr	Leisure Centre	Univ	University
LC	Level Crossing	Wks	Works
Liby	Library	YH	Youth Hostel

Key to map pages

58 Atlas pages at 7 inches to 1 mile

42 Atlas pages at 4½ inches to 1 mile

Scale: 0 1 2 3 4 5 km; 0 1 2 3 miles

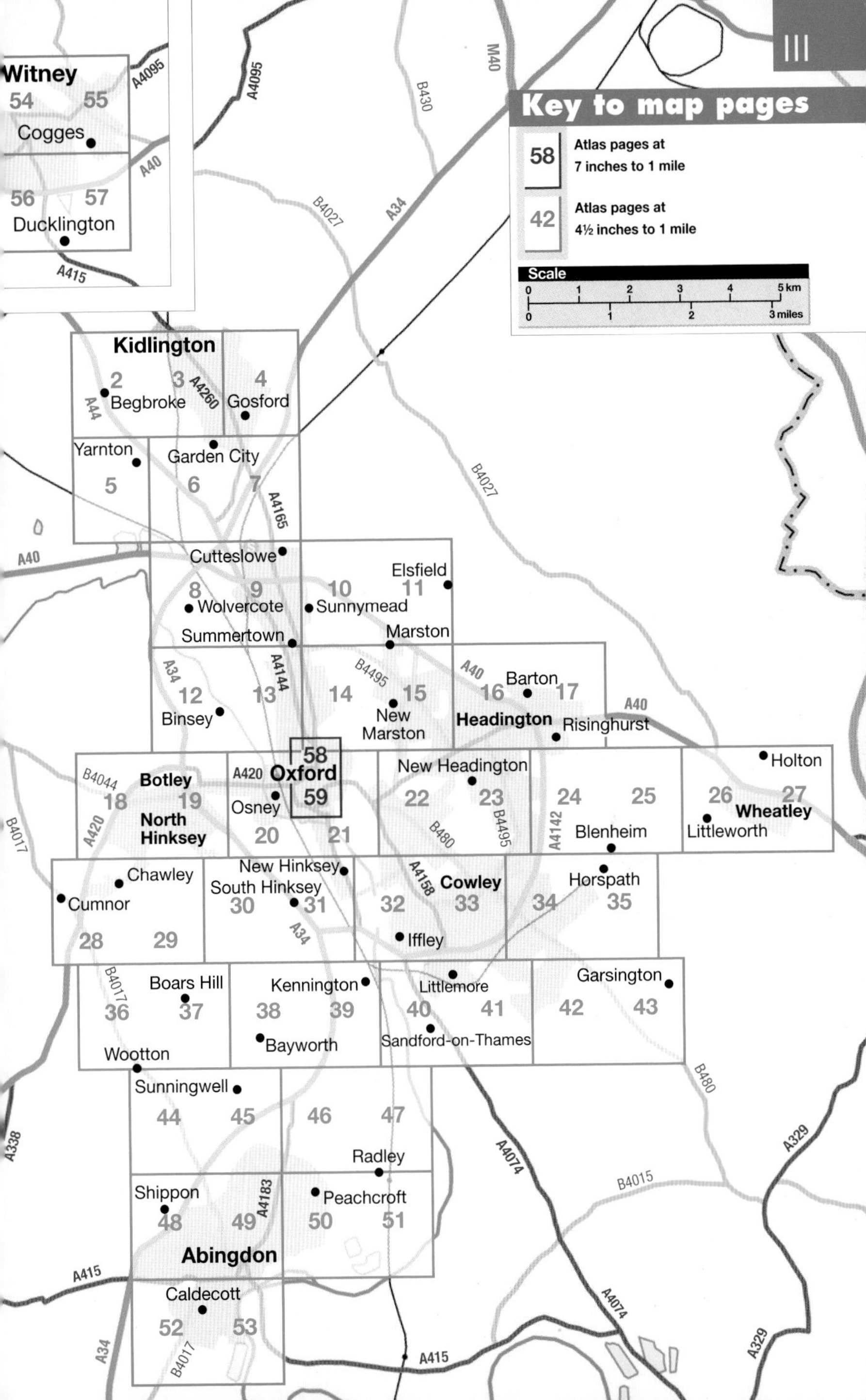

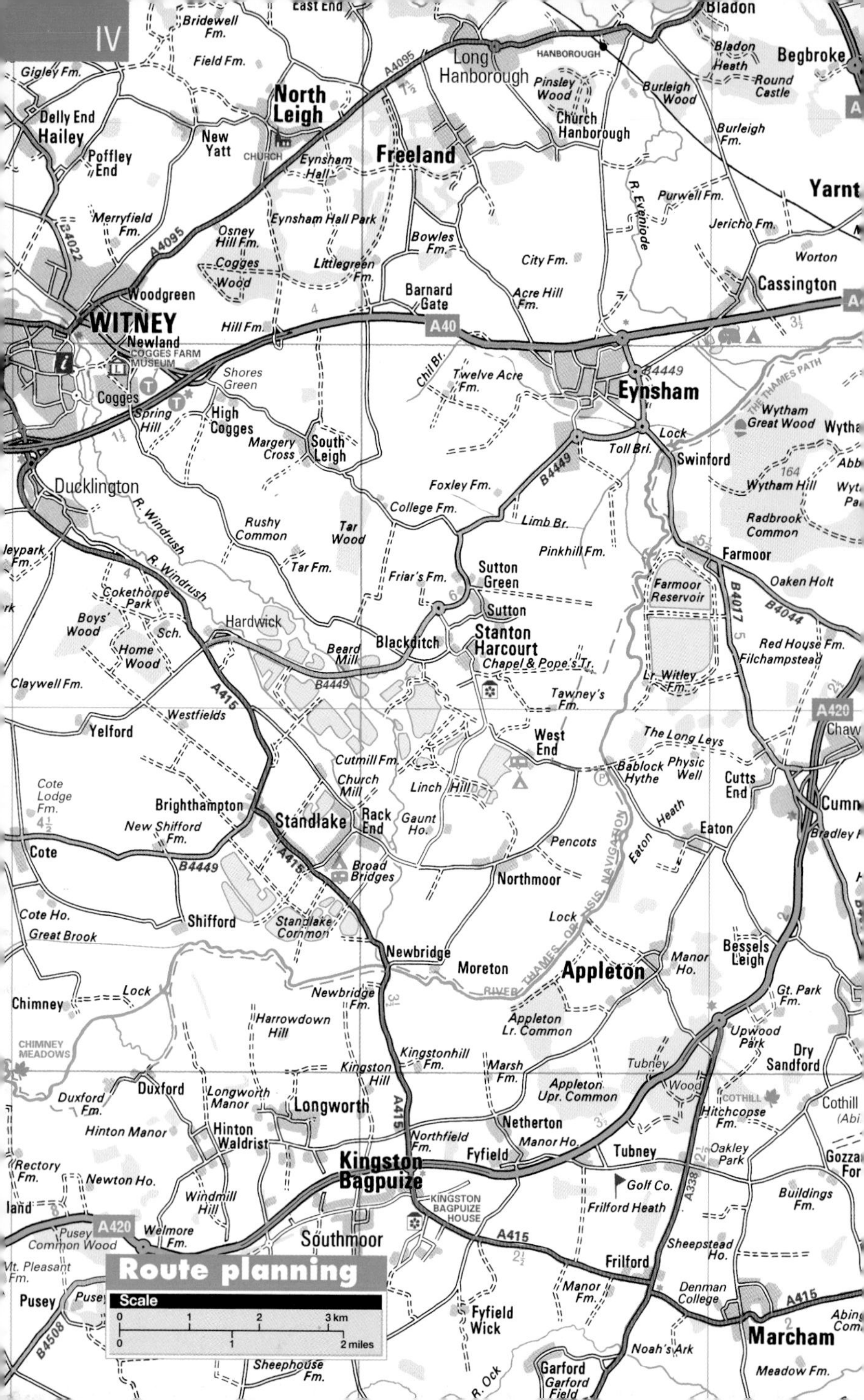
IV
East End
Bridewell Fm.
Field Fm.
Gigley Fm.
Delly End
Hailey
Poffley End
New Yatt
North Leigh
CHURCH
Eynsham Hall
Freeland
Long Hanborough
HANBOROUGH
Pinsley Wood
Church Hanborough
Bladon
Bladon Heath
Begbroke
Round Castle
Burleigh Wood
Burleigh Fm.
Yarnt
Purwell Fm.
Jericho Fm.
Worton
Cassington
R. Evenlode
A4095
Merryfield Fm.
B4022
Eynsham Hall Park
Osney Hill Fm.
Cogges Wood
Littlegreen Fm.
Bowles Fm.
City Fm.
Barnard Gate
Acre Hill Fm.
Woodgreen
WITNEY
Hill Fm.
A40
Newland
COGGES FARM MUSEUM
Shores Green
Cogges
Spring Hill
High Cogges
Margery Cross
South Leigh
Chil Br.
Twelve Acre Fm.
B4449
Eynsham
THE THAMES PATH
Wytham Great Wood
Wytha
Lock
Toll Bri.
Swinford
Ducklington
R. Windrush
Foxley Fm.
College Fm.
Limb Br.
Wytham Hill
164
Radbrook Common
Rushy Common
Tar Wood
Tar Fm.
Pinkhill Fm.
Farmoor
Friar's Fm.
Sutton Green
Sutton
Farmoor Reservoir
B4017
Oaken Holt
B4044
Cokethorpe Park
Boys' Wood
Sch.
Home Wood
Hardwick
Beard Mill
Blackditch
Stanton Harcourt
Chapel & Pope's Tr.
Red House Fm.
Filchampstead
Claywell Fm.
A415
Tawney's Fm.
Lr. Witley Fm.
A420
Chaw
Westfields
Yelford
West End
The Long Leys
Cutmill Fm.
Church Mill
Linch Hill
Bablock Hythe
Physic Well
Cutts End
Cumn
Cote Lodge Fm.
Brighthampton
Standlake
Rack End
Gaunt Ho.
THAMES OR ISIS NAVIGATION
Eaton Heath
Eaton
Bradley
New Shifford Fm.
Cote
Pencots
Broad Bridges
Northmoor
Cote Ho.
Shifford
Standlake Common
Lock
Great Brook
Newbridge
Moreton
Appleton
Manor Ho.
Bessels Leigh
Lock
Chimney
Newbridge Fm.
RIVER
Gt. Park Fm.
CHIMNEY MEADOWS
Harrowdown Hill
Appleton Lr. Common
Upwood Park
Dry Sandford
Kingstonhill Fm.
Kingston Hill
Marsh Fm.
Tubney Wood
Duxford
Duxford Fm.
Longworth Manor
Longworth
Appleton Upr. Common
COTHILL
Cothill
(Abi
Hinton Manor
Hinton Waldrist
Northfield Fm.
Netherton
Manor Ho.
Hitchcopse Fm.
Fyfield
Tubney
Oakley Park
Gozza For
Rectory Fm.
Newton Ho.
Kingston Bagpuize
Golf Co.
Buildings Fm.
Windmill Hill
KINGSTON BAGPUIZE HOUSE
Frilford Heath
A338
Pusey Common Wood
Welmore Fm.
Southmoor
Sheepstead Ho.
Mt. Pleasant Fm.
Frilford
Pusey
Manor Fm.
Denman College
A415
Abing Com
Fyfield Wick
Marcham
B4508
Sheephouse Fm.
Noah's Ark
R. Ock
Garford
Garford Field
Meadow Fm.
Route planning
Scale
0 1 2 3 km
0 1 2 miles

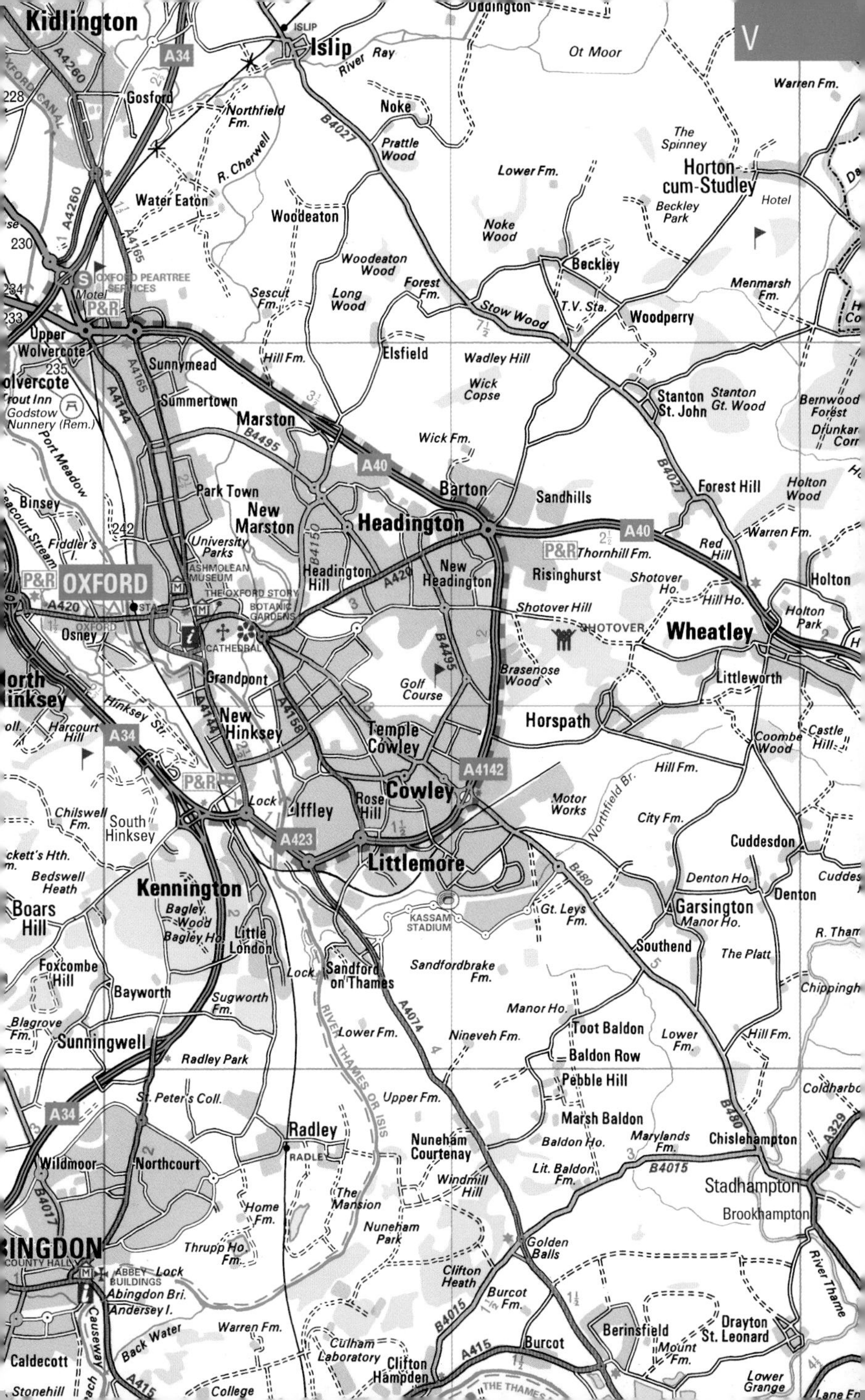

V
Kidlington
Islip
Ot Moor
Gosford
Noke
Water Eaton
Woodeaton
Horton-cum-Studley
Beckley
Woodperry
Upper Wolvercote
Sunnymead
Summertown
Marston
Elsfield
Stanton St. John
OXFORD
Headington
Barton
New Marston
Park Town
Binsey
Osney
Forest Hill
Risinghurst
Wheatley
Holton
Littleworth
Horspath
North Hinksey
Grandpont
New Hinksey
Temple Cowley
Cowley
Iffley
Rose Hill
Littlemore
South Hinksey
Kennington
Boars Hill
Sandford on Thames
Garsington
Southend
Cuddesdon
Denton
Sunningwell
Bayworth
Toot Baldon
Baldon Row
Pebble Hill
Marsh Baldon
Radley
Chislehampton
Stadhampton
Brookhampton
Nuneham Courtenay
Wildmoor
Northcourt
Burcot
Berinsfield
Drayton St. Leonard
Clifton Hampden
Caldecott
Stonehill
A34
A40
A420
A423
A4142
A4074
A415
B4027
B480
B4015
A329
B4017
A4144
A4165
A4260
B4495
A4158
B4150
KASSAM STADIUM
OXFORD PEARTREE SERVICES
ASHMOLEAN MUSEUM
THE OXFORD STORY
BOTANIC GARDENS
CATHEDRAL
SHOTOVER
RIVER THAMES OR ISIS

Sights of Oxford

The University

Not all of the colleges are open to the public and many have restricted or variable opening times. Several also have admission charges. Checking in advance is therefore advised.

All Souls College *High Street, Oxford* Founded in 1438, by Henry VI and Henry Chichele, Archbishop of Canterbury. It is a research institution with no undergraduates. The Front Quad and beautiful chapel are 15th-century while North Quad was built in 1716-34 by Hawksmoor.
☎01865 279 379 59 C2
www.all-souls.ox.ac.uk

Balliol College *Broad Street, Oxford* Founded in 1263 as a hostel and substantially rebuilt in the 19th century, including William Butterfield's candy-striped chapel (1856-57). There are 400 undergraduate and 180 graduate students.
☎01865 277777
www.balliol.ox.ac.uk 58 B3

Bodleian Library *Old Schools Quad, off Radcliffe Square, Oxford* Complex of buildings, including Duke Humfrey's Library (1444), the Proscholium and Arts End (both 1610-12), the Divinity School (1420-83), Convocation House (1632-37, roof 1759) and the Bodleian Library itself (1613-19). In the east of Old Schools Quad is the Tower of the Five Orders, with (from the base up) Doric, Tuscan, Ionic, Corinthian and Composite columns. Other parts of the collection are held elsewhere in the city and rotating exhibitions of some of the libraries' treasures are shown in the Exhibition Room (☎01865 277213, www.bodley.ox.ac.uk/users/jd/exhibitions). Guided tours to parts of complex, university ceremonies permitting.
☎01865 277224 59 C2
www.bodley. ox.ac.uk

Brasenose College *Radcliffe Square, Oxford* Founded in 1509 by William Smythe, Bishop of Lincoln, and Sir Richard Sutton. There are 120 graduate and 350 undergraduate students.
☎01865 277510 www.bnc.ox.ac.uk 59 C2

Bridge of Sighs *see Hertford College*

Christ Church College *St Aldates, Oxford* Founded by Thomas Wolsey as Cardinal's College in 1524, taking over St Frideswide's monastery. Refounded in 1546 by Henry VIII, who made the old monastery church the cathedral of the new diocese of Oxford. Most of the architecture is 17th- and 18th-century. There are 150 graduate and 450 undergraduate students. See also Christ Church Cathedral and Christ Church College Picture Gallery. Guided tours from Tourist Information Centre ☎01865 726871) ☎01865 276518
www.chch.ox.ac.uk 59 B2

Corpus Christi College *Merton Street, Oxford* Founded in 1517, at the beginning of the Renaissance in England, by Richard Foxe, Bishop of Winchester. This small, intimate college retains much of its original architecture and atmosphere, as well as its reputation for Classics. There are 110 graduate and 230 undergraduate students.
☎01865 276700
www.ccc.ox.ac.uk 59 C2

Exeter College *Turl Street, Oxford* Founded in 1314 as Stapledon Hall by Walter de Stapledon, Bishop of Exeter. George Gilbert Scott's Chapel (1856-59) is one of the best Victorian buildings in Oxford: it is richly adorned and houses outstanding stained glass and a tapestry of 'The Adoration of the Magi' by Edward Burne-Jones and William Morris. There are 180 graduate and 330 undergraduate students. ☎01865 279600
www.exeter.ox.ac.uk 59 B2

Green College *Woodstock Road, Oxford* This graduate college was founded in 1979 and is centred around the Radcliffe Observatory (1772-94), which was based on the design of the Hellenestic Tower of the Winds in Athens. There are 300 students. Visits by appointment only. ☎01865 274770
www.green.ox.ac.uk 58 A4

Harris Manchester College *Mansfield Road* Founded in 1786, it is Oxford's institution for full-time education of mature students with 50 graduates and 100 undergraduates. Only the chapel is open to the public. ☎01865 271012
www.hmc.ox.ac.uk 58 C3

Hertford College *Catte Street, Oxford* Refounded in 1874 on the site of the 13th-century Hart Hall. The chapel has interesting Arts and Crafts furnishings. Hertford Bridge (known as the Bridge of Sighs after the Venetian prototype), over New College Lane, links the two parts of the college. There are 200 graduate and 360-370 undergraduate students.
☎01865 279400 59 C2
www.hertford.ox.ac.uk

Jesus College *Turl Street, Oxford* Founded in 1571 by Hugh Price, Treasure of St David's Cathedral, under the patronage of Elizabeth I for the education of prospective clergymen. There are now 140 graduates and 340 undergraduates studying a wide range of subjects.
☎01865 279700
www.jesus.ox.ac.uk 59 B2

Keble College *Parks Road, Oxford* Founded in 1870 in memory of Rev. John Keble, one of the leading lights in the Oxford movement. It is the epitome of high Victorian Gothic. The interior of the chapel abounds with polychrome bricks, tiles, mosaics and stained glass. Among its treasure is William Holman Hunt's 'The Light of the World'. There are 430 undergraduate and 230 graduate students. ☎01865 272727
www.keble.ox.ac.uk 58 B4

Kellogg College *Wellington Square, Oxford* The centre for part-time mature students, with nearly 300 part- and full-time graduate and research students, chiefly in the sciences.
☎01865 270383
www.kellogg.ox.ac.uk 58 B3

Lady Margaret Hall *Norham Gardens, Oxford* Founded in 1878 as a women's hall of residence – men were admitted in 1979. It is housed in a collection of neo-Georgian and Classical buildings. Giles Gilbert Scott's neo-Byzantine chapel houses Taddeo Gaddi's 'Flagellation of Christ' (14th century). The peaceful gardens stretch out towards the river Cherwell. There are 160 graduate and 440 undergraduate students. ☎01865 274300
www.clients.networks/co.uk/ladymargarethall 14 B2

Linacre College *St Cross Road, Oxford* This postgraduate college, founded in 1926, took over this Queen Anne building in 1977. The later buildings are broadly sympathetic – the Abraham Wing has won awards for energy-efficiency. There are 300 students. By appointment only. ☎01865 271650
www.linacre.ox.ac.uk 58 C3

Lincoln College *Turl Street, Oxford* Founded in 1427 by Robert Fleming, Bishop of Lincoln, in reaction against the teachings of John Wycliffe. Many of the 15th-century buildings retain their original character. The chapel has lovely 17th-century woodwork and excellent stained glass. There are 230 graduate and 300 undergraduate students. ☎01865 279800
www.lincoln.ox.ac.uk 59 B2

Magdalen College *High Street, Oxford* Founded in 1458 by William Wayneflete on the site of the former Hospital of St John. The Bell Tower was built in 1492 for Thomas Wolsey, and is the scene of May Day celebrations (see events). Original buildings include the Founder's Tower. The college grounds are spacious and include Magdalen Grove – a deer park – and the meadow across the Cherwell bounded by Addison's walk, which follows the town's civil-war defences for part of the way. There are 220 graduate and 400 undergraduate students.
☎01865 276000 21 C3
www.magd.ox.ac.uk

Mansfield College *Mansfield Road, Oxford* Founded in Birmingham as a non-conformist theological college in 1838, it moved to Oxford in 1886 and the late Victorian Gothic-style buildings by Basil Champneys date from 1887-88. There are 40-70 graduate and 200 undergraduate students.
01865 270999 58 C3
www.mansfield.ox.ac.uk

Merton College *Merton Street, Oxford* Founded in 1264 by Walter de la Merton for a small number of fellows. The buildings, such as Mob Quad, are amongs the oldest in Oxford. The chapel is a mixture of Decorated and Perpendicular Gothic, with a stunning east window. The medieval library (guided tours, limited times and numbers) is adjoined by the Max Beerbohm Room, which contains several of his acidic late 19th-century cartoons. There are 320 undergraduate and 190 graduate students. 01865 276310
www.merton.ox.ac.uk 59 C2

New College *New College Lane, Oxford* Founded in 1379 by William of Wykeham, Bishop of Winchester, New College was the first in the town to accept undergraduates. It was built to a coherent plan, and became the prototype for many later colleges. The chapel is a good example of Perpendicular Gothic and in the garden substantial remains of the medieval town wall survive. There are 190 graduate and 440 undergraduate students.
01865 249555
www.new.ox.ac.uk 59 C2

Nuffield College *New Road, Oxford* Founded in 1937 by local car-manufacturer and philanthropist Lord Nuffield for postgraduate students. The building was begun in 1949 in a mock Cotswold-cottage style. It was the first co-educational college in Oxford. There are nearly 80 graduate students.
01865 278500
www.nuffield.ox.ac.uk 59 A2

Oriel College *Oriel Square, Oxford* Founded in 1324 as St Mary's College by Adam de Brome, ractor of the nearby church of St Mary the Virgin (see religious buildings). In 1326 it was refounded by Edward II as King's College. The Front Quad was build in a high Jacobean part-Gothic-part-Romanesque style in 1620-42. During the 19th century, it was one of the main homes of the Oxford Movement. There are 150 graduate and 300 undergraduate students. 01865 276555
www.oriel.ox.ac.uk 59 C2

Pembroke College *Pembroke Square, Oxford* Founded in 1624 by Thomas Tesdale and Richard Wrightwick and named after the Earl of Pembroke. It is a small college with buildings from the 17th-20th centuries. There are 100 graduate and 400 undergraduate students. By appointment only.
01865 276444 59 B1
www.pembroke.ox.ac.uk

The Queen's College *High Street, Oxford* Founded in 1341 by Robert de Eglesfield, chaplain to Queen Philippa. The college was rebuilt between 1671 and 1765. The chapel has fine plasterwork and earlier stained glass. Some student accommodation is in the futuristic Florey Building on St Clement's Street. There are 150 graduate and 300 undergraduate students. Guided tours only, contact the Tourist Information Centre (01865 726871)
01865 279120
www.queens.ox.ac.uk 59 C2

Radcliffe Camera *Radcliffe Square, Oxford* This domed rotunda was built in 1737-48 by James Gibbs. It is the university's literature and history library. Not open to the public. 59 C2

▼ ***The Radcliffe Camera surrounded by (clockwise from foreground) All Souls, Brasenose, Lincoln and Exeter colleges, the Bodleian Library and Hertford College***

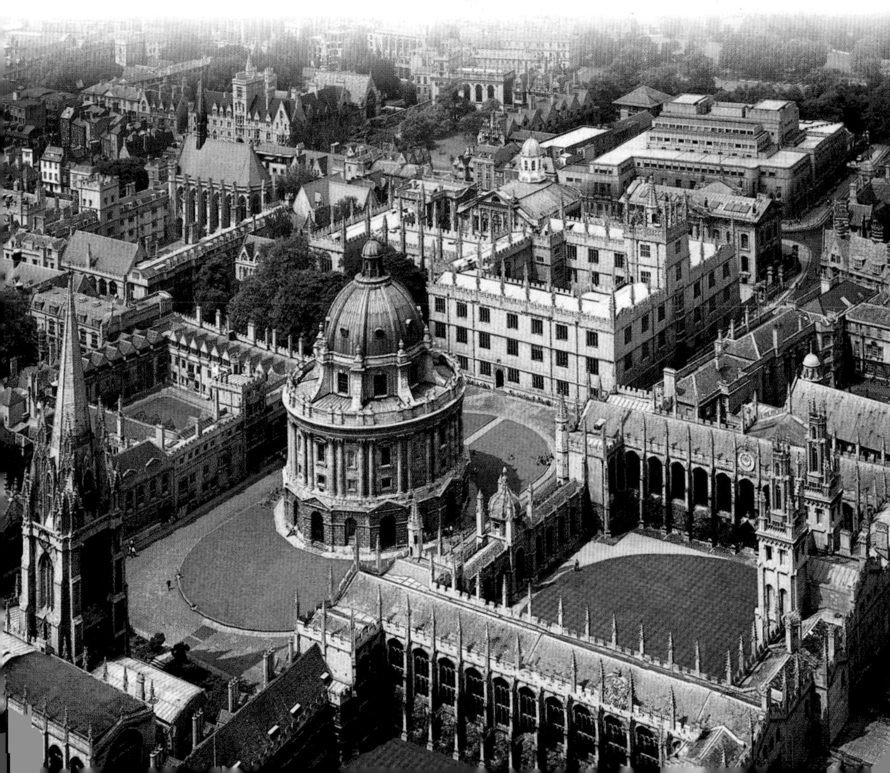

Sackler Library *St John Street, Oxford* Designed by Robert Adam, this Neoclassical building was eventually finished in 2001. It houses the university's archaeological, art historical and Classical books. Not open to the public ☎01865 288190 💻www.saclib.ox.ac.uk 58 B3

St Anne's College *Woodstock Road, Oxford* Traces its origins to the Association for the Education of Women in Oxford, founded in 1878. It is now co-educational, with 420 undergraduate and 160 graduate students. ☎01865 274800 58 B4 💻www.st-annes.ox.ac.uk

St Antony's College *Wodstock Road, Oxford* A graduate college, founded in 1950 and specialising in international studies. By appointment only. ☎01865 284700 💻www.sant.ox.ac.uk 58 A4

St Catherine's College *Manor Road, Oxford* Founded in 1868 as a society for graduate and undergraduate non-collegiate students, Cats became a college in 1963. Built mainly in 1960-64 by Arne Jacobsen, it is a coherent collection of buildings of the Modern Movement. Now one of the larger colleges, with 440 undergraduate and 210 graduate students, its fellows include a high proportion of scientists. ☎01865 271700 💻www.stcatz.ox.ac.uk 21 C4

St Cross College *St Giles', Oxford* Founded in 1965 for graduate students, St Cross has shared this site with Pusey House since 1981. Pusey House's chapel was built in 1912-16 and is the last Gothic Revival building erected in Oxford. There are 300 students. Not open to the public ☎01865 278415 💻www.stx.ox.ac.uk 58 B3

St Edmund Hall *Queen's Lane, Oxford* The foundation is believed to date back to the 1190s. Despite its diminutive size, St Edmund Hall has a large number of students, with 110 graduates and 420 undergraduates. ☎01865 279000 💻www.seh.ox.ac.uk 59 C2

St Hilda's College *Cowley Place, Oxford* Founded for women in 1893 by Dorothea Beal, principal of Cheltenham Ladies' College. Now the only remaining women-only college, with 116 graduate and 420 undergraduate students. See also Jacqueline du Pré Music Building (under entertainment). ☎01865 276884 💻www.sthildas.ox.ac.uk 21 C2

St Hugh's College *St Margaret's Road, Oxford* A former women-only college, founded in 1886, now with 200 graduate and 410 undergraduates. ☎01865 274900 13 C2 💻www.st-hughs.ox.ac.uk

St John's College *St Giles', Oxford.* Founded in 1555 by Sir Thomas White, former mayor of London. It is one of the richest colleges in Oxford, with 185 graduate and 400 undergraduate students. The baroque Canterbury Quad is its architectural claim to fame and the gardens are magnificent. ☎01865 277300 💻www.sjc.ox.ac.uk 58 B3

St Peter's College *New Inn Hall Street, Oxford* Founded as a private hall in 1928 for men who wished to be ordained in the Church of England and for those of limited means. Its 400 undergraduate and 120 graduate students now study a wide range of subjects. ☎01865 278900 💻www.spc.ox.ac.uk 59 B2

Sheldonian Theatre *off Catte Street, Oxford* Built in 1664-69 at the expense of Gilbert Sheldon, former warden of All Souls and Archbishop of Canterbury, this was Wren's first major building. Degree ceremonies, other university occasions, concerts and lectures are held here. May close at short notice for concerts and university functions. ☎01865 277299 59 C2 💻www.sheldon.ox.ac.uk

Somerville College *Woodstock Road, Oxford* Founded in 1879 as a non-demoninational hall for women students. Male students were admitted in 1994. There are 100 graduate and 400 undergraduate students. ☎01865 270600 58 A3 💻www.somerville.ox.ac.uk

Templeton College *Off Kennington Road, Oxford* Founded in 1965, Templeton College specialises in management studies for its 110 graduate students. ☎01865 422500 31 C1 💻www.templeton.ox.ac.uk

Trinity College *Broad Street, Oxford* Monks from Durham founded a college here in 1286 and it was refounded in 1555 by Sir Thomas Pope. It is a small-scale and intimate institution. The chapel interior is a beautiful example of post-Restoration work. There are 130 graduate and 300 undergraduate students. ☎01865 279900 58 B3 💻www.trinity.ox.ac.uk

University College *High Street, Oxford* Despite claims that it was established by Alfred the Great, Univ. was founded in the 13th century, completely rebuilt in 1634. The Radcliffe Quad was added in the early 18th century. There are 160 graduate and 420 undergraduate students. By appointment only. ☎01865 276602 💻www.univ.ox.ac.uk 59 C2

Wadham College *Parks Road, Oxford* Founded in 1610 and the most complete example in Oxford of an early 17th-century college. The Gothic chapel and hall both deliberately hark back to an earlier era. The garden is lovely. There are 160 graduate and 450 undergraduate students. ☎01865 277900 58 C3 💻www.wadham.ox.ac.uk

Wolfson College *Linton Road, Oxford* Originally called Iffley College, a society for graduates reading for (usually) science degrees, it changed its name in 1966 and the present buildings were erected between 1969 and 1974. There are 400 graduate students. ☎01865 273100 14 A3 💻www.wolfson.ox.ac.uk

Worcester College *Walton Street, Oxford* Founded in 1714 on the site of Gloucester College. Its eclectic mix of architecture includes the 15th-century houses of Gloucester College

▼ ***The Bridge of Sighs***

and the Sainsbury Building of 1979-83. The beautiful gardens run down to the ornamental lake and the Oxford Canal. There are 190 graduate and 410 undergraduate students. 01865 278300 58 A3 www.worcester.ox.ac.uk

Religious buildings

Christ Church Cathedral *St Aldates, Oxford (entry via Christ Church College)* The original priory church was built 1160-1200 and there are additions in almost every style of British architecture. There are lovely stained-and painted-glass windows of a variety of eras, large numbers of memorials and good furnishings. The roofs of the nave and sanctuary are particularly fine. 59 B1/C1 01865 286573 www.chch.ox.ac.uk/cathedral

St Barnabas' Church *Cardigan Street, Oxford* Built to the designs of Arthur Blomfield in 1869, this Italian Romanesque Anglo-Catholic church is highly unusual for the Victorian period. It was paid for by Thomas Combe, one of the leading patrons of the Pre-Raphaelites. The interior is richly decorated. Rarely open outside times of worship. www.sbarnabas.co.uk 58 A3

St Ebbe's Church *Pennyfarthing Place, Oxford* A small, 12th-century church and evangelical centre. Substantial parts were rebuilt in the 19th century, but its chief claim to fame is the richly carved Norman west doorway. www.stebbes.org.uk 59 B2

St Mary the Virgin *Church Green, Witney* Largely 13th-century village church with attractive and highly decorative 14th-century chantry chapels. The stone spire is early 13th-century. Among the monuments is a good brass of 1501. 57 A4

St Mary the Virgin *Radcliffe Square, Oxford* At the heart of the oldest parts of the university, this church is largely 15th-century, although the tower is from the original 12th-century building. In the 16th century, Thomas Cranmer, the third of the Oxford Martyrs (see Martyrs Memorial), was tried here, but refused to denounce the Reformation and was condemned to death. The views from the tower across the city are spectacular. 01865 279111 www.university-church.ox.ac.uk 59 C2

St Mary the Virgin, Iffley *Church Way, Iffley, Oxford* One of the best-preserved Norman parish churches in England, built in 1170-80. The west and south doorways, windows and arches are covered in a riot of carvings:, such as chevron, signs of the zodiac, symbols of the Evangelists, beasts, beakheads, flowers and fruit. The chancel dates from the following century. www.iffley.co.uk 32 B1

St Michael's Church *Ship Street, Oxford* Although much-restored, St Michael's is Oxford's oldest building, and once formed part of the town's fortifications. Some 13th- and 15th-century glass remains and the mid 11th-century tower offers views over the centre of the city. 59 B2

Museums and Galleries

Abingdon Museum *The County Hall, Market Place, Abingdon* A small museum, in a beautiful 1670s building, dedicated to the history of England's oldest continuously inhabited town, with both permanent and changing exhibitions. 01235 523703 49 B1

Ashmolean Museum *Beaumont Street, Oxford* Based around the collections of Elias Ashmole, with antiquities from Egypt, Greece, Rome, Saxon Britain, Dark-Age Europe, India and Japan, as well as ancient and modern Chinese art, English porcelain, curiosities from the new world, coins, old musical instruments and western art of all eras. An offshoot in Pusey Place holds the cast gallery, which has more than 900 casts of ancient Greek and Roman sculptures. 01865 278000 www.ashmol.ox.ac.uk 58 B3

Bate Collection of Musical Instruments *St Aldates* A comprehensive collection of antique musical instruments, including woodwind, brass, early keyboard and percussion, as well as a gamelan and a harpsichord said to have been played by Handel. (university term-times only) 01865 276139 59 B1 www.bate.ox.ac.uk

Christ Church Picture Gallery *Oriel Square, Oxford* A good collection of Italian medieval, Renaissance and Baroque art (Filippino Lippi, Tintoretto, Annibale Caracci, Veronese and Domenichino), Old Master drawings (Leonardo, Raphael, Michelangelo, Titian, Hugo van der Goes, Rubens, Rambrandt and Claude Lorraine) and works from the Flemish and Dutch Schools (Van Dyck, Frans Hals). 01865 276172 www.chch.ox.ac.uk/gallery 59 C2

Cogges Manor Farm Museum, Witney *Church Lane, Cogges, Witney* Housed in the old manor house and its outbuildings, with hand-milking and butter-making demonstrations, farm animals and vehicles and occasional cooking and craft demonstrations. Although the hall is a mixture of 13th- and 17th-century buildings, the interiors are set up as they would have been in the late 19th/early 20th century. 01993 722602 www.cogges.org 55 B1

Hands-on *George Street, Oxford* Housed within the Old Fire Station Arts Centre (see entertainment) is an interactive science exhibition with more than 30 different gadgets for children of all ages to try out. www.oxtrust.org.uk/handson 01865 247004 59 B2

Modern Art Oxford *Pembroke Street, Oxford* Located in an old brewery warehouse, this small gallery hosts changing exhibitions of thought-provoking, avant-garde work. www.modernartoxford.org.uk 01865 722733 59 B2

Museum of Oxford *St Aldates, Oxford* Housed in the former public library, this local museum charts the history of the city and surrounding area from prehistoric times to the modern day, with sections including the university, motor manufacture and Alice Liddell ('Alice in Wonderland'). 01865 252761 www.oxford.gov.uk/museum 59 B2

Museum of the History of Science *Broad Street, Oxford* Housed in the original home of the Ashmolean, this museum has an outstanding collection of early astronomical instruments, microscopes, clocks, sundealis, equipment used for physics and chemistry experiments, and a blackboard used by Albert Einstein. 01865 277280 59 B2 www.mhs.ox.ac.uk

The Oxford Story *Broad Street, Oxford* Visitors to this small museum explore the development and history of the university from the comfort of a motorised medieval desk. The Innovate section is an interactive display relating to some of the latest research undertaken by the university's scientists. 01865 728822 www.oxfordstory.co.uk 59 B2

Oxford University Museum of Natural History *South Parks Road, Oxford* Housed in a splendid Gothic Revival building (note the carvings of birds and cats round the inner doorway), is the university's zoological and geological collection, including birds, insects, a working beehive, the Oxford dodo and casts of a 'Tyrannosaus rex' and an 'Iguanodon bernissartensis'. 01865 272950 www.oum.ox.ac.uk 58 B3

Pitt Rivers Museum *South Parks Road, Oxford* Based around the ethnograpical collections of General A.H. Lane-Fox Pitt-Rivers this musuem holds over a million items of anthropological interest from all over the world. 01865 270927 www.prm.ox.ac.uk 58 B3

Witney and District Museum *Gloucester Court Mews, Witney* This local museum has displays relating to the history, people and industries of the town and surrounding area. 01993 775915 www.witney.net/witney-and-district-museum.htm 55 A2

Other sites of interest

Carfax Tower *Cornmarket Street, Oxford* The tower of the 13th-century St Martin's Church. The Quarterboys on the clock are a replica although the clock is original. The top of the tower (99 steps) affords good views over the colleges to the east. 01865 792653 59 B2

Martyrs' Memorial *St Giles', Oxford* The Oxford Martyrs – Thomas Cranmer, Archbishop of Canterbury; Nicholas Ridley, Archbishop of London; and High Latimer, Bishop of Worcester – were martyred in the mid 1550s for their refusal to return to the Catholic faith after Queen Mary gained the throne. In 1843, when fears of a Catholic resurgence were widespread, this memorial to the three men was paid for by public subscription and erected to the designs of George Gilbert Scott to serve as a reminder that the founding fathers of the Church of England had been martyred by a Catholic queen. 58 B3

Oxford Castle *Tidmarsh Lane, Oxford* Only the motte survives of the castle built by Robert d'Oilly in 1071. The nearly contemporary St George's Tower provides good views over the city. The buildings of the late 18th-century gaol serve as a stark reminder of the harshness of prison life. (Now preserved with a residential, retail and hotel complex) www.oxfordcastle.com/home.html 59 A2

Entertainment

Burton Taylor Theatre *Gloucester Street, Oxford* An intimate 50-seater studio theatre. During university terms, productions are put on by students; during vacations it is host to professional touring companies or local small-scale community theatre groups. 01865 305350 59 B2 www.oxfordplayhouse.com/BurtonTaylor

Holywell Music Room *Holywell Street, Oxford* This classical concert venue is among one of the oldest in England. A wide range of classical music is played here. 01865 305305 (Playhouse booking office) 58 C3

Jacqueline du Pré Music Building *St Hilda's College, off Cowley Place, Oxford* New venue hosting classical concerts, readings, lectures and plays. 01865 305 305 (booking) www.st-hildas.ox.ac.uk/jdp 21 C2

New Theatre *George Street, Oxford* Large theatre hosting musicals, comedy and plays. 0870 606 3500 www.newburytheatre.co.uk/theatres/apollo.htm 59 B2

Odeon *George Street, Oxford* www.odeon.co.uk 0871 2244007 59 B2

Odeon *Magdalen Street, Oxford* www.odeon.co.uk 0871 2244007 59 B2

Old Fire Station Arts Centre *George Street, Oxford* Part of the new Arts Centre based in the Old Fire Station. A variety of plays, from writers such as Shakespeare and Marlow to David Hare and Anthony Burgess, are performed here. 01865 297170 www.newburytheatre.co.uk/theatres/oldfire.htm 59 B2

Oxford Playhouse *Beaumont Street, Oxford* Performances range from classics to modern plays and musicals. www.oxfordplayhouse.com 01865 305305 59 B2

Ozone Multiplex *Ozone Leisure Park, Grenoble Road, Oxford* www.ozonemultiplex.com0870 4443030 41 B3

Phoenix Cinema *Walton Street/Cranham St, Oxford* 01865 512526 58 A4 www.picturehouses.co.uk

Screen at the Square *Market Square, Witney* www.screenwitney.co.uk 01865 880645 55 A1

Sheldonian Theatre *See under University*

Ultimate Picture Palace *Jeune Street, Oxford* 01865 245288 www.ultimatepicturepalace.co.uk/ 22 A2

Other activities

Golf courses

Hinksey Heights Golf Club *South Hinksey, Oxford (off southern bypass)* 18-hole inland Championship links course. 01865 237775 www.oxford-golf.co.uk 30 C3

North Oxford Golf Club *Banbury Road, Oxford* 18-hole course www.nogc.co.uk 01865 554924 7 B1

Southfield Golf Club *Hilltop Road, Oxford* 18-hole course set in beautiful undulating parkland. www.southfieldgolf.com 01865 244258 23 A2

Guided Tours

Oxford Tourist Information Centre *15-16 Broad Street, Oxford* Open-top bus, Oxford Past and Present, Inspector Morse, Ghost and many others 59 B2 01865 726871 www.oxfordcity.co.uk/info/tours

◀ ***The cloisters at Magdalen College***

Leisure facilities

Barton Pool *Wayneflete Road, Barton, Headington* A 25-metre indoor pool, opening in 2006. www.oxford.gov.uk 01865 249 811 (council switchboard) 17 A2

Blackbird Leys Leisure Centre *Pegasus Road, Blackbird Leys, Oxford* Small leisure centre with a fitness suite, gym and pool. Open to the public outside office hours. 01865 467020 www.oxford.gov.uk/services/blackbird-leys-leisure-centre.cfm 41 C4

Ferry Sports Centre *Diamond Place, Ferry Pool Road, Summertown, Oxford* Facilities include main and learner pools, a fitness suite and dance studio, squash courst and a multi-use sports hall. Open to public outside school hours. www.oxford.gov.uk/services/ferry-sports-centre.cfm 01865 467060 14 A4

Hinksey Pool *Lake Street, Oxford* Heated outdoor pool, open in summer outside school hours. 01865 467079 31 B4 www.oxford.gov.uk/services/hinksey-swimming-pool.cfm

Kidlington and Gosford Sports Centre *Oxford Road, Kidlington* Facilities include a sports hall, squash courts, a pool, sauna and steam rooms, an all-weather pitch and a fitness studio. 01865 376368 www.cherwell-dc.gov.uk/leisure/gosford.cfm 4 A1

Oxford Ice Rink *Oxpens Road, Oxford* Popular attraction offering skating lessons, disco and open sessions and home to clubs. Is also the home to Oxford Stars Ice Hockey team. www.oxford.gov.uk/services/oxford-ice-rink.cfm 01865 467002 59 A1

Peers Sports Centre *Peers School Campus, Sandy Lane West, Littlemore, Oxford* Facilities include a pool, a sports hall, squash and tennis courts and a variety of clubs and classes. Open to public outside school hours. 01865 467095 www.oxford.gov.uk/services/peers-sports-centre.cfm 41 A4

Temple Cowley Pool *Temple Road, Cowley, Oxford* Within this small complex are main and learner pools, a gym and sauna and steam rooms. Open to public outside school hours. 01865 467124 www.oxford.gov.uk/services/temple-cowley-swimming-pool.cfm 33 B3

White Horse Leisure and Tennis Centre *Audlett Drive, Abingdon* Facilities include a fitness suite, dance studio, indoor and outdoor tennis courts, squash courts and a swimming pool. 01235 540700 50 B2

Windrush Leisure Centre *Witan Road, Witney* Outside school hours, the public have access to main and learner pools, aerobics and fitness studios, a snooker room, squash courts and a sports hall. 01993 202020 www.wll.co.uk 55 A1

Football

Oxford City Football Club *Court Place Farm, Marsh Road, Marston, Oxford* www.oxfordcityfc.co.uk 01865 744493 15 B4

Oxford United Football Club *Kassam Stadium, Grenoble Road, Oxford* 01865 337500 www.oufc.premiumtv.co.uk/page/Home/0,,10342,00.html 41 B3

Open spaces

Christ Church Meadow *St Aldates, Oxford* More tranquil during vacations than in term-times, although it is a good spot to watch college boat races. 59 C1

Port Meadow (and Wolvercote Common) *off Walton Well Road, Oxford* Large area of west meadow and common land grazed traditionally by cattle and horses. Good for birdwatching in summer, but prone to flooding in winter and spring. 12 C4

Shotover Country Park *Old Road, Oxford* Some 250 acres of open common land and woodland and other varied habitats. As well as being an increasingly important site for local wildlife (part of it is an SSSI), it provides views over the city to the west, picnic areas and a giant natural sandpit. 0800 0521455 www.oxford.gov.uk/services/nature-reserves.cfm/text/1 24 B2

University Botanic Garden *Rose Lane, Oxford* Founded in 1621 by the botanist Harry Danvers, this is the oldest scientific garden in the UK. It is divided into three sections: the walled garden with plants grouped by geographical origin or use, the glass houses and the more open area which has such features as a water garden, bog garden, bog garden and themed borders. www.botanic-garden.ox.ac.uk 01865 286690 59 C2

University Parks *Parks Road, Oxford* Home of the university's cricket team 58 B4/C4

Boat hire

Cherwell Boathouse *Bardwell Road, Oxford* Punt and rowing-boat hire on the Cherwell 01865 515978 14 B2

IPG Marine *Boat Station, Head of the River Pub, Folly Bridge, Oxford* Punt hire on the Isis. 0961 115369 59 B1

Magdalen Bridge Boathouse *High Street, Oxford* Punt hire on the Cherwell in the area around the University Botanic Gardens 01865 202643 21 C3

Salters Steamers *Folly Bridge, Oxford* Boats for pleasure and charter trips, as well as self-drive boats. 01865 243421 www.salterssteamers.co.uk 59 B1

Events

Eights week Four-day inter-collegiate rowing contest, held on the Isis in the fifth week of Trinity (summer) term, usually in late May.

May Day The morning starts with a Latin Grace being sung from Magdalen College's Bell Tower, followed by the bells ringing. and other activities such as Morris dancing.

Oxford Literary Festival Held for one week in early April www.sundaytimes-oxfordliterary-festival.co.uk

St Giles' Fair Annual fair held in St Giles on the first Monday and Tuesday after 1 September.

Torpids College boat races held in late February

General information

Abingdon Tourist Information Centre *Abbey House, Abbey Close, Abingdon* 01235 522711 49 B1

Oxford Tourist Information Centre *15-16 Broad Street, Oxford* 01865 726871 59 B2

Witney Tourist Information Centre *26a Market Square, Witney* 01993 775802 www.oxfordshirecotswolds.org 55 A1

Abingdon Town Council 01235 522642

Oxford City Council 01865 249 811 www.oxford.gov.uk

West Oxfordshire District Council 01933 861000 www.westoxon.gov.uk

Oxford City Car Parks www.oxford.gov.uk/services/parking.cfm

Park and Ride 01865 785400 www.oxfordbus.co.uk

Chiltern Railways 08456 005165 www.chilternrailways.co.uk

First Great Western 01457 000125 www.firstgreatwestern.co.uk

First Great Western Link 01457 000125 www.firstgreatwestern.co.uk/link

National Express 08705 808080 www.nationalexpress.com

National Rail Enquiries 08457 48 49 50 www.nationalrail.co.uk/

The Oxford Bus Company 01865 785400 www.oxfordbus.co.uk

Stagecoach Oxford (local and Oxford Tube) 01865 727000 www.stagecoachbus.com/oxfordshire

Sustrans Charitable organisation that promotes cycling and cycle networks www.sustrans.org.uk

Travelline Public Transport Information 08706 6082608 www.travelline.co.uk

Virgin Cross Country 0870 7891234 www.virgintrains.co.uk

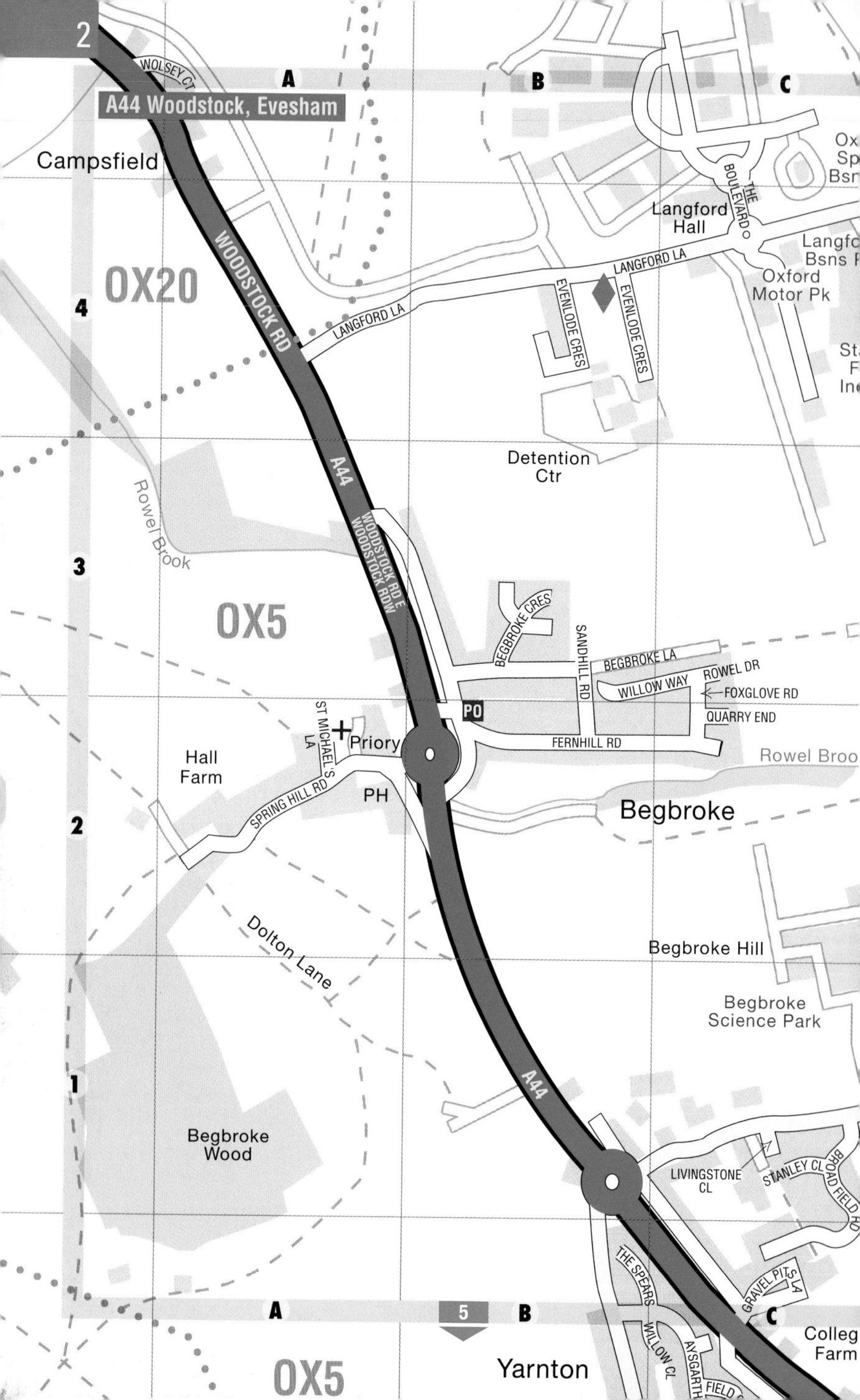
A44 Woodstock, Evesham
WOLSEY CT
A
B
C
Campsfield
OX20
WOODSTOCK RD
Langford Hall
THE BOULEVARD
LANGFORD LA
EVENLODE CRES
EVENLODE CRES
Oxford Motor Pk
4
Detention Ctr
A44
Rowel Brook
3
WOODSTOCK RD E
WOODSTOCK RDW
OX5
BEGBROKE CRES
SANDHILL RD
BEGBROKE LA
WILLOW WAY
ROWEL DR
FOXGLOVE RD
QUARRY END
PO
FERNHILL RD
ST MICHAEL'S LA
Priory
Hall Farm
SPRING HILL RD
PH
Rowel Broo
Begbroke
2
Dolton Lane
Begbroke Hill
Begbroke Science Park
1
A44
Begbroke Wood
LIVINGSTONE CL
STANLEY CL
BROAD FIELD RD
THE SPEARS
GRAVEL PITS LA
WILLOW CL
AYSGARTH
FIELD
A
5
B
C
Yarnton
OX5
Colleg Farm

A4260 Banbury
A
B
C
A4260
BANBURY RD
OX5
Cherwell Bsns Ctr
Roundham Lock
LC
Parker's Farm
Sandy Lane Crossing
SANDY LA
BEGBROKE LA
BRIAR END
BRIAR CL
STATION APP
BANKSIDE
CHARLBURY CL
MARLBOROUGH CL
BLANDFORD RD
LEE CL
MARLBOROUGH AVE
THE MOORS
PARK AVE
HELWYS PL
THE MOORLANDS
MEADOW VIEW
MEAD WAY
BEN CL
WISE AVE
CHERWELL CT
FLATFORD PL
THE RIDINGS
COT'S GN
WILSDON WAY
THORNE CL
AXTELL CL
CHAMBERLAIN PL
PARTRIDGE PL
LYNE RD
ROUNDHAM CL
CHOREFIELDS
GREYSTONES CT
THE ROOKERY 1
HEYFORD MEAD 2
CROWN RD 3
ANDERSONS CL
THE HOMESTEAD
BARN CL
RUTTERS CL
NURSERIES RD
COURT CL
CROWN RD
JUDGES CL
THE PHELPS
PLOUGHLEY CL
LANE CL
GROVELANDS
HARTS CL
CALVES CL
BELLENGER WAY
BRANDON CL
SCOTT CL
BOWERMAN CL
BROAD CL
YARNTON CT
YARNTON RD
FERNHILL CL 1
MORRELL CL 2
BELGROVE CL 3
OSBORNE CL
NEWPORT CL
1 WATTS WAY
2 The Kidlington Ctr
BENMEAD RD
CURTIS RD
Sch
P
DEAUFORT CL
HOME CL
THE CLOSES
HIGH ST
FOXDOWN CL
DALE PL
STERLING ROAD APP
Liby
PO
STERLING CL
STERLING RD
EXETER RD
TREEGROUND PL
MORTON CL
CHURCHILL RD
WINSTON CL
MORTON AVE
COPTHORNE RD
CHERRY CL
ROWAN CL
SPRUCE RD
MAGNOLIA CL
LINCRAFT CL
HARDWICK AVE
HOLLY CL
ASH CL
Schs
POPLAR CL
MAPLE AVE
HAWTHORN WAY
MAPLE CT
LABURNUM CRES
ALMOND AVE
AZALEA AVE
HAZEL CRES
BEECH CRES
STRATFIELD
LOCK CRES
ELM GR
HAZEL WLK
OXFORD RD
Kidlington Green Lock
YARNTON LA
6
LAMBS CL
FREEBORN CL
ST MARY'S CL
MANOR WAY
FARM CL
CHURCH ST
THE ALMSHOUSES
SPINDLERS
FRANKLIN CL
FRANK COOK CT
OLD CHAPEL CL
THE TOWN GN
VICARAGE RD
SCHOOL RD
GREEN RD
ST JOHNS DR
BRASENOSE DR
OAK DR
4
DUKES RD
MULCASTER AVE
BASSET WAY
FIELD CL
CROFT AVE
HONOR CL
WHITE WAY
FLORENCE CL
BLENHEIM RD
PRESTIDGE PL
TURNER CT
BICESTER
BUCKLAND CT
Gosf
Gos

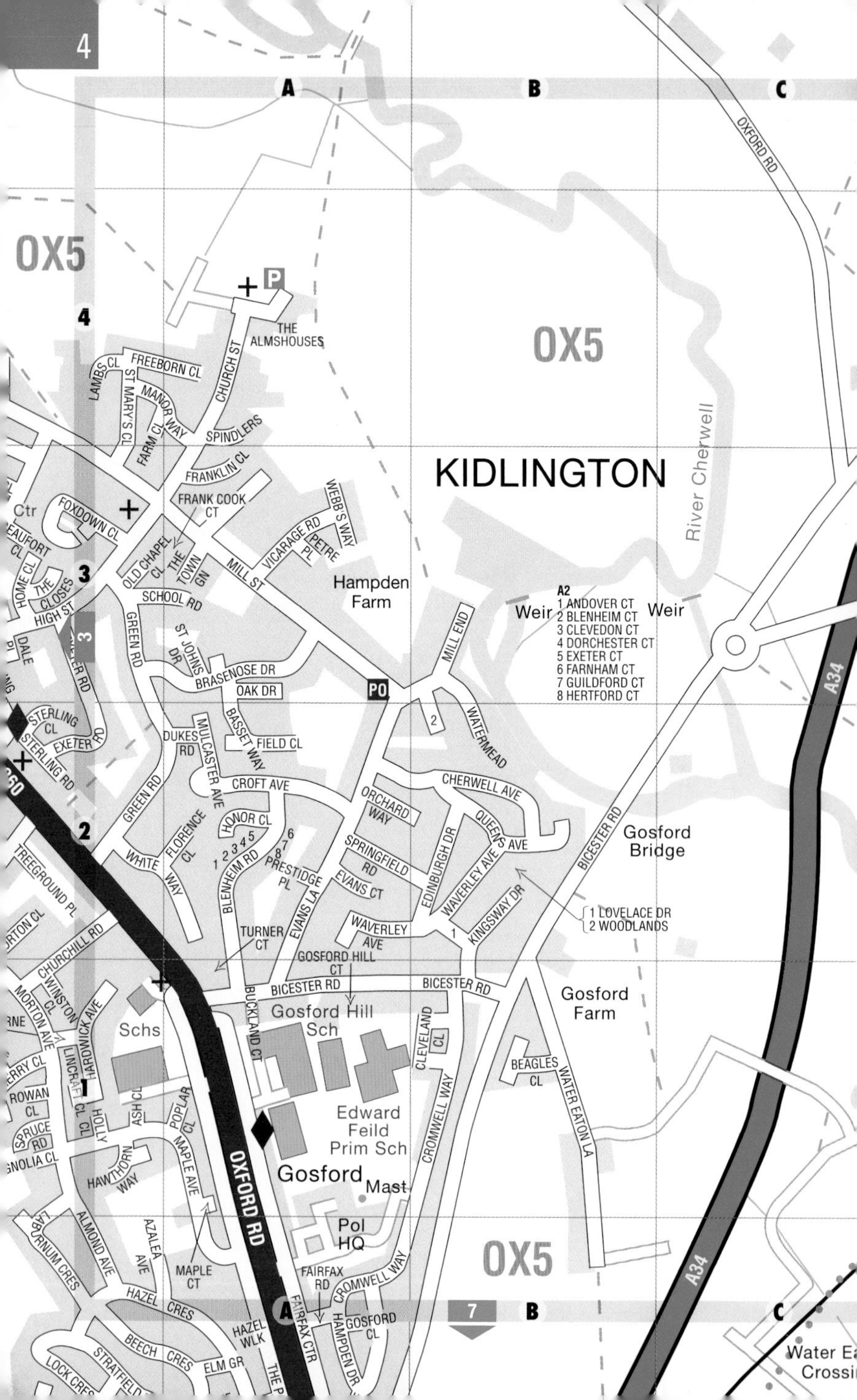

KIDLINGTON
OX5
OX5
OX5
A
B
C
4
3
2
1
THE ALMSHOUSES
FREEBORN CL
LAMBS CL
ST MARY'S CL
MANOR WAY
CHURCH ST
FARM CL
SPINDLERS
FRANKLIN CL
FRANK COOK CT
FOXDOWN CL
Ctr
BEAUFORT CL
HOME CL
THE CLOSES
HIGH ST
OLD CHAPEL CL
THE TOWN GN
MILL ST
VICARAGE RD
WEBB'S WAY
PETRE PL
Hampden Farm
SCHOOL RD
GREEN RD
ST JOHNS DR
BRASENOSE DR
OAK DR
PO
MILL END
Weir
Weir
A2
1 ANDOVER CT
2 BLENHEIM CT
3 CLEVEDON CT
4 DORCHESTER CT
5 EXETER CT
6 FARNHAM CT
7 GUILDFORD CT
8 HERTFORD CT
River Cherwell
OXFORD RD
A34
A34
DALE
STERLING CL
STERLING RD
EXETER RD
DUKES RD
MULCASTER AVE
BASSET WAY
FIELD CL
WATERMEAD
2
CROFT AVE
GREEN RD
HONOR CL
ORCHARD WAY
CHERWELL AVE
QUEEN'S AVE
FLORENCE CL
WHITE WAY
BLENHEIM RD
PRESTIDGE PL
SPRINGFIELD RD
EDINBURGH DR
WAVERLEY AVE
EVANS CT
EVANS LA
KINGSWAY DR
BICESTER RD
Gosford Bridge
1 LOVELACE DR
2 WOODLANDS
TREEGROUND PL
CHURCHILL RD
TURNER CT
WAVERLEY AVE
GOSFORD HILL CT
BICESTER RD
BICESTER RD
Gosford Farm
WINSTON CL
MORTON AVE
HARDWICK AVE
Schs
Gosford Hill Sch
BUCKLAND CT
CLEVELAND CL
BEAGLES CL
WATER EATON LA
ROWAN CL
LINCRAFT CL
HOLLY CL
ASH CL
POPLAR CL
CROMWELL WAY
SPRUCE RD
HAWTHORN WAY
MAPLE AVE
OXFORD RD
Edward Feild Prim Sch
Gosford
Mast
Pol HQ
ALMOND AVE
AZALEA AVE
MAPLE CT
LABURNUM CRES
HAZEL CRES
FAIRFAX RD
CROMWELL WAY
FAIRFAX CTR
HAMPDEN DR
GOSFORD CL
HAZEL WLK
BEECH CRES
ELM GR
STRATFIELD
LOCK CRES
7
Water Eaton Crossing

A
B
2
C
SAND
Begbroke
Wood
A44
LIVINGSTONE
CL
STANLEY CL
BROAD FIELD RD
RYDER CL
THE SPEARS
GRAVEL PITS LA
College
Farm
4
WILLOW CL
AYSGARTH RD
FIELD CL
Yarnton
OX5
RUTTEN LA
THE GARTH
FLETCHER
CL
Yarnton
House
MEADOW WAY
BARTHOLOMEW
AVE
SPENCER AVE
DASHWOOD AVE
William Fletcher
Prim Sch
Frogwelldown Lane
FOLLETS CL
A44
Gra
STOUTSFIELD CL
MERTON WAY
GREAT CLOSE RD
MARSH CL
Little Blenheim
3
LITTLE
BLENHEIM
BERNARD CL
Hill
Farm
POUND CL
THE PADDOCKS
9
STOCKS
TREE CL
CASSINGTON RD
PARK CL
Ind Est
The Red Lion
(PH)
CHURCH LA
CASSINGTON RD
2
Manor
House
Mead
Farm
1
OX5
OX29
Oxey Mead
A
B
C
A40

SANDY LA
A
3
B
C
CHERRY CL
ROWAN CL
LINCRAFT CL
HOLLY CL
SPRUCE RD
MAGNOLIA CL
HAWTH
STANLEY CL
BROAD FIELD RD
RYDER CL
Sandy Lane Crossing
OX5
LABURNUM CRES
ALMOND AVE
GRAVEL PITS LA
Kidlington Green Lock
College Farm
4
YARNTON LA
LOCK CRES
Towing Path
CROXFORD G
FLETCHER CL
ASHWOOD AVE
MEADOW WAY
A44
FOLLETS CL
The Grapes Inn (PH)
LC
Oxford Canal
Garden C
Oxford Canal Walk
MERTON WAY
GREAT CLOSE RD
MARSH CL
3
BERNARD CL
THE PADDOCK
5
CASSINGTON RD
MEAD RD
Ind Est
WOODSTOCK RD
Ickworth
CHURCH LA
2
Stonehouse Farm
OX5
Kingsbridge Brook
Mead Farm
Frieze F
Swing Bridge
Loop Farm
1
A44
A4260
OX5
Peartree Hill
A44
Oxey Mead
OX2
PEARTREE INTERCHANGE
A34
A
8
B
C
A40
Duke's Lock

A
B
C
4
Edward Feild Prim Sch
Gosford
Mast
Pol HQ
OXFORD RD
CROMWELL WAY
BEAGLES CL
OX5
FAIRFAX RD
CROMWELL WAY
HAZEL WLK
FAIRFAX CTR
HAMPDEN DR
GOSFORD CL
ELM GR
THE PARADE
THE BROADWAY
ASTLEY AVE
PO
SOUTH CL
AVE
A34
Water Eaton Crossing
Middle Farm
Superstore
A4260
A4165
P&R
FRIEZE WAY
OX2
St Frideswide Farm
North Oxford Golf Club
OXFORD RD
CH
Mast
JORDAN HILL
Oxford Bsns Pk
9
Cutteslowe
LAKESIDE
HASLEMERE GDNS
Cemy
HAYWARD RD
4
3
2
1

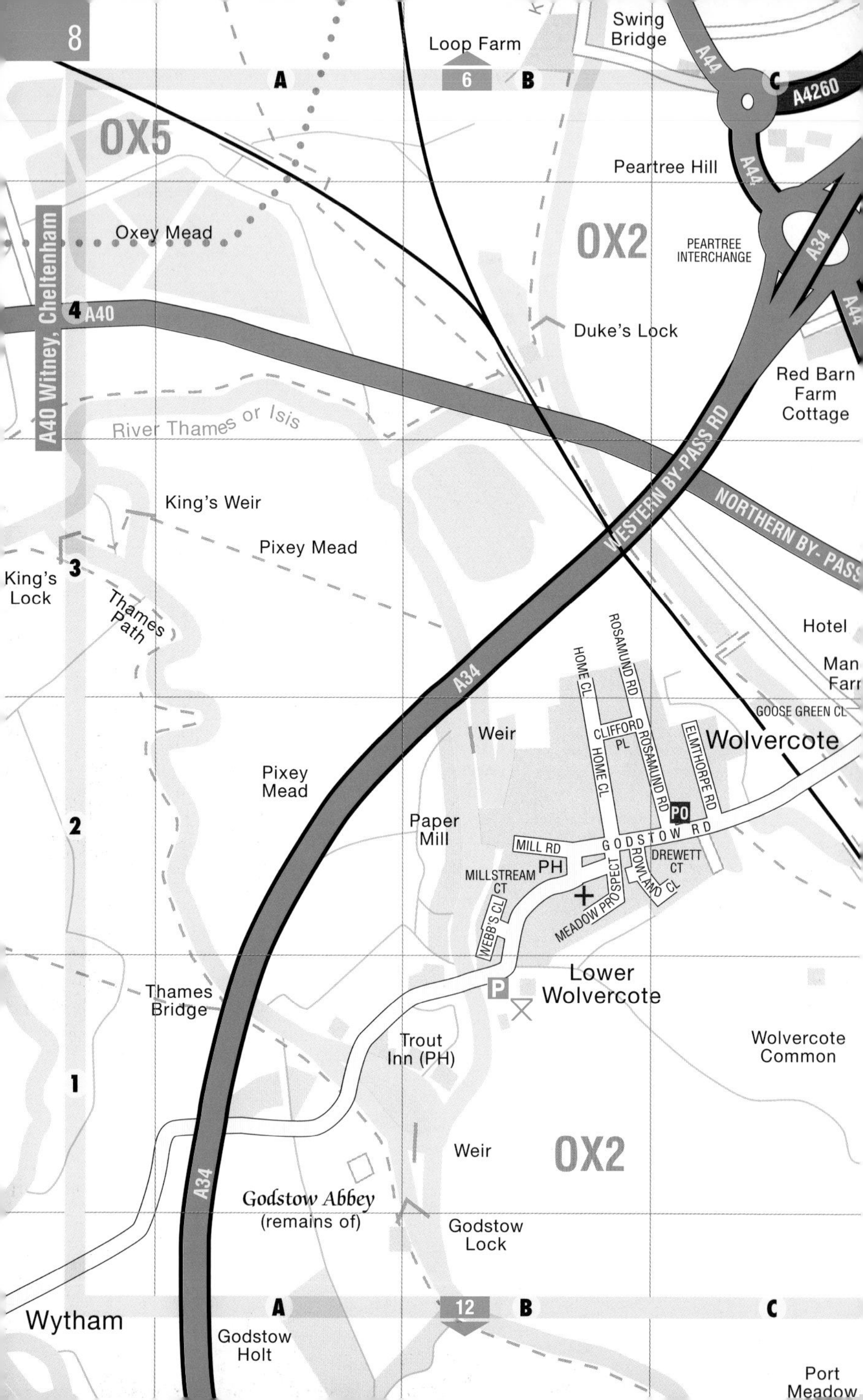

Loop Farm
6
Swing Bridge
A
B
C
A44
A4260
OX5
Peartree Hill
A44
Oxey Mead
OX2
PEARTREE INTERCHANGE
A34
A40 Witney, Cheltenham
4
A40
Duke's Lock
A44
Red Barn Farm Cottage
River Thames or Isis
WESTERN BY-PASS RD
NORTHERN BY-PASS
King's Weir
Pixey Mead
3
King's Lock
Thames Path
Hotel
ROSAMUND RD
HOME CL
A34
Weir
GOOSE GREEN CL
CLIFFORD PL
HOME CL
ROSAMUND RD
ELMTHORPE RD
Wolvercote
Pixey Mead
PO
Paper Mill
2
MILL RD
GODSTOW RD
ROWLAND CL
DREWETT CT
MILLSTREAM CT
PH
WEBB'S CL
MEADOW PROSPECT
Lower Wolvercote
P
Thames Bridge
Trout Inn (PH)
Wolvercote Common
1
Weir
OX2
A34
Godstow Abbey (remains of)
Godstow Lock
A
12
B
C
Wytham
Godstow Holt
Port Meadow

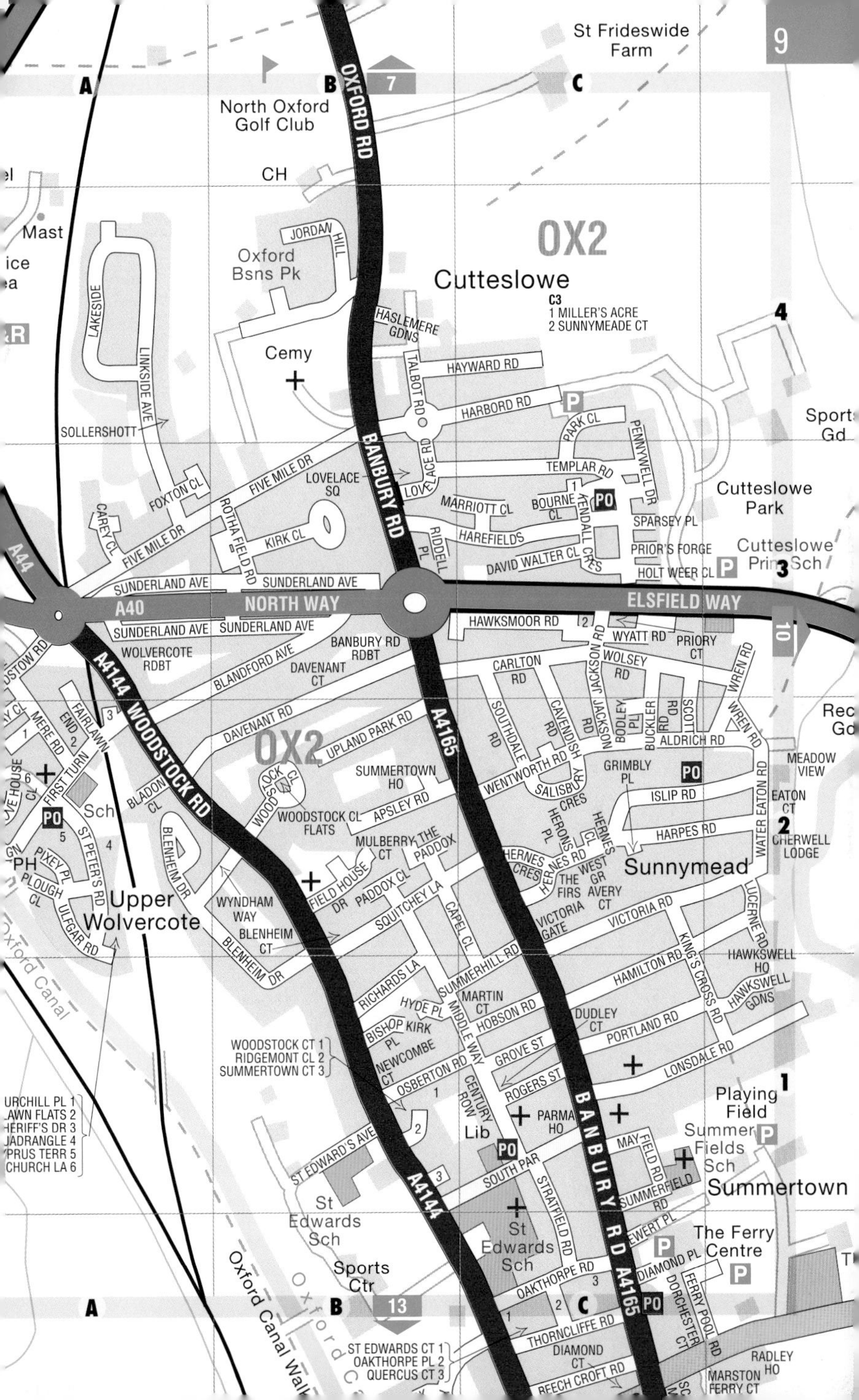

St Frideswide Farm
North Oxford Golf Club
CH
Mast
OX2
Cutteslowe
C3
1 MILLER'S ACRE
2 SUNNYMEADE CT
Oxford Bsns Pk
JORDAN HILL
HASLEMERE GDNS
Cemy
LAKESIDE
LINKSIDE AVE
SOLLERSHOTT
HAYWARD RD
TALBOT RD
HARBORD RD
PARK CL
PENNYWELL DR
TEMPLAR RD
LOVELACE SQ
LOVELACE RD
FIVE MILE DR
FOXTON CL
CAREY CL
ROTHA FIELD RD
KIRK CL
MARRIOTT CL
BOURNE CL
KENDALL CRES
SPARSEY PL
HAREFIELDS
RIDDELL PL
DAVID WALTER CL
PRIOR'S FORGE
HOLT WEER CL
Cutteslowe Park
Cutteslowe Prim Sch
Sports Gd
SUNDERLAND AVE
A40
NORTH WAY
ELSFIELD WAY
OXFORD RD
BANBURY RD
A44
A4144
WOODSTOCK RD
A4165
WOLVERCOTE RDBT
BANBURY RD RDBT
HAWKSMOOR RD
WYATT RD
PRIORY CT
WOLSEY RD
CARLTON RD
JACKSON RD
BLANDFORD AVE
DAVENANT CT
DAVENANT RD
UPLAND PARK RD
SOUTHDALE RD
CAVENDISH RD
BODLEY PL
BUCKLER RD
SCOTT RD
WREN RD
ALDRICH RD
MEADOW VIEW
EATON CT
CHERWELL LODGE
Rec Gd
FAIRLAWN END
MERE RD
FIRST TURN
SUMMERTOWN HO
WENTWORTH RD
SALISBURY CRES
GRIMBLY PL
ISLIP RD
HARPES RD
WATER EATON RD
BLADON CL
WOODSTOCK CL
WOODSTOCK CL FLATS
APSLEY RD
HERONS PL
HERNES CL
HERNES CRES
HERNES RD
Sunnymead
Sch
PH
PIXEY PL
ST PETER'S RD
PLOUGH CL
ULFGAR RD
Upper Wolvercote
BLENHEIM DR
WYNDHAM WAY
BLENHEIM CT
MULBERRY CT
THE PADDOX
FIELD HOUSE DR
PADDOX CL
SQUITCHEY LA
CAPEL CL
THE FIRS
WEST GR
AVERY CT
VICTORIA GATE
VICTORIA RD
LUCERNE RD
KING'S CROSS RD
HAWKSWELL HO
HAWKSWELL GDNS
Oxford Canal
RICHARDS LA
SUMMERHILL RD
HAMILTON RD
HYDE PL
MARTIN CT
MIDDLE WAY
HOBSON RD
DUDLEY CT
PORTLAND RD
BISHOP KIRK PL
NEWCOMBE CT
GROVE ST
LONSDALE RD
WOODSTOCK CT 1
RIDGEMONT CL 2
SUMMERTOWN CT 3
OSBERTON RD
CENTURY ROW
ROGERS ST
Playing Field
URCHILL PL 1
AWN FLATS 2
HERIFF'S DR 3
UADRANGLE 4
PRUS TERR 5
CHURCH LA 6
PARMA HO
Lib
Summer Fields Sch
ST EDWARD'S AVE
MAYFIELD RD
SUMMERFIELD RD
Summertown
SOUTH PAR
STRATFIELD RD
St Edwards Sch
EWERT PL
The Ferry Centre
Oxford Canal Walk
Sports Ctr
OAKTHORPE RD
DIAMOND PL
DORCHESTER CT
FERRY POOL RD
THORNCLIFFE RD
DIAMOND CT
BEECH CROFT RD
RADLEY HO
MARSTON FERRY CT
ST EDWARDS CT 1
OAKTHORPE PL 2
QUERCUS CT 3
PO
P
A
B
C
1
2
3
4
7
10
13

A
B
C
OX2
OX3
4
Sports Gd
Cutteslowe Park
Cutteslowe Prim Sch
PARK CL
PENNYWELL DR
TEMPLAR RD
KENDALL CRES
SPARSEY PL
PRIOR'S FORGE
HOLT WEER CL
3
ELSFIELD WAY
9
PRIORY CT
WOLSEY RD
JACKSON RD
CAVENDISH RD
BODLEY PL
BUCKLER RD
SCOTT RD
WREN RD
ALDRICH RD
GRIMBLY PL
ISLIP RD
HARPES RD
2
Sunnymead
HERNES CL
WEST GR
AVERY CT
THE FIRS
VICTORIA RD
WATER EATON RD
MEADOW VIEW
EATON CT
CHERWELL LODGE
LUCERNE RD
Recn Gd
Cherwell Bridge
A40
New Manor Farm
Hill Farm
Sescut Farm
MILL LA
NORTHERN BY-PASS RD
HAMILTON RD
KING'S CROSS RD
HAWKSWELL HO
HAWKSWELL GDNS
DUDLEY CT
PORTLAND RD
LONSDALE RD
1
BANBURY RD A4165
Playing Field
Summer Fields Sch
MAYFIELD RD
SUMMERFIELD RD
Summertown
EWERT PL
The Ferry Centre
DIAMOND PL
DORCHESTER CT
FERRY POOL RD
The Cherwell Sch
Northern Meadow Farm
The Victoria Arms (PH)
Hill View Farm
Cumberlege House
CUMBERLEGE
MARSTON FERRY RD
14
RADLEY HO
MARSTON FERRY CT
PO
P

A
B
C
Woodeaton Wood
OX3
4
Long Wood
Sewage Works
Little Wood
Home Farm
3
Manor House
swater Brook
Elsfield
Church Farm
Pennywell Wood
Vicarage
Hill Farm
Marston Common
2
1
ST NICHOLAS PK (CVN PK)
Marston
LODGE CL
A40
W WAY
CHURCH LA
BUTTS LA
B4150
PONDS LA
LITTLE ACREAGE
ELSFIELD RD
A
B
15
C
PH
WHITE HART
CANNONS FIELD
SOUTHCROFT
PO
Cemy
OX3

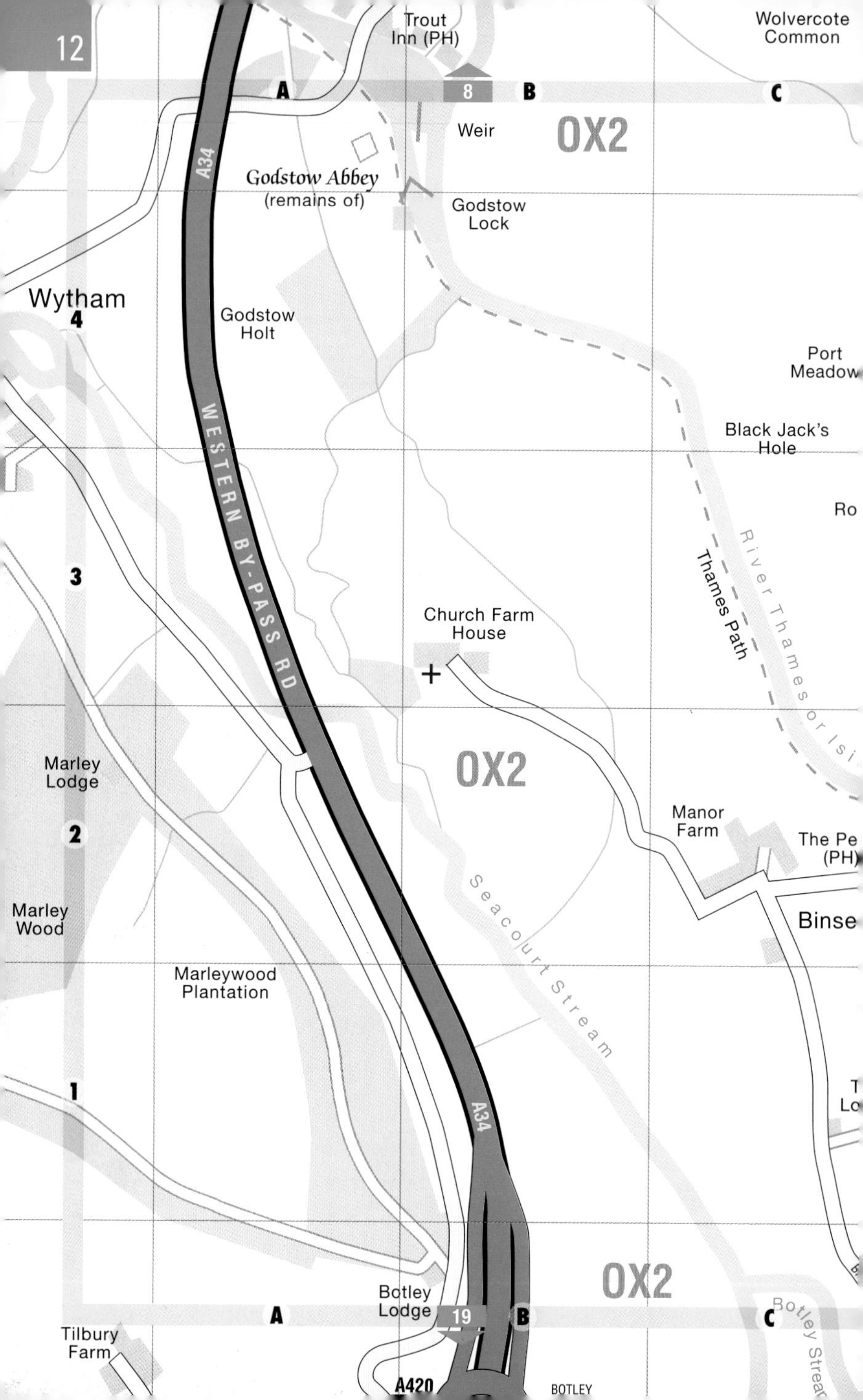

Trout Inn (PH)
Wolvercote Common
A
8
B
C
Weir
OX2
A34
Godstow Abbey
(remains of)
Godstow Lock
Wytham
4
Godstow Holt
Port Meadow
Black Jack's Hole
WESTERN BY-PASS RD
River Thames or Isis
Thames Path
3
Church Farm House
OX2
Marley Lodge
2
Manor Farm
The Pe (PH)
Seacourt Stream
Marley Wood
Binse
Marleywood Plantation
1
A34
OX2
Botley Lodge
A
19
B
C
Botley Stream
Tilbury Farm
A420
BOTLEY

WOODSTOCK CT 1
RIDGEMONT CL 2
SUMMERTOWN CT 3
Summertown
Playing Field
Summer Fields Sch
St Edwards Sch
Sports Ctr
Oxford Canal Walk
Oxford Canal
The Ferry Centre
ST EDWARDS CT 1
OAKTHORPE PL 2
QUERCUS CT 3
MORETON RD
B4495
A4144
A4165
WOODSTOCK RD
BANBURY RD
OX2
Univ Coll Oxford (Annexe)
SS Philip & James' CE Prim Sch
St Aloysius RC Prim Sch
St Hugh's Coll
PARK TOWN
MERRIVALE SQ
BALLIOL CT 1
MERTON CT 2
THE CRESCENT 3
Willow Walk
Fiddler's Island
Walton Manor
Cemy
Castle Mill Stream
River Thames or Isis
St Anne's Coll
Radcliffe
Somerville Coll
Arts Ctr
Jericho
Keble Coll
OX1
9
14
20
58

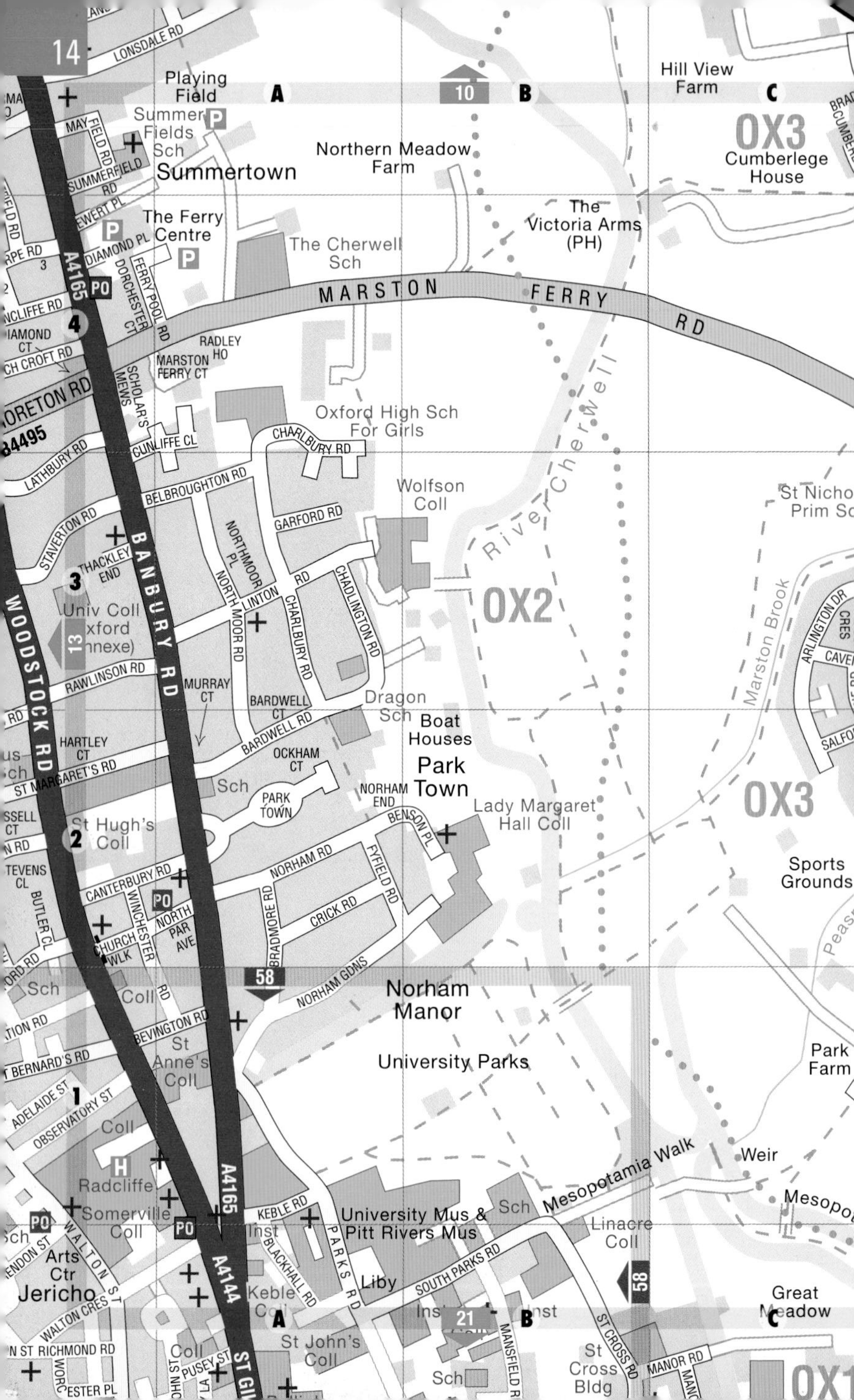

LONSDALE RD
Playing Field
A
10
B
Hill View Farm
C
OX3
Cumberlege House
MAYFIELD RD
Summer Fields Sch
Summertown
Northern Meadow Farm
SUMMERFIELD RD
EWERT PL
The Ferry Centre
The Victoria Arms (PH)
DIAMOND PL
The Cherwell Sch
A4165
DORCHESTER CT
FERRY POOL RD
MARSTON FERRY RD
RADLEY HO
MARSTON FERRY CT
SCHOLAR'S MEWS
Oxford High Sch For Girls
CHARLBURY RD
GUNLIFFE CL
LATHBURY RD
BELBROUGHTON RD
Wolfson Coll
GARFORD RD
River Cherwell
STAVERTON RD
THACKLEY END
BANBURY RD
NORTHMOOR PL
NORTH MOOR RD
LINTON RD
CHADLINGTON RD
OX2
Marston Brook
ARLINGTON DR
St Nicho Prim Sc
Univ Coll Oxford Annexe
WOODSTOCK RD
13
RAWLINSON RD
MURRAY CT
BARDWELL CT
BARDWELL RD
Dragon Sch
Boat Houses
HARTLEY CT
ST MARGARET'S RD
OCKHAM CT
Park Town
Sch
PARK TOWN
NORHAM END
BENSON PL
Lady Margaret Hall Coll
OX3
St Hugh's Coll
CANTERBURY RD
NORHAM RD
FYFIELD RD
Sports Grounds
BUTLER CL
PO
NORTH PARADE AVE
CRICK RD
BRADMORE RD
CHURCH WLK
WINCHESTER RD
58
NORHAM GDNS
Norham Manor
BEVINGTON RD
University Parks
Park Farm
ST BERNARD'S RD
St Anne's Coll
ADELAIDE ST
OBSERVATORY ST
Coll
H
Radcliffe
Weir
Mesopotamia Walk
KEBLE RD
Somerville Coll
University Mus & Pitt Rivers Mus
Sch
Linacre Coll
WALTON ST
Arts Ctr
Jericho
A4144
BLACKHALL RD
PARKS RD
Liby
SOUTH PARKS RD
Keble Coll
Inst
58
Great Meadow
WALTON CRES
21
MANSFIELD RD
ST CROSS RD
St John's Coll
St Cross Bldg
MANOR RD
RICHMOND RD
PUSEY ST
ST GILES

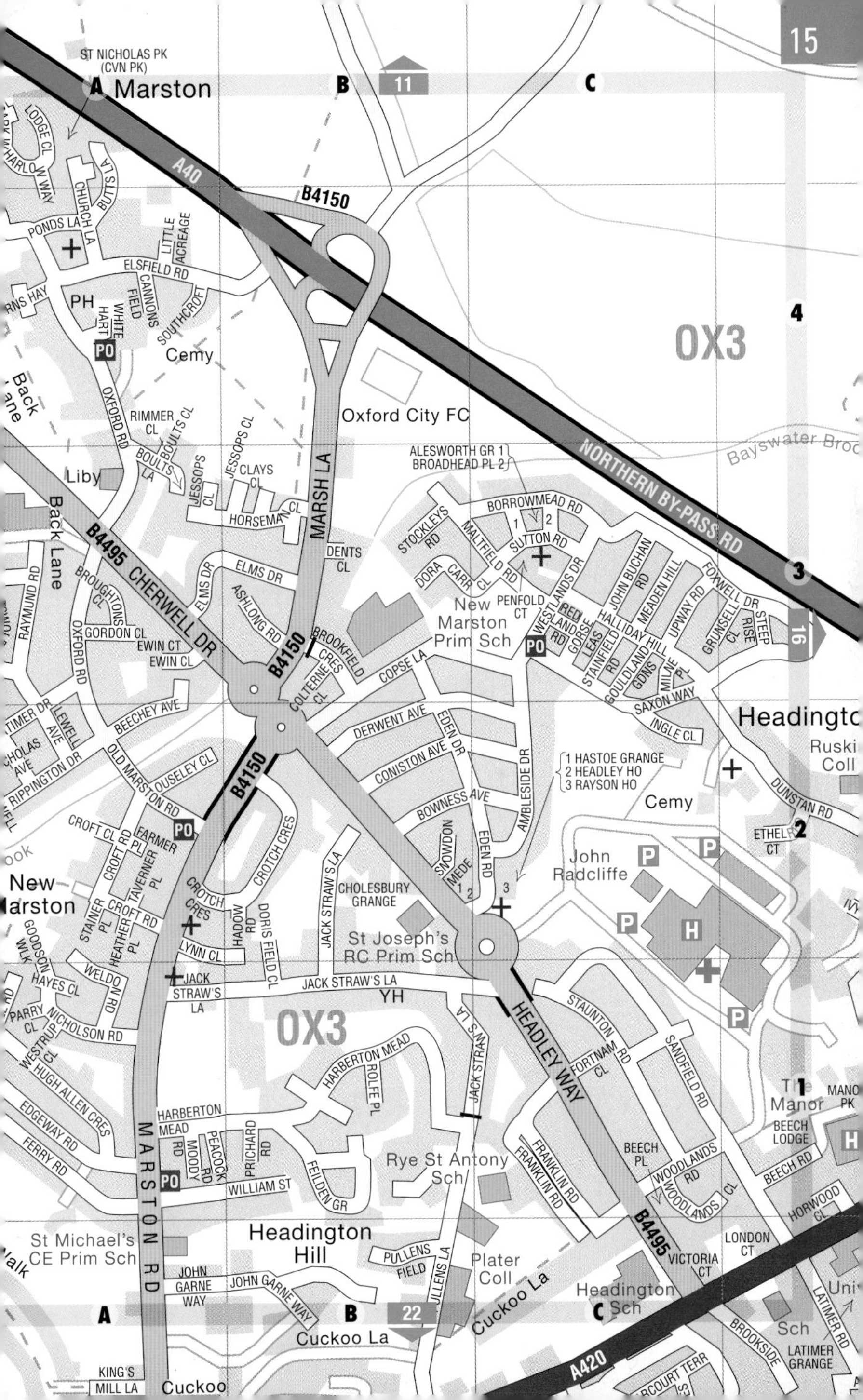

Marston
ST NICHOLAS PK (CVN PK)
A
B
C
11
A40
B4150
OX3
4
3
16
2
1
Oxford City FC
NORTHERN BY-PASS RD
Bayswater Brook
Cemy
Liby
PH
PO
Back Lane
B4495 CHERWELL DR
MARSH LA
New Marston Prim Sch
Headington
Ruskin Coll
John Radcliffe
Cemy
New Marston
St Joseph's RC Prim Sch
YH
JACK STRAW'S LA
HEADLEY WAY
MARSTON RD
Rye St Antony Sch
Headington Hill
St Michael's CE Prim Sch
Plater Coll
Headington Sch
Cuckoo La
B4495
A420
The Manor
MANOR PK
BEECH LODGE
1 HASTOE GRANGE
2 HEADLEY HO
3 RAYSON HO
ALESWORTH GR 1
BROADHEAD PL 2
22

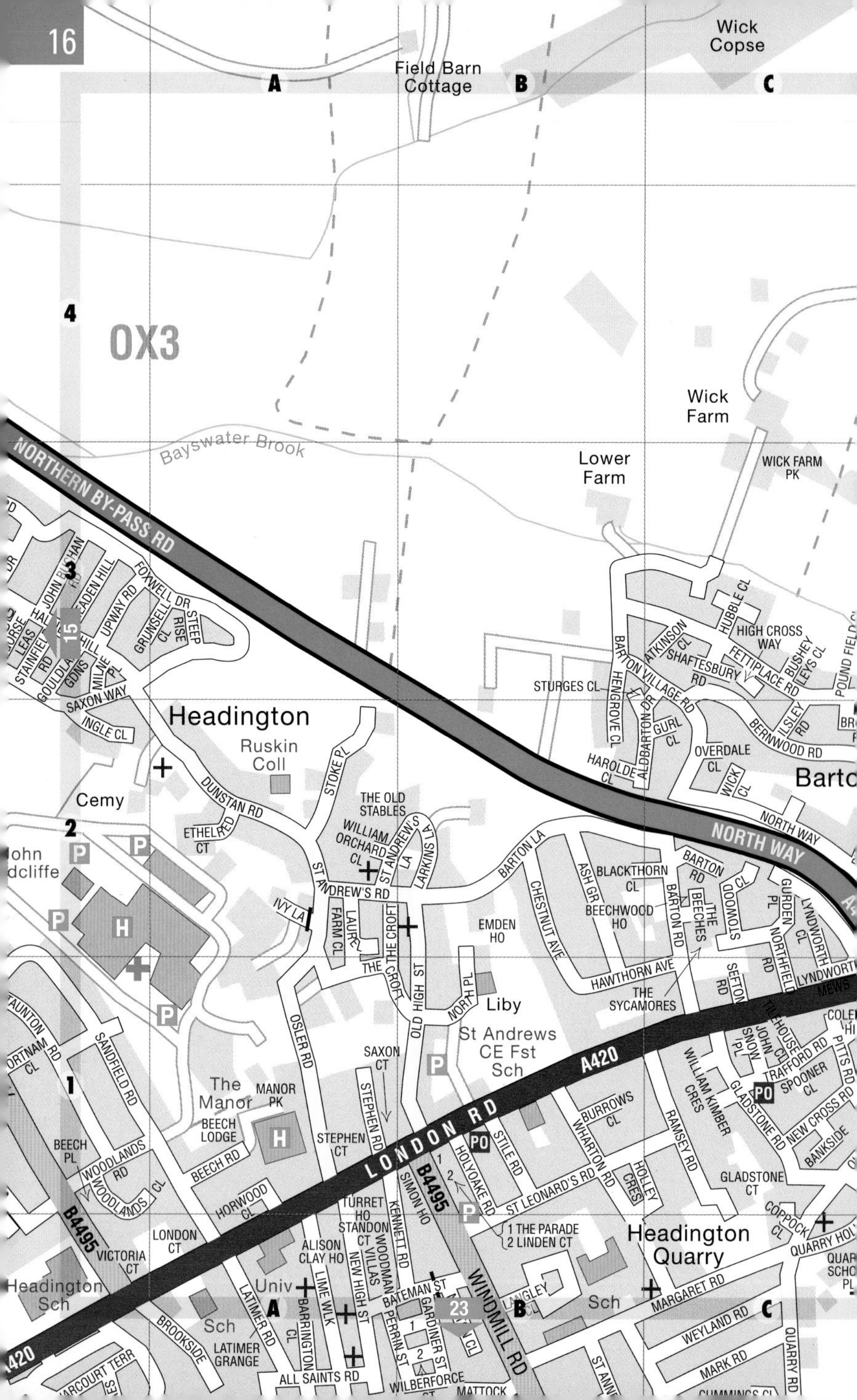
Field Barn
Cottage
Wick
Copse
OX3
Bayswater Brook
NORTHERN BY-PASS RD
Wick
Farm
Lower
Farm
WICK FARM
PK
Headington
Ruskin
Coll
Cemy
John
Radcliffe
The
Manor
St Andrews
CE Fst
Sch
Liby
LONDON RD
A420
B4495
NORTH WAY
Headington
Quarry
Barton
Headington
Sch
Univ
Sch
WINDMILL RD
23
15

A
B
C
OX3
Shepherd's Pit
OX33
4
Ashen Copse
Crem
STOWFORD CT
3
Bayswater Mill
Stowford Farm
STAGGS GATE
BAYSWATER RD
WAYNFLETE RD
STOWFORD RD
HANDLO PL
MATHER RD
ROUTH RD
HUMFREY RD
BAYSWATER FARM
BASSETT RD
WATERMILL WAY
BAYSWATER FARM RD
CRANLEY RD
MALFORD RD
CLAYMOND RD
THE DALE
COLWELL DR
ROBERTS CL
HILL VIEW
BURDELL AVE
DELBUSH AVE
Sandhills
Sandhills Com Prim Sch
2
MEREWOOD AVE
GREEN RIDGES
ELTON CL
TERRETT AVE
SWEET GREEN CL
CRESS HILL PL
HEADINGTON RDBT
LYDIA CL
THE ROUNDWAY
Sch
BURLINGTON CRES
HOSKER CL
BURSILL CL
A40
LONDON RD
OX3
A40 M40 Juncs 8a,8
A4142
FOREST RD
GREEN RD
RIDGEWAY RD
THE LINK
STANWAY RD
THE LARCHES
DOWNSIDE END
ROWLANDS HO
P&R
DOWNSIDE RD
POND CL
RINGWOOD RD
COLLINWOOD CL
COLLINWOOD RD
PO
Risinghurst
Swilly
1
Thornhill Farm
GROVELANDS RD
SHELLEY CL
KILN LA
BAKER CL
CARTER CL
RICHARDS WAY
Liby
NETHERWOODS RD
LEWIS CL
WYCHWOOD LA
SERMON CL
SLAYMAKER CL
SPRING LA

24

A
B
C
Cowleaze Copse
Oaken Holt
Bean Wood
4
Higgins's Copse
Tilbury Farm
Hill End (Field Studies Ctr)
Hill End Farm House
OX2
EYNSHAM RD
Stimpson's Cottages
3
HOMESTALL CL
POTTLE CL
STONE CL
STIMPSONS CL
FOGWELL RD
BUSHY CL
B4044
Red House Farm
A420
ASHCROFT CL
LONG CL
BROAD CL
NOBLES LA
TUDOR CT
FOGWELL RD
GRANGE CT
EYNSHAM RD
2
NOBLES CL
GREEN LA
PINNOCKS WAY
ORCHARD RD
THIRD ACRE RISE
QUEENS CL
Dean Court
STUBBLE CL
DENTON CL
BROWNS CL
SONGERS CL
DEAN COURT RD
Denman's Farm
Hid's Copse
CUMNOR HILL
1
A420
Saddle Copse
HID'S COPSE RD
DELAMARE WAY
OX2
COTSWOLD RD
HILLSIDE
BARN CL
Long Copse
COLEGROVE DOWN
CLOVER CL
Chawley

28
29

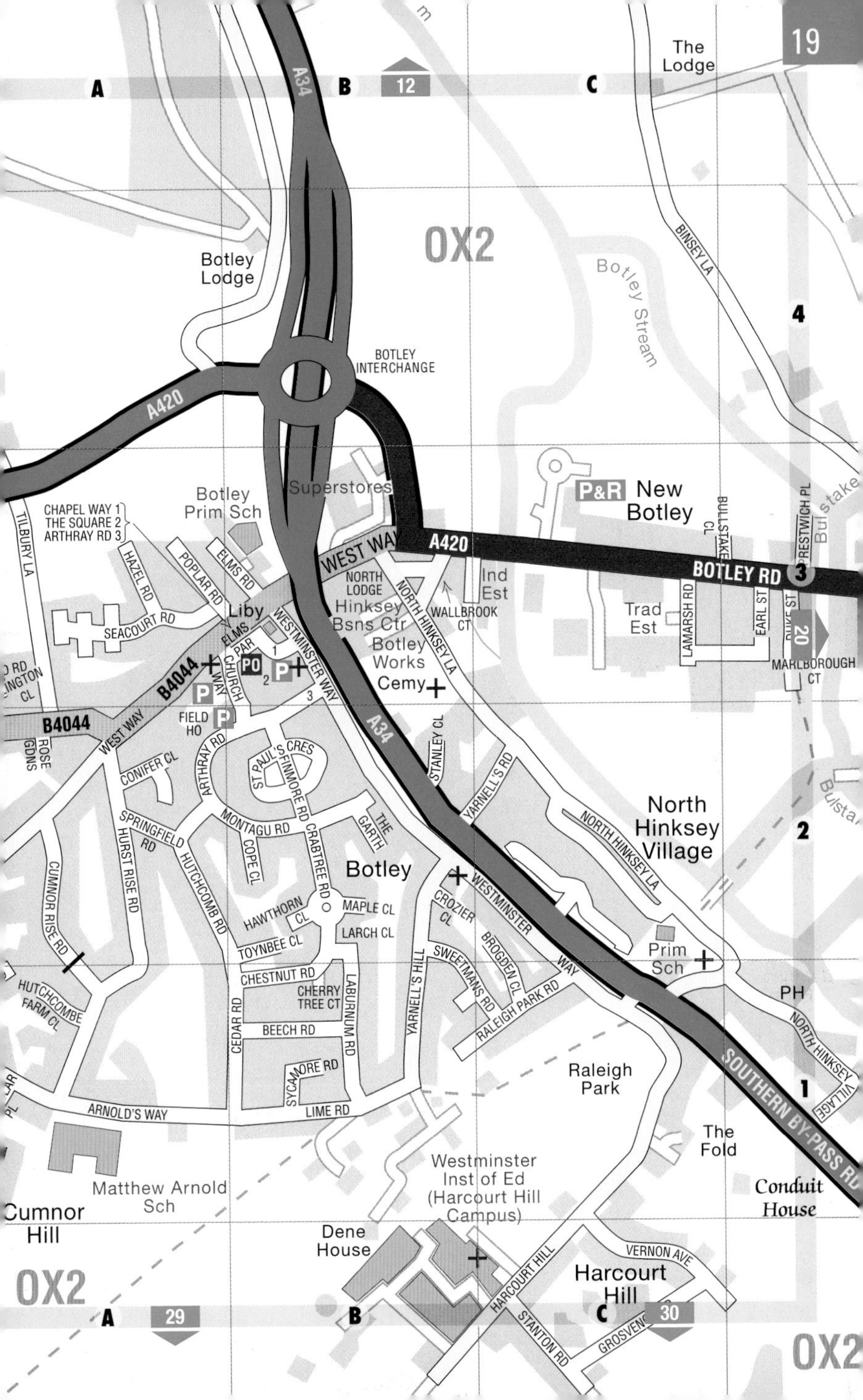
The Lodge
A
B
12
C
A34
OX2
Botley Lodge
Botley Stream
BINSEY LA
4
BOTLEY INTERCHANGE
A420
Superstores
P&R
New Botley
Botley Prim Sch
CHAPEL WAY 1
THE SQUARE 2
ARTHRAY RD 3
TILBURY LA
HAZEL RD
POPLAR RD
ELMS RD
WEST WAY
A420
BULLSTAKE CL
PRESTWICH PL
Bulstake
BOTLEY RD
3
NORTH LODGE
Ind Est
Trad Est
LAMARSH RD
EARL ST
DUKE ST
20
SEACOURT RD
Liby
ELMS PAR
WESTMINSTER WAY
Hinksey Bsns Ctr
NORTH HINKSEY LA
WALLBROOK CT
MARLBOROUGH CT
Botley Works
Cemy
B4044
CHURCH WAY
PO
1
2
3
FIELD HO
B4044
WEST WAY
ROSE GDNS
A34
STANLEY CL
YARNELL'S RD
CONIFER CL
ARTHRAY RD
ST PAUL'S CRES
FINMORE RD
North Hinksey Village
NORTH HINKSEY LA
Bulstake
2
SPRINGFIELD RD
HURST RISE RD
HUTCHCOMB RD
MONTAGU RD
COPE CL
CRABTREE RD
THE GARTH
CUMNOR RISE RD
Botley
WESTMINSTER WAY
HAWTHORN CL
MAPLE CL
CROZIER CL
LARCH CL
TOYNBEE CL
SWEETMANS RD
BROGDEN CL
Prim Sch
HUTCHCOMBE FARM CL
CHESTNUT RD
CHERRY TREE CT
RALEIGH PARK RD
PH
CEDAR RD
BEECH RD
LABURNUM RD
YARNELL'S HILL
Raleigh Park
NORTH HINKSEY VILLAGE
SOUTHERN BY-PASS RD
1
SYCAMORE RD
ARNOLD'S WAY
LIME RD
The Fold
Westminster Inst of Ed (Harcourt Hill Campus)
Conduit House
Matthew Arnold Sch
Cumnor Hill
Dene House
VERNON AVE
HARCOURT HILL
Harcourt Hill
OX2
A
29
B
C
30
STANTON RD
GROSVENOR RD
OX2

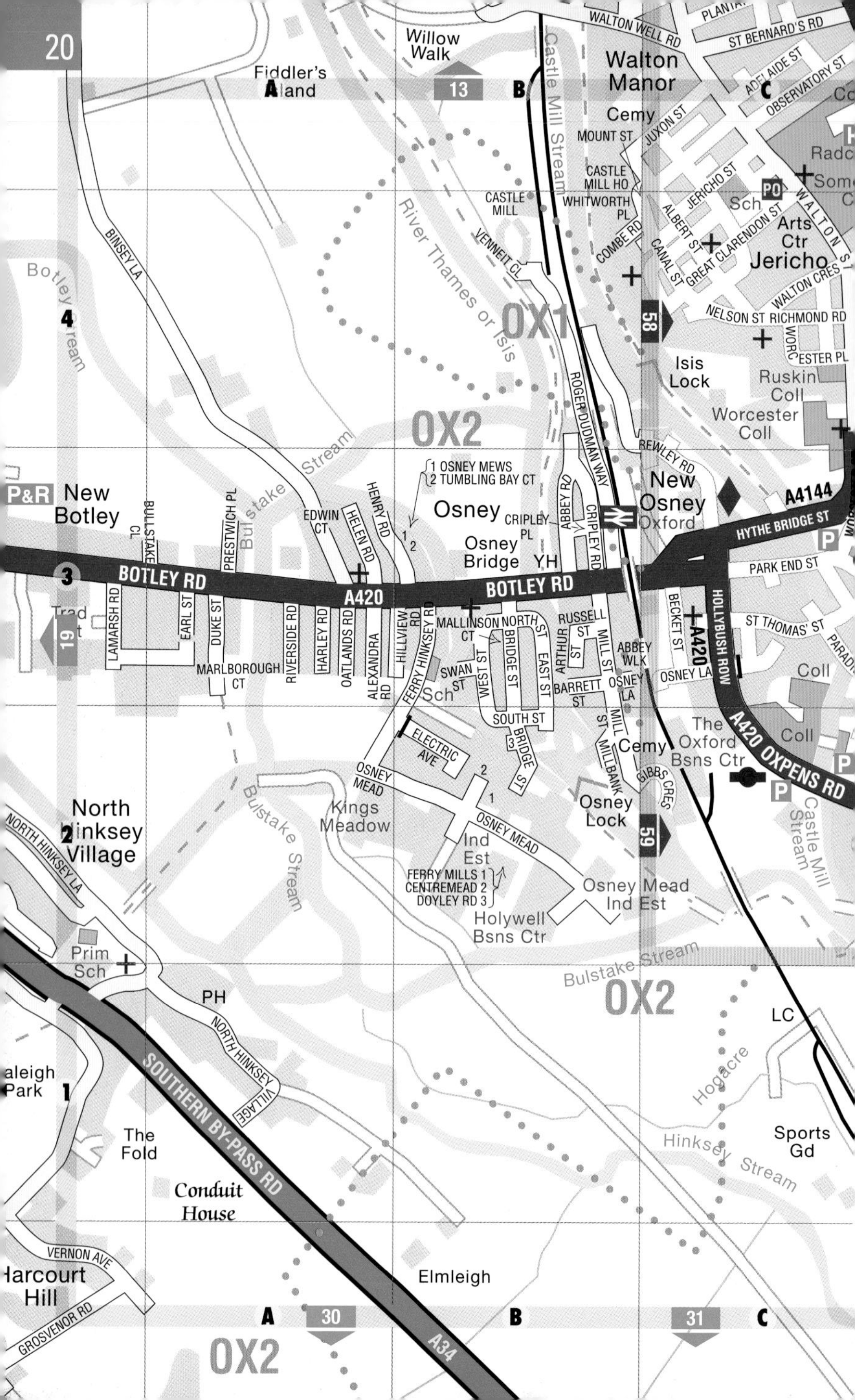
Willow Walk
Fiddler's Island
13
Walton Well Rd
St Bernard's Rd
Walton Manor
Adelaide St
Observatory St
Cemy
Juxon St
Mount St
Castle Mill Ho
Castle Mill Stream
Castle Mill
Whitworth Pl
Jericho St
Sch
PO
Radc
Albert St
Great Clarendon St
Arts Ctr
Jericho
Combe Rd
Canal St
Walton St
Walton Cres
Venneit Cl
River Thames or Isis
OX1
58
Nelson St
Richmond Rd
Worcester Pl
Isis Lock
Ruskin Coll
Worcester Coll
Roger Dudman Way
OX2
Botley Stream
Binsey La
Bulstake Stream
1 Osney Mews
2 Tumbling Bay Ct
Rewley Rd
New Osney
P&R
New Botley
Osney
Cripley Pl
Abbey Rd
Cripley Rd
Oxford
A4144
Hythe Bridge St
Bullstake Cl
Prestwich Pl
Edwin Ct
Helen Rd
Henry Rd
Osney Bridge
YH
Botley Rd
A420
Park End St
Lamarsh Rd
Earl St
Duke St
Riverside Rd
Harley Rd
Oatlands Rd
Alexandra Rd
Hillview Rd
Ferry Hinksey Rd
Mallinson Ct
North St
Russell St
Beckett St
Hollybush Row
St Thomas' St
19
Marlborough Ct
Swan St
West St
Bridge St
East St
Arthur St
Mill St
Abbey Wlk
Osney La
Barrett St
Sch
Coll
Electric Ave
South St
The Oxford Bsns Ctr
A420 Oxpens Rd
Osney Mead
Kings Meadow
Gibbs Cres
Millbank
Cemy
Osney Lock
North Hinksey Village
North Hinksey La
Ind Est
59
Ferry Mills 1
Centremead 2
Doyley Rd 3
Osney Mead Ind Est
Holywell Bsns Ctr
Prim Sch
PH
Bulstake Stream
LC
Hogacre
Raleigh Park
Southern By-Pass Rd
The Fold
Sports Gd
Hinksey Stream
Conduit House
Vernon Ave
Harcourt Hill
Elmleigh
Grosvenor Rd
30
31
A34
OX2

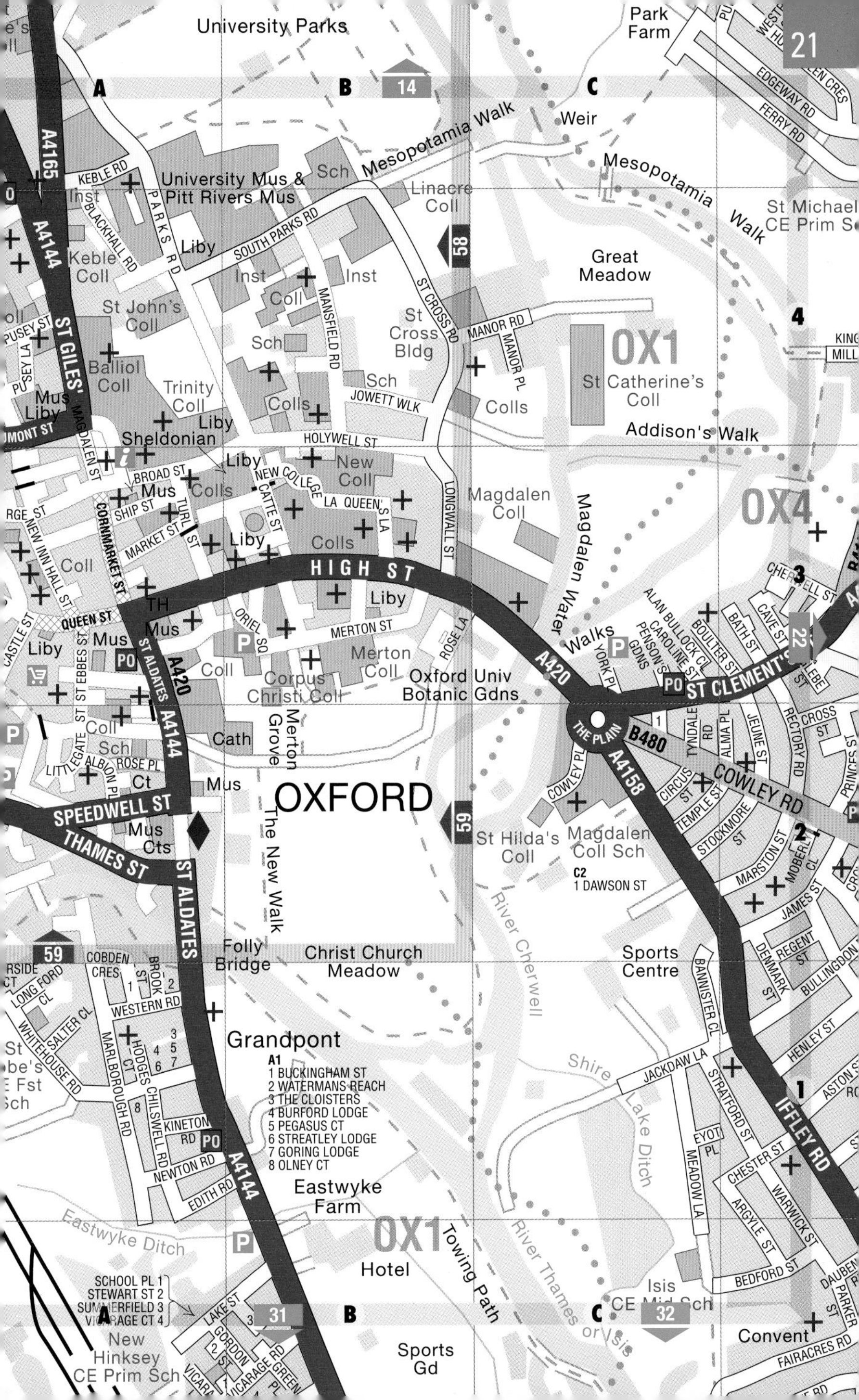
University Parks
Park Farm
A
B
C
14
Mesopotamia Walk
Weir
KEBLE RD
University Mus &
Pitt Rivers Mus
Sch
Linacre Coll
Inst
BLACKHALL RD
PARKS RD
SOUTH PARKS RD
Liby
Keble Coll
Inst
Coll
Inst
MANSFIELD RD
ST CROSS RD
58
Great Meadow
St Michael CE Prim Sch
St John's Coll
St Cross Bldg
MANOR RD
MANOR PL
OX1
St Catherine's Coll
PUSEY ST
Balliol Coll
Trinity Coll
Sch
Sch
JOWETT WALK
Colls
Colls
Addison's Walk
ST GILES'
A4165
A4144
Mus
Liby
MAGDALEN ST
Liby
Sheldonian
HOLYWELL ST
BROAD ST
Liby
NEW COLLEGE LA
New Coll
QUEEN'S LA
CATTE ST
LONGWALL ST
Magdalen Coll
Magdalen Water Walks
OX4
Mus
SHIP ST
Colls
TURL ST
CORNMARKET ST
MARKET ST
Liby
Colls
NEW INN HALL ST
Coll
HIGH ST
Liby
CHERWELL ST
QUEEN ST
TH
Mus
ORIEL SQ
MERTON ST
ROSE LA
ALAN BULLOCK CL
CAROLINE ST
PENSON'S GDNS
BOULTER ST
BATH ST
CAVE ST
22
CASTLE ST
Liby
Mus
PO
ST ALDATES
A420
Coll
Corpus Christi Coll
Merton Coll
Oxford Univ Botanic Gdns
YORK PL
PO
ST CLEMENT'S
ST EBBES ST
LITTLEGATE ST
Coll
Sch
Merton Grove
THE PLAIN
B480
TYNDALE RD
ALMA PL
JEUNE ST
RECTORY RD
CROSS ST
PRINCES ST
ALBION PL
ROSE PL
Ct
Cath
Mus
COWLEY PL
A4158
CIRCUS ST
TEMPLE ST
COWLEY RD
SPEEDWELL ST
OXFORD
The New Walk
59
Mus
Cts
St Hilda's Coll
Magdalen Coll Sch
STOCKMORE ST
MARSTON ST
MOBERLY CL
THAMES ST
ST ALDATES
C2
1 DAWSON ST
JAMES ST
River Cherwell
59
COBDEN CRES
BROOK ST
LONGFORD CL
Folly Bridge
Christ Church Meadow
Sports Centre
BANNISTER CL
DENMARK ST
REGENT ST
BULLINGDON RD
WESTERN RD
SALTER CL
WHITEHOUSE RD
MARLBOROUGH RD
HODGES CT
Grandpont
A1
1 BUCKINGHAM ST
2 WATERMANS REACH
3 THE CLOISTERS
4 BURFORD LODGE
5 PEGASUS CT
6 STREATLEY LODGE
7 GORING LODGE
8 OLNEY CT
Shire Lake Ditch
JACKDAW LA
STRATFORD ST
HENLEY ST
ASTON ST
IFFLEY RD
CHILSWELL RD
KINETON RD
PO
NEWTON RD
EDITH RD
A4144
EYOT PL
MEADOW LA
CHESTER ST
WARWICK ST
ARGYLE ST
Eastwyke Farm
Eastwyke Ditch
OX1
Towing Path
Hotel
River Thames or Isis
BEDFORD ST
Isis CE Mid Sch
SCHOOL PL 1
STEWART ST 2
SUMMERFIELD 3
VICARAGE CT 4
LAKE ST
31
32
DAUBENY RD
PARKER ST
New Hinksey CE Prim Sch
GORDON ST
VICARAGE RD
GREEN PL
Sports Gd
Convent
FAIRACRES RD

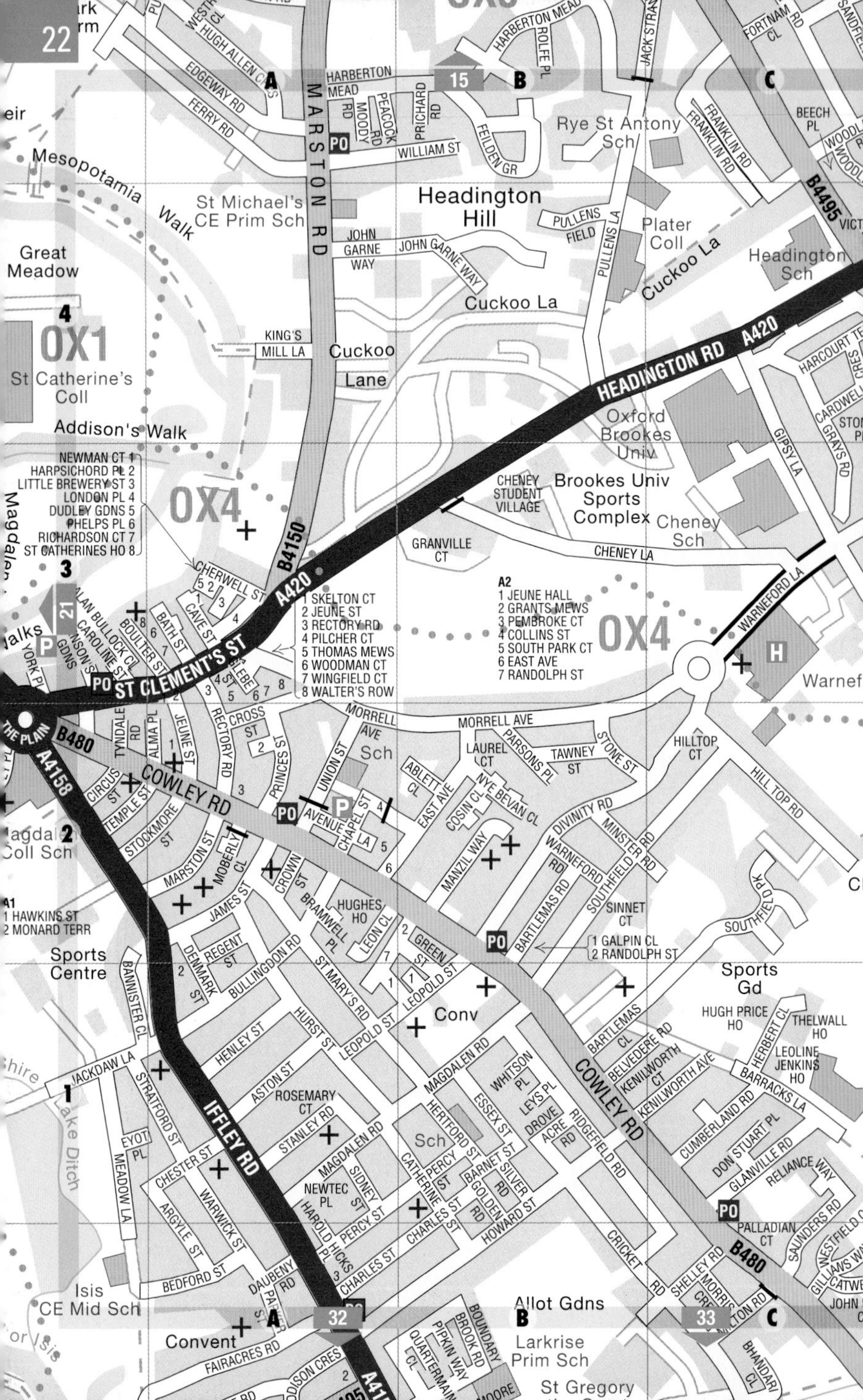

15
A
B
C
Harberton Mead
Rolfe Pl
Jack Straw's La
Fortnam Cl
Hugh Allen Cres
Edgeway Rd
Ferry Rd
Marston Rd
Moody Rd
Peacock Rd
Prichard Rd
William St
PO
Feilden Gr
Rye St Antony Sch
Franklin Rd
Beech Pl
B4495
Mesopotamia Walk
St Michael's CE Prim Sch
Headington Hill
Pullens Field
Pullens La
Plater Coll
Headington Sch
Great Meadow
John Garne Way
Cuckoo La
4
OX1
St Catherine's Coll
King's Mill La
Cuckoo Lane
Headington Rd
A420
Harcourt Ter
Cardwell Cres
Grays Rd
Gipsy La
Addison's Walk
Oxford Brookes Univ
Cheney Student Village
Brookes Univ Sports Complex
Cheney Sch
Cheney La
Granville Ct
OX4
B4150
NEWMAN CT 1
HARPSICHORD PL 2
LITTLE BREWERY ST 3
LONDON PL 4
DUDLEY GDNS 5
PHELPS PL 6
RICHARDSON CT 7
ST CATHERINES HO 8
3
21
Cherwell St
Cave St
Bath St
Boulter St
Caroline St
York Pl
1 SKELTON CT
2 JEUNE ST
3 RECTORY RD
4 PILCHER CT
5 THOMAS MEWS
6 WOODMAN CT
7 WINGFIELD CT
8 WALTER'S ROW
A2
1 JEUNE HALL
2 GRANTS MEWS
3 PEMBROKE CT
4 COLLINS ST
5 SOUTH PARK CT
6 EAST AVE
7 RANDOLPH ST
Warneford La
H
St Clement's St
The Plain
B480
A4158
Tyndale Rd
Alma Pl
Jeune St
Rectory Rd
Cross St
Princes St
Morrell Ave
Union St
Sch
Laurel Ct
Parsons Pl
Tawney St
Stone St
Hilltop Ct
Hill Top Rd
Cowley Rd
Circus St
Temple St
Stockmore St
Ablett Cl
East Ave
Cosin Cl
Nye Bevan Cl
Avenue La
Chapel St
Manzil Way
Divinity Rd
Minster Rd
Warneford Rd
Southfield Rd
Southfield Pk
Magdalen Coll Sch
2
Marston St
Moberly Cl
Crown St
Bramwell Pl
Hughes Ho
Leon Cl
Green St
Bartlemas Rd
Sinnet Ct
1 GALPIN CL
2 RANDOLPH ST
A1
1 HAWKINS ST
2 MONARD TERR
James St
Regent St
Denmark St
Bullingdon Rd
St Mary's Rd
Leopold St
Sports Centre
Sports Gd
Bannister Cl
Conv
Bartlemas Cl
Belvedere Rd
Kenilworth Ct
Kenilworth Ave
Hugh Price Ho
Herbert Cl
Thelwall Ho
Leoline Jenkins Ho
Henley St
Hurst St
Magdalen Rd
Whitson Pl
Essex St
Leys Pl
Drove Acre Rd
Ridgefield Rd
Barracks La
Cumberland Rd
Jackdaw La
1
Stratford St
Iffley Rd
Aston St
Rosemary Ct
Stanley Rd
Hertford St
Don Stuart Pl
Glanville Rd
Reliance Way
Lake Ditch
Eyot Pl
Meadow La
Chester St
Warwick St
Sidney St
Newtec Pl
Catherine St
Percy St
Barnet St
Silver Rd
Golden Rd
Howard St
Charles St
Harold Hicks Pl
Cricket Rd
Shelley Rd
Morris Cres
PO
Palladian Ct
Saunders Rd
Westfield Cl
B480
Argyle St
Bedford St
Daubeny Rd
Parker St
Isis CE Mid Sch
Allot Gdns
32
33
Convent
Fairacres Rd
Boundary Brook Rd
Pipkin Way
Quartermain Cl
Larkrise Prim Sch
St Gregory
Bhandari Cl
A4158
Moore

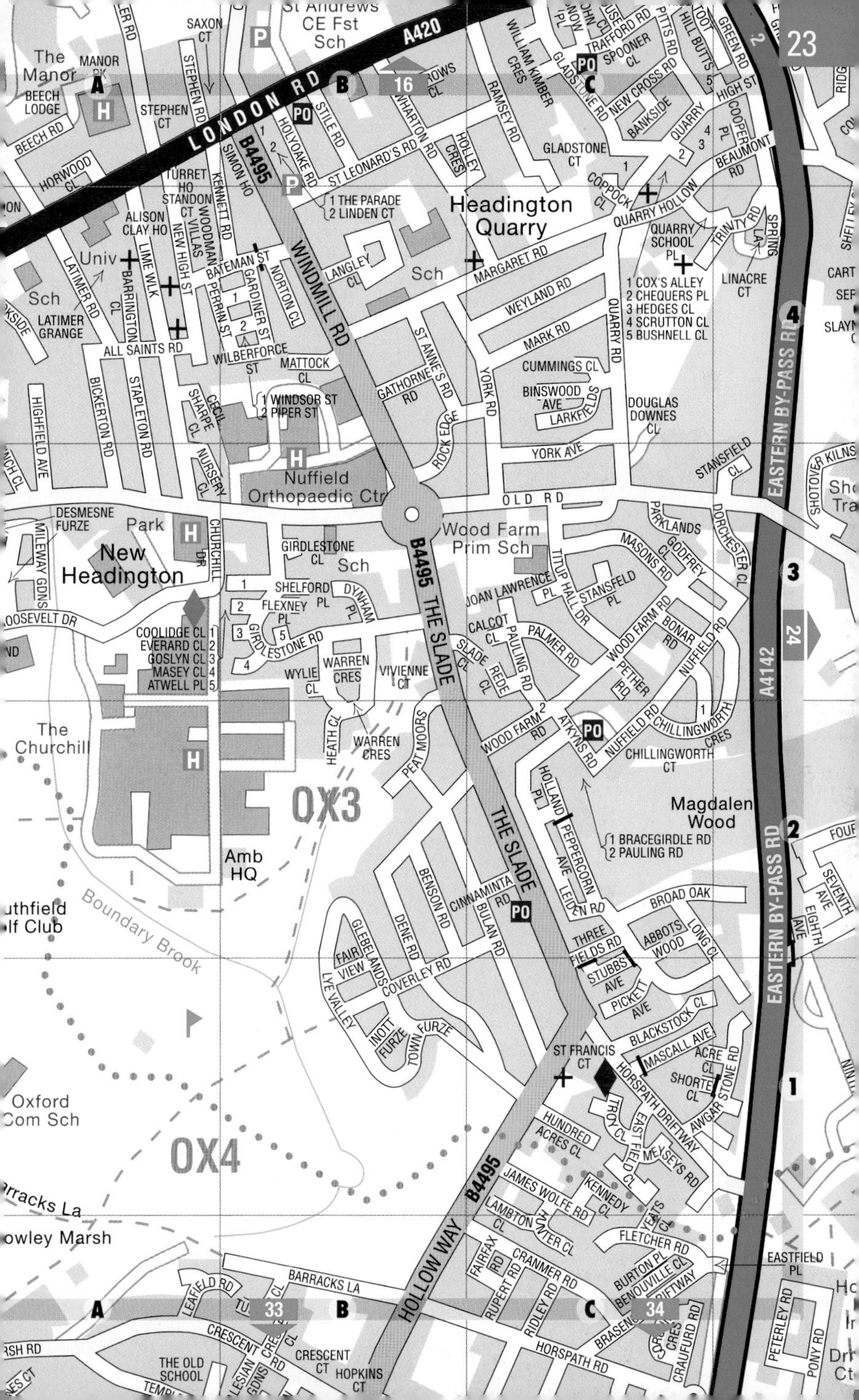

Headington Quarry
New Headington
Nuffield Orthopaedic Ctr
Wood Farm Prim Sch
Magdalen Wood
The Churchill
Amb HQ
Oxford Com Sch
OX3
OX4
LONDON RD
A420
B4495
WINDMILL RD
THE SLADE
HOLLOW WAY
OLD RD
EASTERN BY-PASS RD
A4142
Boundary Brook
Barracks La
Cowley Marsh
St Andrews CE Fst Sch
The Manor
1 THE PARADE
2 LINDEN CT
1 COX'S ALLEY
2 CHEQUERS PL
3 HEDGES CL
4 SCRUTTON CL
5 BUSHNELL CL
1 WINDSOR ST
2 PIPER ST
COOLIDGE CL
EVERARD CL
GOSLYN CL
MASEY CL
ATWELL PL
1 BRACEGIRDLE RD
2 PAULING RD

16
24
33
34

Risinghurst
Swilly
P&R
DOWNSIDE END
ROWLANDS HO
STANWAY RD
THE LINK
COLLINWOOD RD
COLLINWOOD CL
DOWNSIDE RD
GROVELANDS RD
KILN LA
SHELLEY CL
BAKER CL
CARTER CL
SERMON CL
SLAYMAKER CL
RICHARDS WAY
NETHERWOODS RD
LEWIS CL
WYCHWOOD LA
Liby
HAROLD WHITE CL 1
KNIGHTS HO 2
PO
NEW CROSS RD
BANKSIDE
QUARRY
HIGH ST
COOPER PL
BEAUMONT RD
QUARRY HOLLOW
COPPOCK CL
QUARRY SCHOOL PL
TRINITY RD
SPRING LA
LINACRE CT
QUARRY RD
DOUGLAS DOWNES CL
STANSFIELD CL
EASTERN BY-PASS RD
A4142
SHOTOVER KILNS
Shotover Trad Est
Monk's Wood
Monk's Farm
Shotover Hill
Forest Farm
OLD RD
Shotover Plain
PARKLANDS
DORCHESTER CL
MASONS RD
GODFREY CL
STANSFIELD PL
BONAR RD
NUFFIELD RD
PETHER RD
1 BRACEGIRDLE RD
2 CHILLINGWORTH CRES
3 FORESTERS TOWER
THE RIDINGS
CHILLINGWORTH CRES
CHILLINGWORTH CT
Shotover Cleve
Shotover Country Park
Magdalen Wood
FOURTH AVE
SEVENTH AVE
EIGHTH AVE
FIRST AVE
BROAD OAK
ABBOTS WOOD
LONG CL
THREE FIELDS RD
STUBBS AVE
PICKETT AVE
BLACKSTOCK CL
MASCALL AVE
ACRE CL
SHORTE CL
STONE RD
AWGAR
HORSPATH DRIFTWAY
FRANCIS CT
TROY CL
EAST FIELD CL
MEYSEYS RD
KENNEDY CL
YEATS CL
FLETCHER RD
BURTON PL
BENOUVILLE CL
BRASENOSE DRIFTWAY
CORUNNA CRES
CRAUFURD RD
OX3
Westhill Farm
Brasenose Wood
NINTH AVE
1 OLD BARN GROUND
2 NETHER DURNFORD CL
Open Brasnose
OX33
Brasenose Farm
EASTFIELD PL
OX4
Horspath Ro Ind Est
PETERLEY RD
PONY RD
Drift Ctr
Sports Ground
17
34
35
23
A
B
C
1
2
3
4

A40 Oxford (A420)
A
B
C
Thornhill Farm
Lodge
A40
Pointed Covert
Shotover House
4
Obelisk
Thorn Hill
OX3
The Spinney
3
Home Farm
26
OX33
Ochre Pits
The Common
Shotover Plain
2
OLD RD
Horspath Common
KEYDALE RD
ACREMEAD RD
KELLY'S RD
Piggery
Shotover Orchards
Three Acre
Sandy La
BLENHEIM ROAD
Blenheim
Littlew
1
Ways Farm
BLENHEIM WAY
SPRING LA
Horspath CE Prim Sch
PROSPECT PK
COLLCUTT CL
GIDLEY WAY
GATELEY
MANOR FARM RD
FORDS CL
CHURCH RD
WRIGHTSON CL
BUTTS RD
MANOR DR
HORSEPATH PARK CVN SITE
HILL RISE
CENTRE RISE
SUNNY RISE
VALLEY RD
35
Green Gates
PO
PH
Horspath
THE GREEN

A
B
C
Red Hill
Keeper's Cottage
Warren Farm
Warren Wood
Lodge
A40
Lyehill Quarries (dis)
Shotover House
B4027
4
Obelisk
OX33
Wheatley Park Sch
Recn Gd
Liby
Sports Ctr
John Watson Sch
3
Home Farm
25
PARK HILL
WESTFIELD RD
LONDON RD
MORLAND CL
WESTFIELD RD
KILN LA
TEMPLARS CL
GARDINER CL
ST MARY'S CL
The Common
BLENHEIM LA
HOLLOWAY RD
ST MARY'S HO
THE GLEBE
Wheatley CE Prim Sch
LITTLEWORTH RD
CHURCH RD
2
LITTLEWORTH RD
Liby
BARLOW CL
HIGH ST
PO
BELL LA
FRIDAY LA
CROWN SQ
WREN RD
KEYDALE RD
BEECHING WAY
HATHAWAYS
STATION RD
SIMON'S CL
CL
FARM CLOSE
FARM CLOSE RD
ACREMEAD RD
KELLY'S RD
COOPERS CT
Wheatley
LA
MULBERRY DR
KIMBER CL
HOWE CL
BEECH RD
ORCHARD CL
Littleworth Ind Est
LITTLEWORTH PK
KELHAM HALL DR
Littleworth Bsns Ctr
Littleworth
Windmill (disused)
WINDMILL LA
1
Ways Farm
WINDMILL LA
LADDER HILL
Coombe House
A
B
C

Pond Farm
A
B
C
Old Park Farm
BURYHOOK CNR
Cottage Copse
Warwick Close Farm
4
OX33
The Rectory
Holton Place
Holton
Church Farm
3
Wheatley Campus (Brookes Univ)
Garden Copse
COLLEGE CL
Bsns Ctr
BISCOE CT
FAIRFAX GATE
SUNNYSIDE
TYNDALE PL
OLD LONDON RD
2
Holton Mill House
ANSON CL
AMBROSE RISE
CULLUM HO
River Thame
CULLUM RD
LEYSHON RD
THE AVENUE
LONDON RD
MILLER RD
HILLARY WAY
ELM CL
WINDOWS CT
ELTON CRES
ROMAN RD
Wheatley Bridge
A40
1
Sewage Works
PH
Hotel
A40 M40 juncs 8a,8
ASHHURST CT
OX33
A
B
C
Castle Hill Farm

A
B
C
18
A420
Denman's Copse
Saddle Copse
OX2
Long Copse
CHAWLEY LA
Chawley
CHAWLEY LA
NORREYS RD
NORREYS RD
BERTIE RD
OXFORD RD
CUMNOR HILL
COLEGROVE DOWN
4
3
2
1
HIGH ST
PO
College Farm
Cumnor CE Prim Sch
DENMAN'S LA
SANDS CL
A420
PH
PH
GLEBE RD
APPLETON RD
Cumnor
THE GLEBE
B4017
THE WINNYARDS
THE PARK
KENILWORTH RD
FORSTER LA
ABINGDON RD
ROBSART PL
OX2
Cross Roads Farm
Bradley Cottages
B4017
Bradley Farm
FARINGDON RD
OX1
OX2
Henwo
Farm
A
B
C
36
A420 Swindon

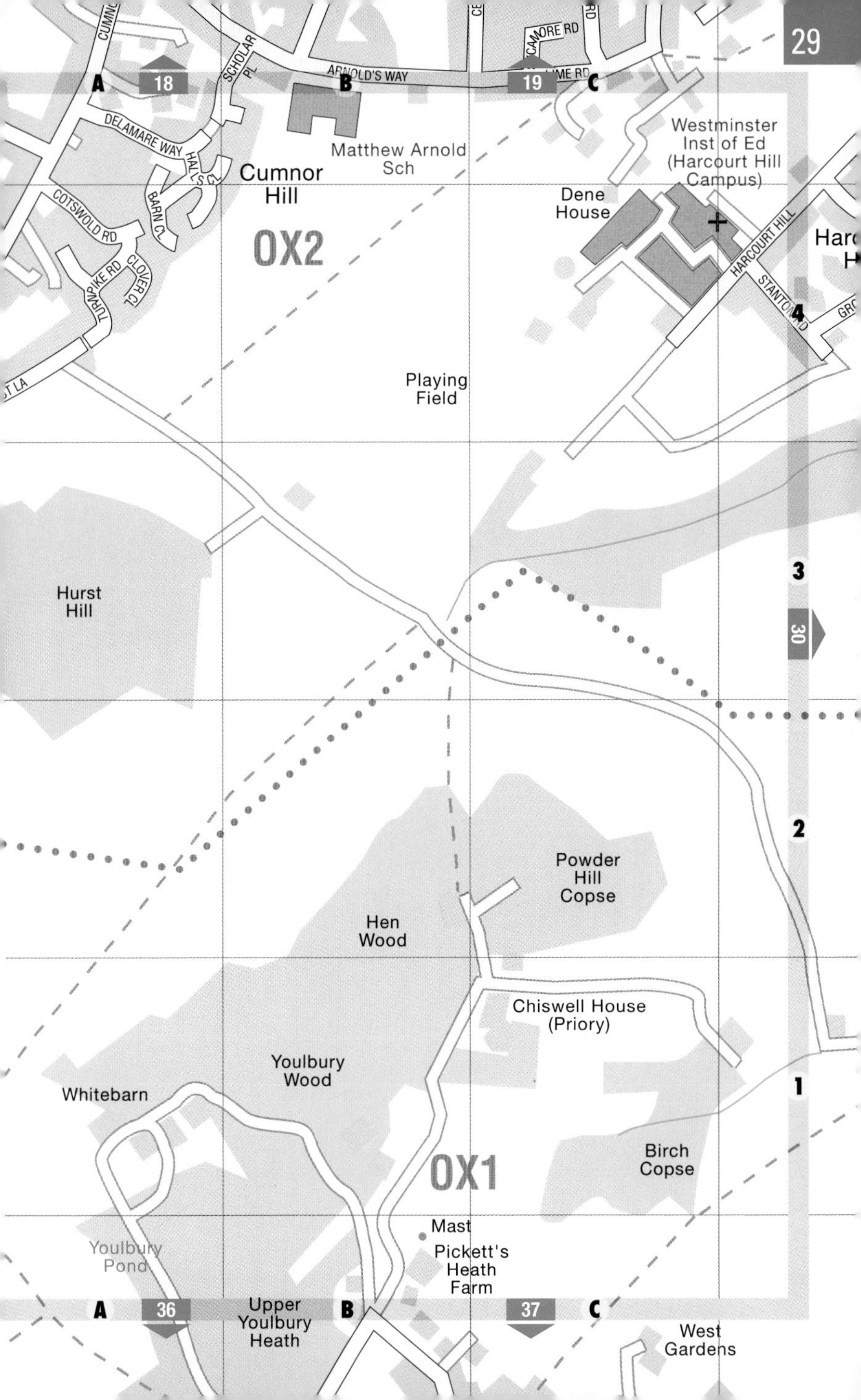
A
18
B
19
C
ARNOLD'S WAY
SCHOLAR PL
DELAMARE WAY
HALL'S CL
BARN CL
COTSWOLD RD
TURNPIKE RD
CLOVER CL
Matthew Arnold Sch
Cumnor Hill
OX2
Westminster Inst of Ed (Harcourt Hill Campus)
Dene House
HARCOURT HILL
STANTON RD
4
Playing Field
Hurst Hill
3
30
2
Powder Hill Copse
Hen Wood
Chiswell House (Priory)
Youlbury Wood
Whitebarn
1
Birch Copse
OX1
Mast
Pickett's Heath Farm
Youlbury Pond
A
36
Upper Youlbury Heath
B
37
C
West Gardens

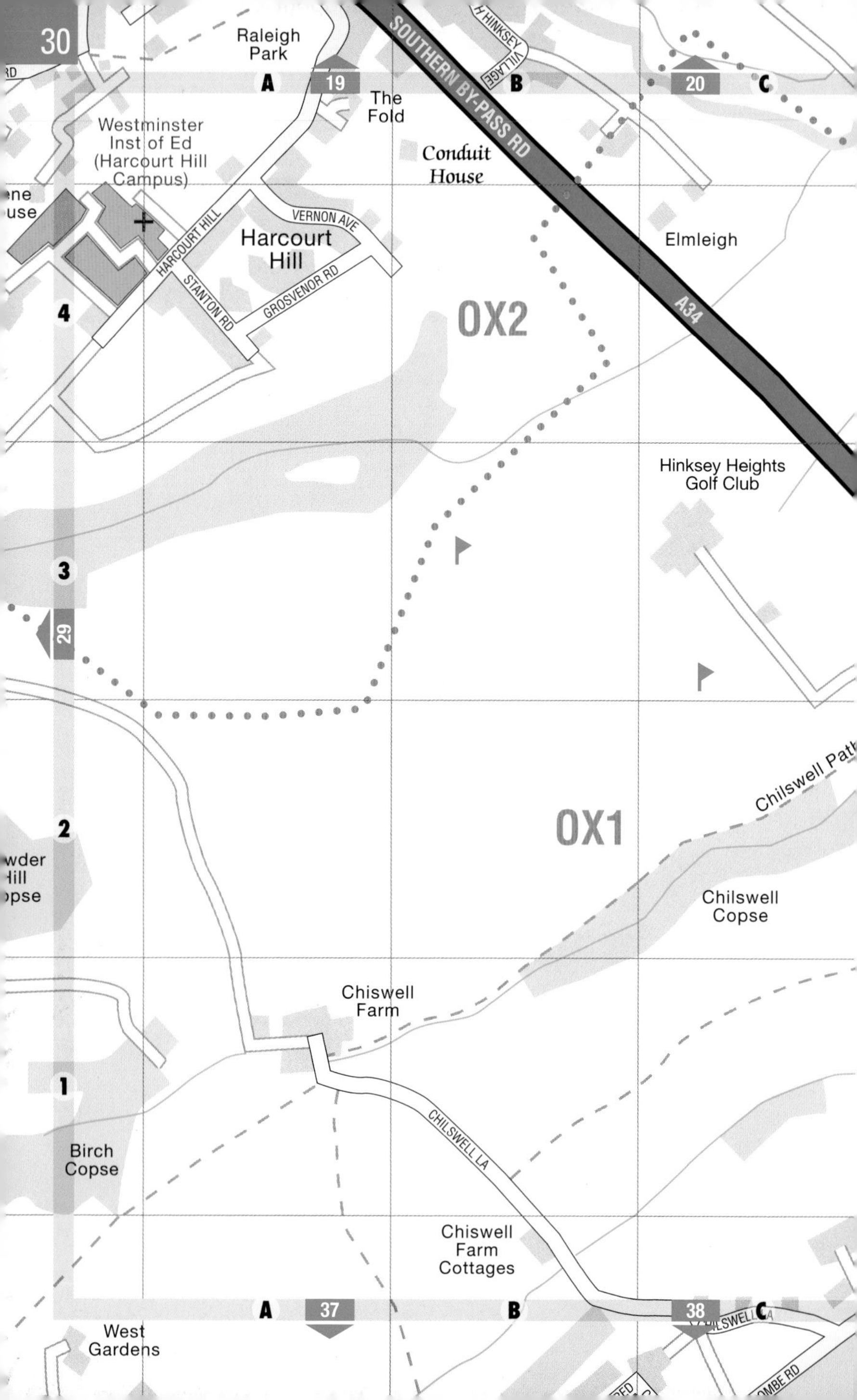

Raleigh Park
A
19
B
20
C
SOUTHERN BY-PASS RD
HINKSEY
VILLAGE
The Fold
Westminster Inst of Ed (Harcourt Hill Campus)
Conduit House
HARCOURT HILL
VERNON AVE
Harcourt Hill
STANTON RD
GROSVENOR RD
Elmleigh
A34
OX2
4
Hinksey Heights Golf Club
3
29
Chilswell Path
OX1
2
Chilswell Copse
Chiswell Farm
1
CHILSWELL LA
Birch Copse
Chiswell Farm Cottages
A
37
B
38
C
West Gardens

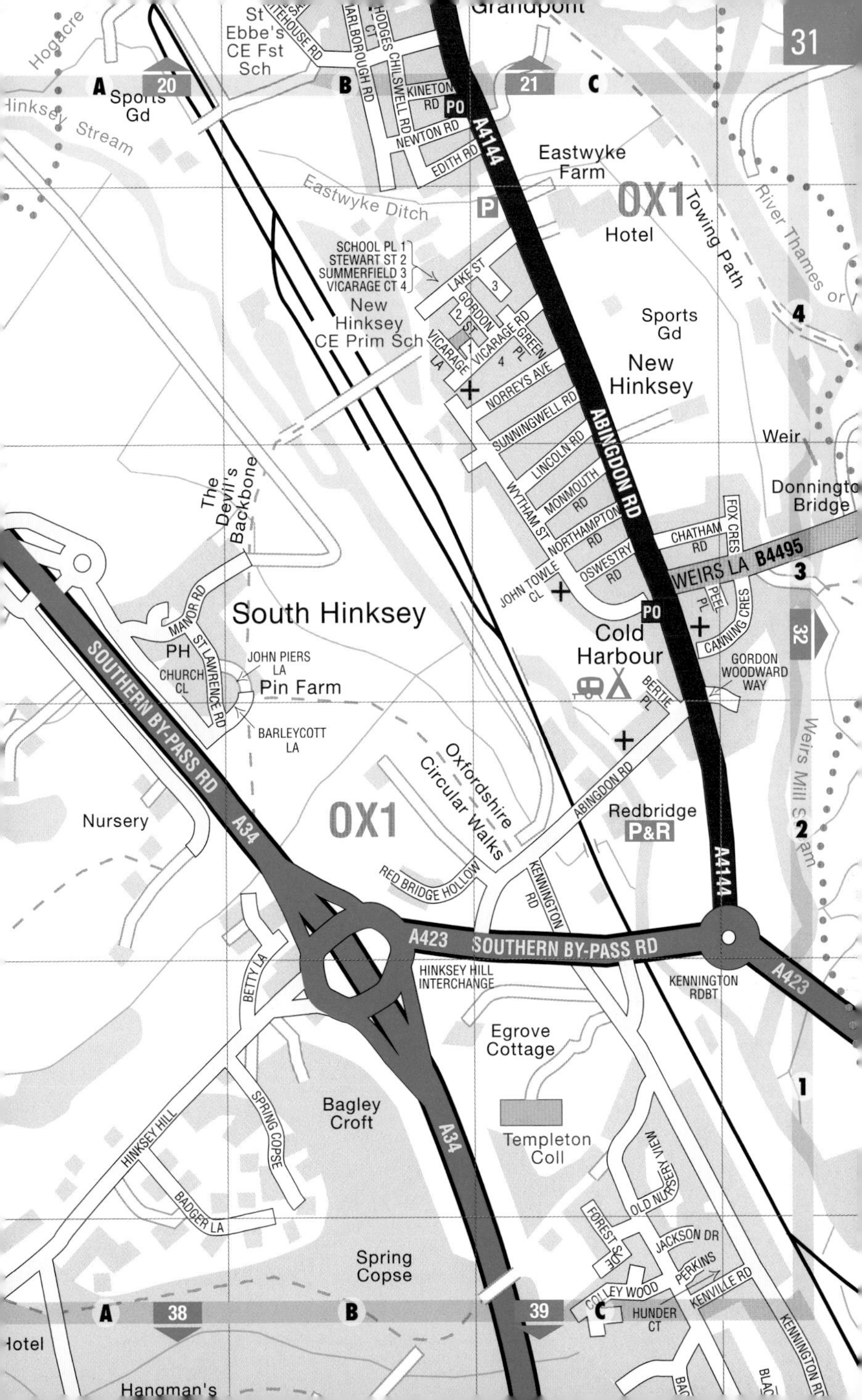

Grandpont
St Ebbe's CE Fst Sch
Hogacre
Sports Gd
Hinksey Stream
A 20 B 21 C
MARLBOROUGH RD
HODGES CT
CHILSWELL RD
KINETON RD
NEWTON RD
EDITH RD
PO
A4144
Eastwyke Farm
Eastwyke Ditch
OX1
Hotel
Towing Path
River Thames or Isis
SCHOOL PL 1
STEWART ST 2
SUMMERFIELD 3
VICARAGE CT 4
New Hinksey CE Prim Sch
LAKE ST
GORDON ST
VICARAGE LA
VICARAGE RD
GREEN PL
NORREYS AVE
SUNNINGWELL RD
LINCOLN RD
MONMOUTH RD
NORTHAMPTON RD
WYTHAM ST
OSWESTRY RD
JOHN TOWLE CL
ABINGDON RD
Sports Gd
New Hinksey
Weir
Donnington Bridge
CHATHAM RD
FOX CRES
WEIRS LA B4495
PEEL PL
CANNING CRES
PO
The Devil's Backbone
South Hinksey
MANOR RD
ST LAWRENCE RD
PH
CHURCH CL
JOHN PIERS LA
Pin Farm
BARLEYCOTT LA
Cold Harbour
BERTIE PL
GORDON WOODWARD WAY
32
Weirs Mill Stream
SOUTHERN BY-PASS RD
A34
Nursery
OX1
Oxfordshire Circular Walks
ABINGDON RD
Redbridge
P&R
RED BRIDGE HOLLOW
KENNINGTON RD
A4144
A423 SOUTHERN BY-PASS RD
HINKSEY HILL INTERCHANGE
KENNINGTON RDBT
A423
BETTY LA
Egrove Cottage
Bagley Croft
A34
Templeton Coll
HINKSEY HILL
SPRING COPSE
OLD NURSERY VIEW
BADGER LA
FOREST SIDE
JACKSON DR
PERKINS
KENVILLE RD
Spring Copse
COLLEY WOOD
HUNDER CT
KENNINGTON RD
A 38 B 39 C
Hotel
Hangman's
4
3
2
1

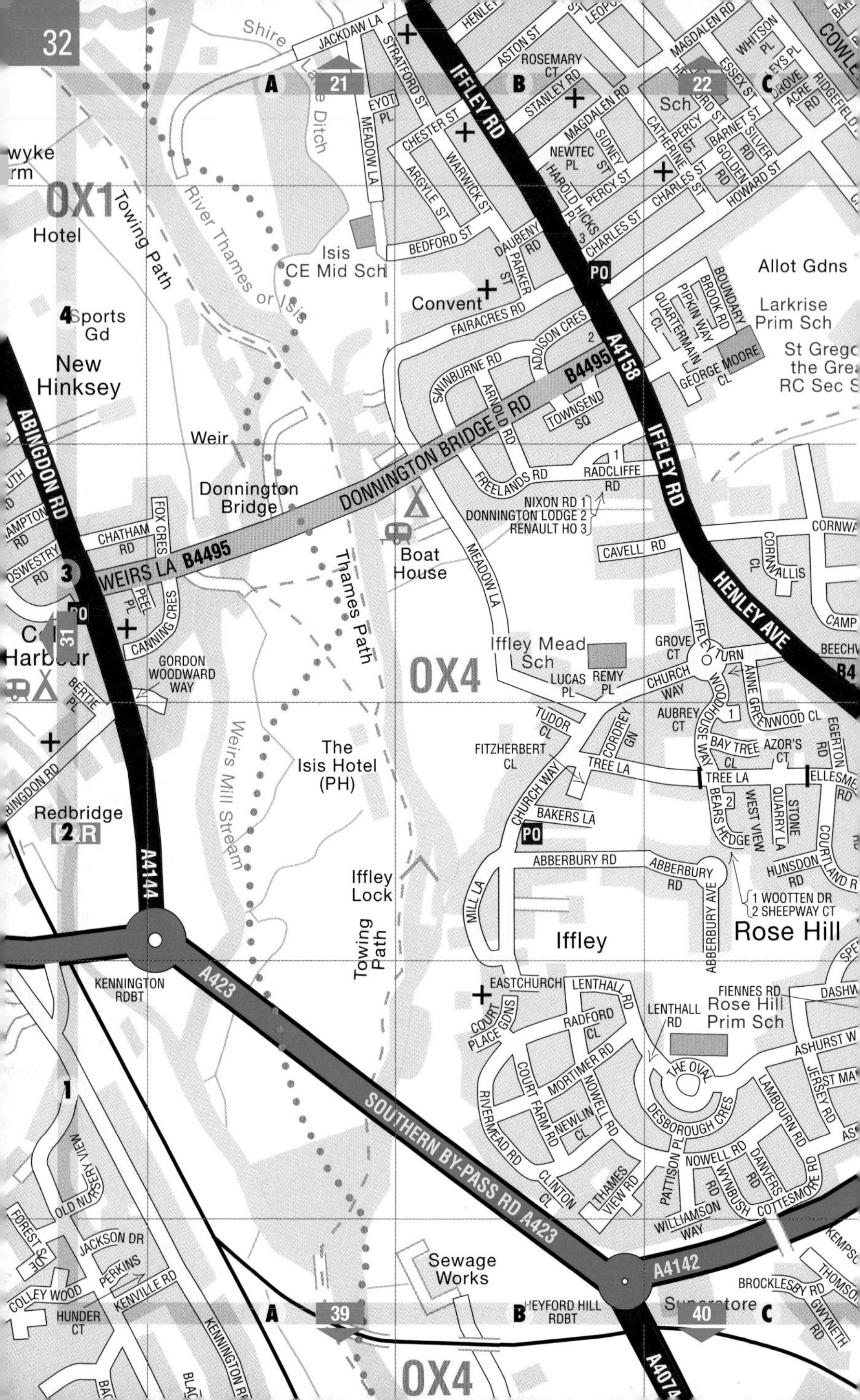
OX1
Hotel
Towing Path
River Thames or Isis
Shire Lake Ditch
Jackdaw La
Stratford St
Meadow La
Eyot Pl
Iffley Rd
Henley
Aston St
Rosemary Ct
Stanley Rd
Magdalen Rd
Whitson Pl
Cowley
Essex St
Leys Pl
Grove
Acre Rd
Ridgefield
Sch
Chester St
Argyle St
Warwick St
Newtec Pl
Sidney St
Harold Hicks Pl
Percy St
Catherine St
Barnet St
Silver Rd
Golden Rd
Charles St
Howard St
Bedford St
Daubeny Rd
Parker St
Isis CE Mid Sch
Convent
PO
Allot Gdns
Boundary
Brook Rd
Pipkin Way
Quartermain Cl
George Moore Cl
Larkrise Prim Sch
St Gregory the Great RC Sec Sch
Fairacres Rd
Addison Cres
Swinburne Rd
Arnold Rd
Townsend Sq
B4495
A4158
Sports Gd
New Hinksey
Abingdon Rd
Weir
Donnington Bridge
Donnington Bridge Rd
Freelands Rd
Radcliffe Rd
Nixon Rd 1
Donnington Lodge 2
Renault Ho 3
Chatham Rd
Fox Cres
Oswestry Rd
Weirs La B4495
Peel Pl
Canning Cres
Thames Path
Boat House
Meadow La
Cavell Rd
Cornwallis Cl
Henley Ave
Cornwallis
Camp
Beechw
Gordon Woodward Way
Bertie Pl
OX4
Iffley Mead Sch
Grove Ct
Iffley Turn
Lucas Pl
Remy Pl
Church Way
Tudor Cl
Cordrey Gn
Aubrey Ct
Woodhouse Way
Anne Greenwood Cl
Egerton Rd
Fitzherbert Cl
Tree La
Bay Tree Cl
Azor's Ct
Ellesmere Rd
Weirs Mill Stream
The Isis Hotel (PH)
Redbridge
Bears Hedge
West View
Quarry La
Stone
Bakers La
Abberbury Rd
Courtland Rd
Hunsdon Rd
Iffley Lock
Mill La
Abberbury Ave
1 Wootten Dr
2 Sheepway Ct
A4144
Iffley
Rose Hill
Towing Path
Kennington Rdbt
A423
Eastchurch
Lenthall Rd
Fiennes Rd
Dashwood
Court Place Gdns
Radford Cl
Rose Hill Prim Sch
Ashurst Way
Mortimer Rd
The Oval
Court Farm Rd
Nowell Rd
Jersey Rd
St Mary's
Lambourn Rd
Rivermead Rd
Newlin Cl
Desborough Cres
Southern By-Pass Rd A423
Clinton Cl
Thames View Rd
Pattison Pl
Wynbush Rd
Danvers Rd
Cottesmore Rd
Williamson Way
Old Nursery View
Forest Side
Jackson Dr
Perkins
Colley Wood
Kenville Rd
Hunder Ct
Kennington Rd
Sewage Works
A4142
Heyford Hill Rdbt
Superstore
Brocklesby Rd
Gwyneth Rd
Thomson
Kempson
A4074
21
22
31
39
40
A
B
C
1
2
3
4

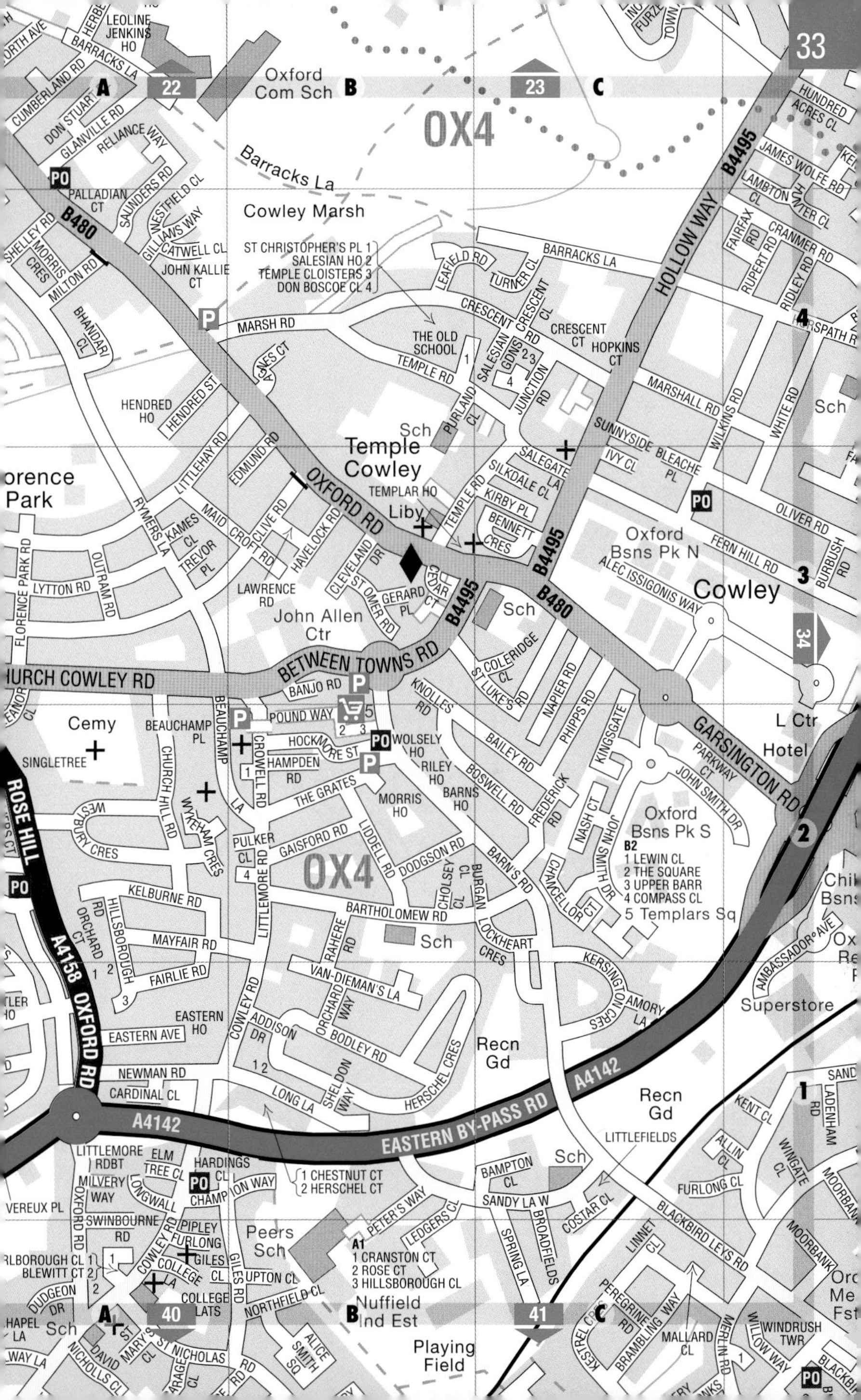

OX4
Oxford Com Sch
Barracks La
Cowley Marsh
Temple Cowley
Cowley
Oxford Bsns Pk N
Oxford Bsns Pk S
John Allen Ctr
OXFORD RD
HOLLOW WAY
BETWEEN TOWNS RD
CHURCH COWLEY RD
GARSINGTON RD
EASTERN BY-PASS RD
ROSE HILL
B480
B4495
A4142
A4158
ST CHRISTOPHER'S PL 1
SALESIAN HO 2
TEMPLE CLOISTERS 3
DON BOSCOE CL 4
B2
1 LEWIN CL
2 THE SQUARE
3 UPPER BARR
4 COMPASS CL
5 Templars Sq
A1
1 CRANSTON CT
2 ROSE CT
3 HILLSBOROUGH CL
1 CHESTNUT CT
2 HERSCHEL CT
Recn Gd
Cemy
Superstore
Peers Sch
Nuffield Ind Est
Playing Field
L Ctr
Hotel

22
23
34
40
41

ST FRANCIS CT
MASCALL AVE
ACRE CL
SHORTE CL
STONE RD
23
A
TROY CL
ST FIELD CL
MEYSEYS RD
AWGAR
HUNDRED ACRES CL
B4495
JAMES WOLFE RD
KENNEDY CL
LAMBTON CL
YEATS CL
FLETCHER RD
HOLLOW WAY
FAIRFAX RD
CRANMER RD
RUPERT RD
BURTON PL
BENOUVILLE CL
BRASENOSE DRIFTWAY
RIDLEY RD
CORUNNA CRES
CRAUFURD RD
HORSPATH RD
HOPKINS CT
MARSHALL RD
WILKINS RD
WHITE RD
Sch
PAGET RD
SUNNYSIDE
IVY CL
BLEACHE PL
FANSHAWE PL
NORMANDY CRES
PO
OLIVER RD
Oxford Bsns Pk N
FERN HILL RD
BURBUSH RD
ALEC ISSIGONIS WAY
Cowley
33
B480
GARSINGTON RD
L Ctr
Hotel
KINGSGATE
PARKWAY CT
JOHN SMITH DR
Oxford Bsns Pk S
EASTERN BY-PASS RD
A4142
B
NINTH AVE
24
C
Open Brasnose
OX4
EASTFIELD PL
Horspath Road Ind Est
PETERLEY RD
PONY RD
Drift Ctr
Isis Bsns Ctr
Sports Ground
Works
ROMAN WAY
OX4
COWLEY JUNC
Works
BOBBY FRYER CL
Chiltern Bsns Ctr
Depot
AMBASSADOR AVE
Oxford Retail Pk
County Trad Est
WATLINGTON RD
PRUNUS CL 1
PINE CL 2
JASMINE CL 3
Superstore
Stadium
ASHVILLE WAY
HARROW RD
HOLLY CT
OXFORD RD
AMORY LA
Recn Gd
SANDY LA
DRUCE WAY
LADENHAM RD
TUCKER RD
LONGLANDS RD
ASHMOLE PL
B480
KENT CL
JOURDAIN RD
Guydens Farm
LITTLEFIELDS
ALLIN CL
WINGATE CL
BALFOUR RD
COMFREY RD
BERRY CL
MOORBANK
BLAY CL
SAWPIT RD
POULTON PL
WARBURG CRES
ERICA CL
SORREL RD
FURLONG CL
HALDANE RD
CUDDESDON WAY
BRIAR WAY
TREFOIL PL
BLACKBIRD LEYS RD
WESLEY CL
JUNIPER DR
LINNET CL
Park
WOODRUFF CL
VETCH PL
BRYONY CL
Orchard Meadow Sch
Blackbird Leys
FIELD AVE
CENTAURY PL
YEW CL
THISTLE DR
PEREGRINE RD
BRAMBLING WAY
41
CLEMATIS PL
42
MALLARD CL
MERLIN RD
WILLOW WAY
WINDRUSH TWR
OX4
Pegasus Sch
HAREBELL RD
Liby
L Ctr
SAMPHIRE
BROOK VIEW

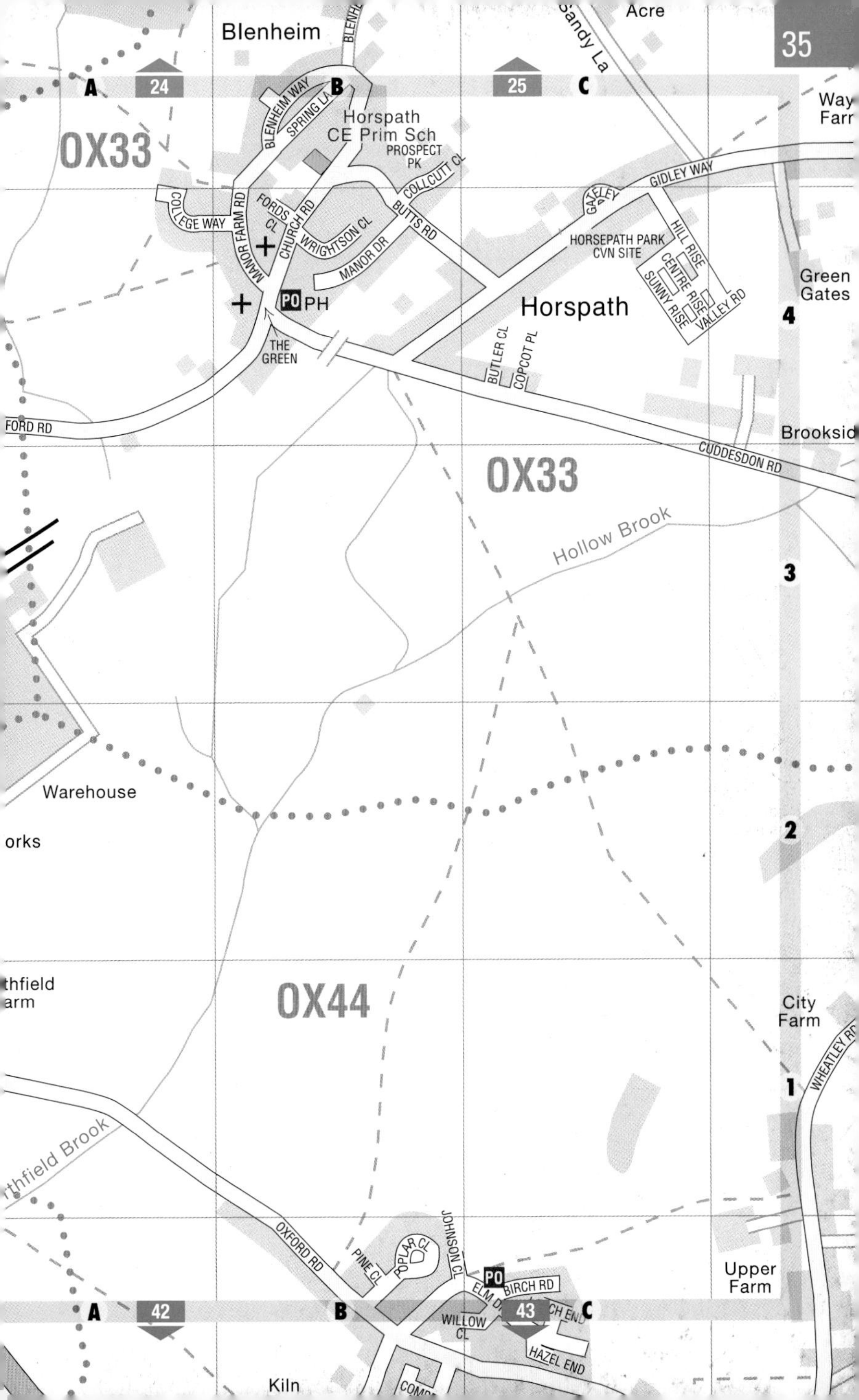
Blenheim
Acre
Sandy La
A
24
B
25
C
OX33
BLENHEIM WAY
SPRING LA
Horspath CE Prim Sch
PROSPECT PK
COLLCUTT CL
GIDLEY WAY
Way Farm
COLLEGE WAY
MANOR FARM RD
FORDS CL
CHURCH RD
WRIGHTSON CL
MANOR DR
BUTTS RD
HORSEPATH PARK CVN SITE
HILL RISE
CENTRE RISE
SUNNY RISE
VALLEY RD
Green Gates
PO
PH
THE GREEN
Horspath
4
BUTLER CL
COPCOT PL
FORD RD
Brookside
CUDDESDON RD
OX33
Hollow Brook
3
Warehouse
orks
2
thfield
arm
OX44
City Farm
WHEATLEY RD
1
thfield Brook
OXFORD RD
JOHNSON CL
PINE CL
POPLAR CL
PO
BIRCH RD
ELM D
Upper Farm
A
42
B
43
C
WILLOW CL
HAZEL END
Kiln

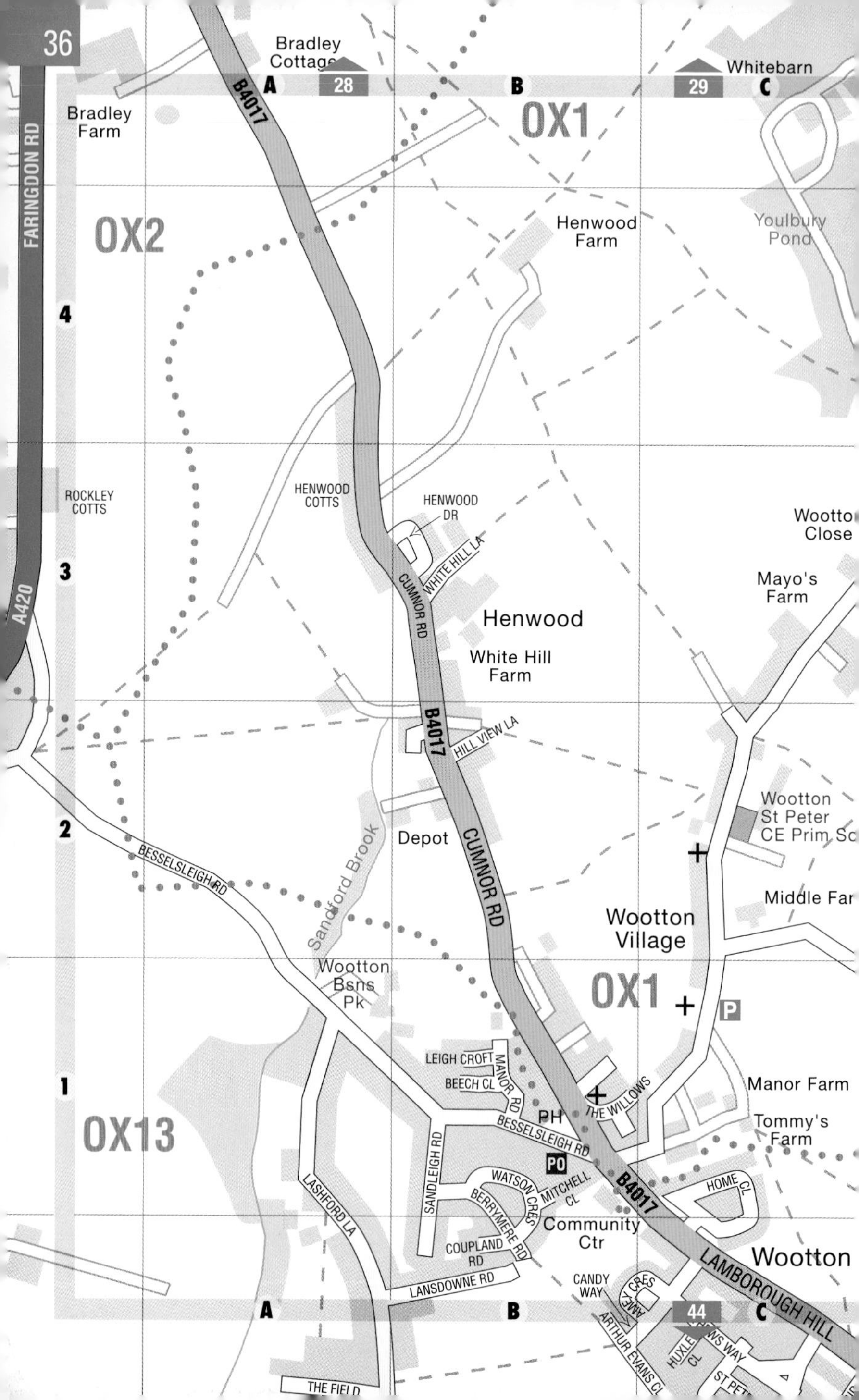
Bradley Cottage
28
Whitebarn
29
A
B
C
Bradley Farm
OX1
FARINGDON RD
OX2
Henwood Farm
Youlbury Pond
4
B4017
ROCKLEY COTTS
HENWOOD COTTS
HENWOOD DR
Wootton Close
3
WHITE HILL LA
CUMNOR RD
Mayo's Farm
Henwood
A420
White Hill Farm
HILL VIEW LA
Wootton St Peter CE Prim Sc
2
Depot
Sandford Brook
BESSELSLEIGH RD
CUMNOR RD
Middle Far
Wootton Village
Wootton Bsns Pk
OX1
P
LEIGH CROFT
MANOR RD
BEECH CL
Manor Farm
1
THE WILLOWS
OX13
PH
Tommy's Farm
SANDLEIGH RD
BESSELSLEIGH RD
PO
WATSON CRES
MITCHELL CL
HOME CL
LASHFORD LA
BERRYMERE RD
Community Ctr
COUPLAND RD
Wootton
LAMBOROUGH HILL
LANSDOWNE RD
CANDY WAY
AMEY CRES
44
ARTHUR EVANS CL
HUXLEY CL
THE FIELD

Youlbury Wood
A
29
B
C
30
CHILSWELL LA
OX1
Birch Copse
Mast
Pickett's Heath Farm
Chiswell Farm Cottages
Upper
oulbury
Heath
West Gardens
4
HITE BARN
SANDY LA
RIDGEWAY
Yatsco
Cops
Jarn Mound
BEDWELLS HEATH
Boars Hill
Oxford Preservation Trust
3
Old Boars Hill
OLD BOARS HILL
JARN WAY
FOXCOMBE
38
ORCHARD LA
Foxcombe Hall
BERKELEY RD
WOODLAND WLK
FOXCOMBE RD
Foxcombe Hill
Old Boars Hill
Blackthorn
2
Duckling's Copse
OLD BOARS HILL
OX1
The Fox Inn (PH)
1
OX13
LINCOMBE LA
FOX LA
Broom Hill Copse
Copse View
Blagrove Copse
A
44
B
C
45
OX13
Sunningwell

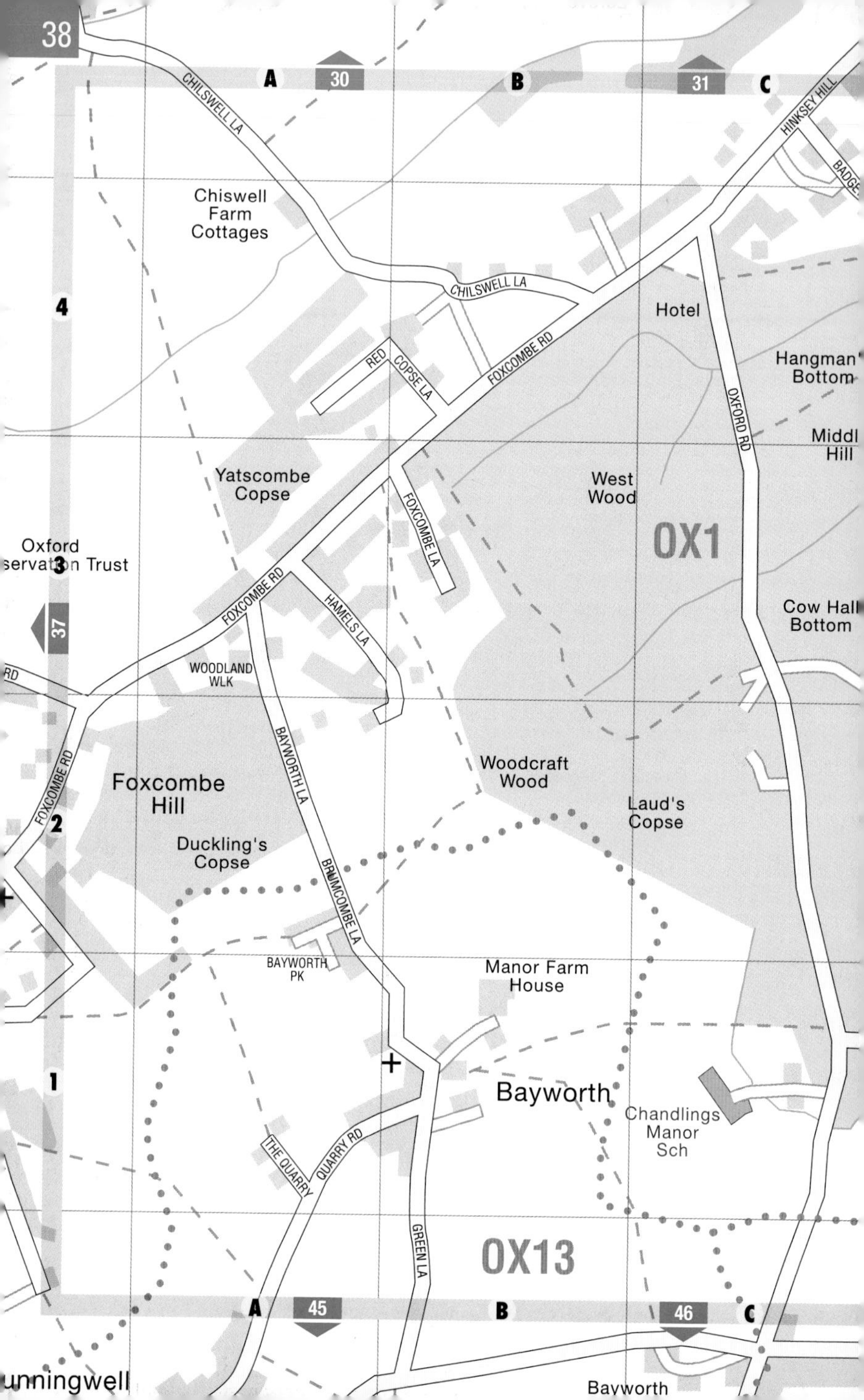
A
30
B
31
C
CHILSWELL LA
HINKSEY HILL
BADGE
Chiswell
Farm
Cottages
CHILSWELL LA
Hotel
4
RED
COPSE LA
FOXCOMBE RD
Hangman
Bottom
OXFORD RD
Middl
Hill
Yatscombe
Copse
West
Wood
FOXCOMBE LA
OX1
Oxford
servation Trust
3
FOXCOMBE RD
HAMELS LA
Cow Hall
Bottom
37
RD
WOODLAND
WLK
BAYWORTH LA
FOXCOMBE RD
Foxcombe
Hill
Woodcraft
Wood
Laud's
Copse
2
Duckling's
Copse
BRUMCOMBE LA
BAYWORTH
PK
Manor Farm
House
1
Bayworth
Chandlings
Manor
Sch
THE QUARRY
QUARRY RD
GREEN LA
OX13
A
45
B
46
C
unningwell
Bayworth

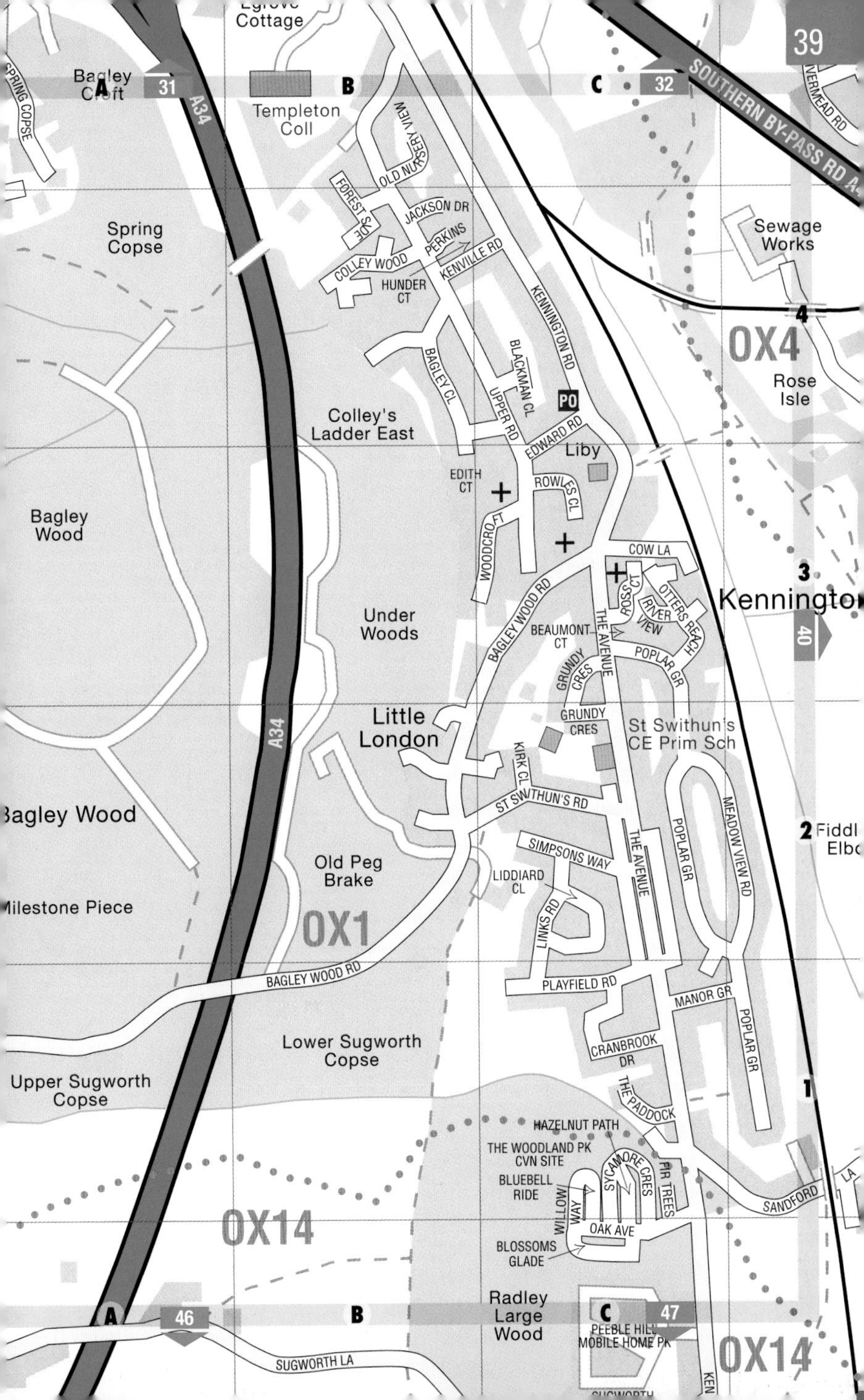

Eglove Cottage
Bagley Croft
A
31
B
C
32
Templeton Coll
SOUTHERN BY-PASS RD A4
VERMEAD RD
SPRING COPSE
A34
OLD NURSERY VIEW
FOREST SIDE
JACKSON DR
PERKINS
COLLEY WOOD
KENVILLE RD
HUNDER CT
KENNINGTON RD
Spring Copse
Sewage Works
4
OX4
Rose Isle
BAGLEY CL
BLACKMAN CL
UPPER RD
PO
Colley's Ladder East
EDWARD RD
Liby
EDITH CT
ROWLES CL
WOODCROFT
Bagley Wood
COW LA
3
Kennington
ROSS CT
OTTERS REACH
RIVER VIEW
Under Woods
BAGLEY WOOD RD
BEAUMONT CT
THE AVENUE
40
POPLAR GR
GRUNDY CRES
Little London
St Swithun's CE Prim Sch
KIRK CL
ST SWITHUN'S RD
MEADOW VIEW RD
Bagley Wood
SIMPSONS WAY
2
LIDDIARD CL
Old Peg Brake
Milestone Piece
LINKS RD
OX1
BAGLEY WOOD RD
PLAYFIELD RD
MANOR GR
Lower Sugworth Copse
CRANBROOK DR
Upper Sugworth Copse
THE PADDOCK
1
HAZELNUT PATH
THE WOODLAND PK CVN SITE
SYCAMORE CRES
FIR TREES
BLUEBELL RIDE
WILLOW WAY
SANDFORD
OAK AVE
OX14
BLOSSOMS GLADE
Radley Large Wood
46
47
PEEBLE HILL MOBILE HOME PK
SUGWORTH LA
OX14

SOUTHERN BY-PASS RD A423
A
32
B
33
C
A4142
A4074
4
3
2
1
39
47
OX4
OX1
OX14
Sewage Works
HEYFORD HILL RDBT
Superstore
Rose Isle
Kennington
St Swithun's CE Prim Sch
Fiddler's Elbow
River Thames or Isis
Sandford Pool
Hotel
Orchard House
Catherine Wheel (PH)
Sandford-on-Thames
PH
Lock
Ind Est
Lower Farm
Sch
Littlemore Brook
MORTIMER RD
COURT FARM RD
RIVERMEAD RD
CLINTON CL
THAMES VIEW RD
THE OVAL
DESBOROUGH CRES
PATTISON PL
NOWELL RD
WILLIAMSON WAY
WYNBUSH RD
DANVERS RD
LAMBOURN RD
JERSEY RD
ST MARTIN'S RD
ASQUITH RD
COTTESMORE RD
DEVEREUX PL
NEWMAN RD
CARDINAL CL
LITTLEMORE RDBT
ELM TREE CL
MILVERY WAY
OXFORD RD
LONGWALL
SWINBOURNE RD
COWLEY RD
COLLEGE LA
MARLBOROUGH CL 1
BLEWITT CT 2
DUDGEON DR
KEMPSON CRES
THOMSON TERR
BROCKLESBY RD
GWYNETH RD
CHAPEL LA
RAILWAY LA
ST DAVID CL
ST MARY'S CL
NICHOLLS CL
LANHAM WAY
VICARAGE
MORRELL CRES
SANDFORD RD
MANDLEBROTE DR
ARMSTRONG RD
EDMUND RD
HEYFORD HILL LA
PHEASANT WLK
YEFTLY DR
BROADHURST GDNS
BATTEN PL
JANAWAY 1
BUCKLER PL 2
FOX FURLONG 3
ROCK FARM LA
KEENE CL
CHURCH RD
HENLEY RD
RIVER VIEW
BURRA CL
SANDFORD LA
COW LA
BOSSOM
RIVER VIEW
OTTERS REACH
THE AVENUE
POPLAR GR
MEADOW VIEW RD
MANOR GR
CRANBROOK DR
THE PADDOCK
SYCAMORE CRES
FIR TREES
OAK AVE
PEEBLE HILL MOBILE HOME PK
SUGWORTH
LOWER FARM LA

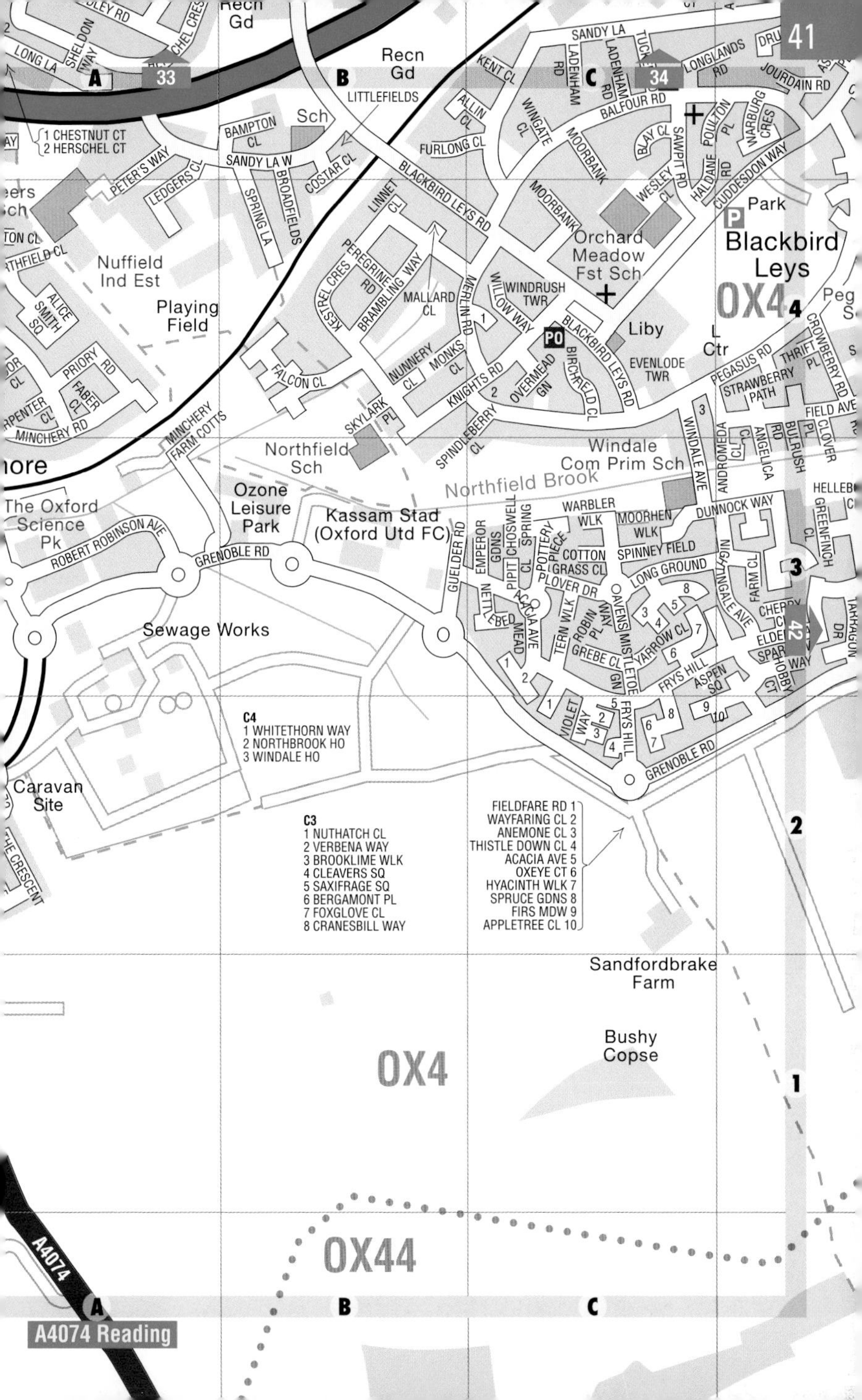
A
B
C
33
34
42
Recn Gd
LONG LA
SHELDON WAY
1 CHESTNUT CT
2 HERSCHEL CT
PETER'S WAY
LEDGERS CL
BAMPTON CL
Sch
SANDY LA W
SPRING LA
BROADFIELDS
COSTAR CL
LITTLEFIELDS
Nuffield Ind Est
Playing Field
ALICE SMITH SQ
PRIORY RD
FABER CL
MINCHERY RD
MINCHERY FARM COTTS
LINNET CL
PEREGRINE RD
KESTREL CRES
BRAMBLING WAY
MALLARD CL
FALCON CL
SKYLARK PL
NUNNERY CL
MONKS CL
MERLIN RD
KNIGHTS RD
BLACKBIRD LEYS RD
FURLONG CL
ALLIN CL
KENT CL
SANDY LA
LADENHAM RD
WINGATE CL
MOORBANK
BALFOUR RD
BLAY CL
SAWPIT RD
WESLEY CL
HALDANE RD
POULTON PL
WARBURG CRES
CUDDESDON WAY
LONGLANDS RD
JOURDAIN RD
Park
Blackbird Leys
OX4
Orchard Meadow Fst Sch
WILLOW WAY
WINDRUSH TWR
PO
OVERMEAD GN
BIRCHFIELD CL
Liby
EVENLODE TWR
L Ctr
SPINDLEBERRY CL
Windale Com Prim Sch
WINDALE AVE
PEGASUS RD
THRIFT PL
CROWBERRY RD
STRAWBERRY PATH
FIELD AVE
ANDROMEDA CL
ANGELICA CL
BULRUSH RD
CLOVER PL
Northfield Sch
Northfield Brook
Ozone Leisure Park
Kassam Stad (Oxford Utd FC)
The Oxford Science Pk
ROBERT ROBINSON AVE
GRENOBLE RD
GUELDER RD
EMPEROR GDNS
PIPIT CL
CHOSWELL SPRING
POTTERY PIECE
WARBLER WLK
MOORHEN WLK
DUNNOCK WAY
COTTON GRASS CL
SPINNEY FIELD
LONG GROUND
PLOVER DR
NETTLEBED MEAD
ACACIA AVE
TERN WLK
ROBIN PL
RAVENS WAY
MISTLETOE GN
YARROW CL
GREBE CL
FRYS HILL
ASPEN SQ
NIGHTINGALE AVE
FARM CL
GREENFINCH CL
CHERRY CL
ELDER
SPARROW WAY
HOBBY CT
TARRAGON DR
HELLEBORE CL
VIOLET WAY
Sewage Works
Caravan Site
THE CRESCENT
C4
1 WHITETHORN WAY
2 NORTHBROOK HO
3 WINDALE HO
C3
1 NUTHATCH CL
2 VERBENA WAY
3 BROOKLIME WLK
4 CLEAVERS SQ
5 SAXIFRAGE SQ
6 BERGAMONT PL
7 FOXGLOVE CL
8 CRANESBILL WAY
FIELDFARE RD 1
WAYFARING CL 2
ANEMONE CL 3
THISTLE DOWN CL 4
ACACIA AVE 5
OXEYE CT 6
HYACINTH WLK 7
SPRUCE GDNS 8
FIRS MDW 9
APPLETREE CL 10
Sandfordbrake Farm
Bushy Copse
OX4
OX44
A4074
A4074 Reading
4
3
2
1

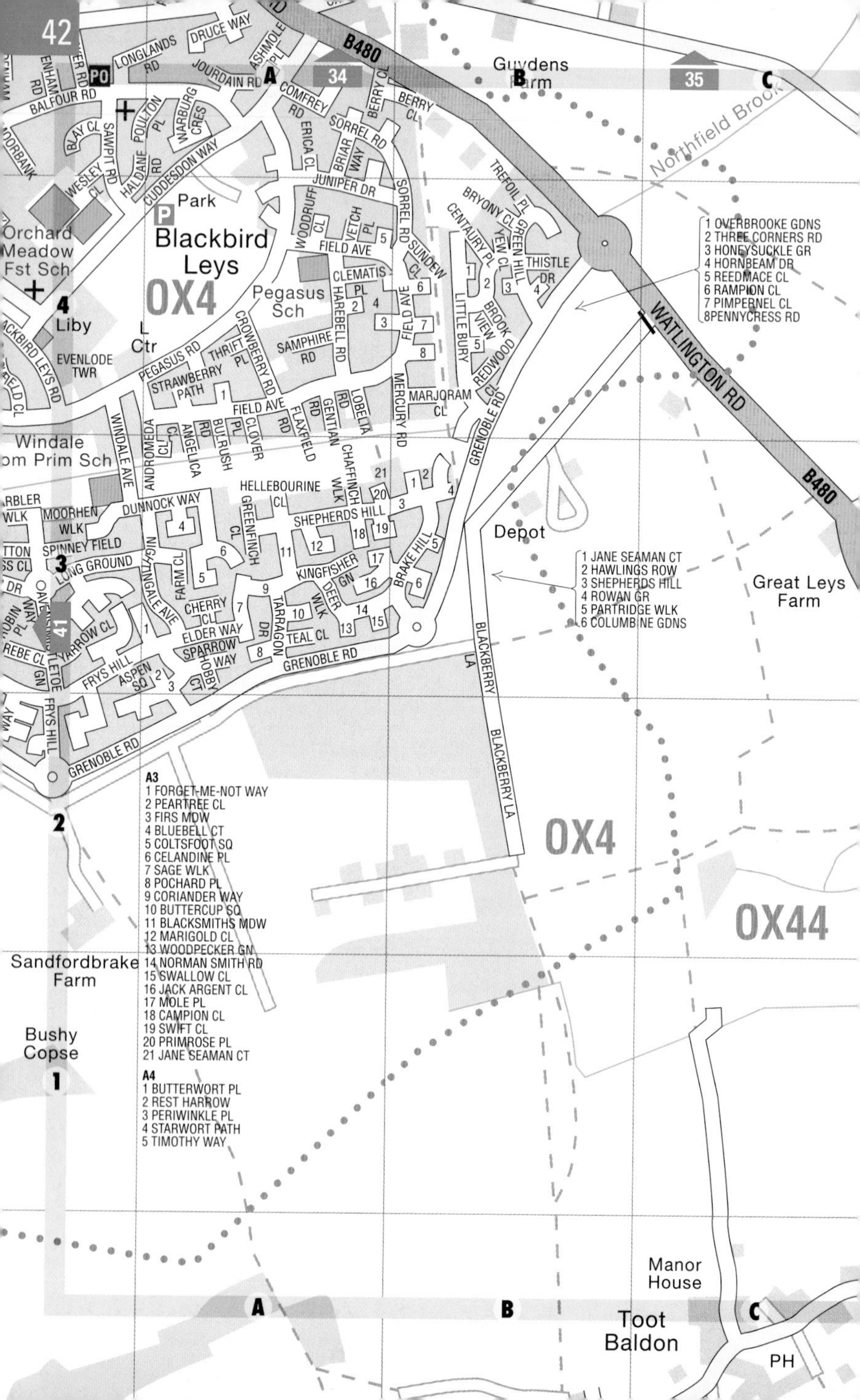

Guydens Farm
34
35
A
B
C
B480
Northfield Brook
Park
Blackbird Leys
OX4
Orchard Meadow Fst Sch
Pegasus Sch
Liby
L Ctr
Windale Com Prim Sch
Depot
Great Leys Farm
WATLINGTON RD
BLACKBERRY LA
GRENOBLE RD
1 OVERBROOKE GDNS
2 THREE CORNERS RD
3 HONEYSUCKLE GR
4 HORNBEAM DR
5 REEDMACE CL
6 RAMPION CL
7 PIMPERNEL CL
8PENNYCRESS RD
1 JANE SEAMAN CT
2 HAWLINGS ROW
3 SHEPHERDS HILL
4 ROWAN GR
5 PARTRIDGE WLK
6 COLUMBINE GDNS
A3
1 FORGET-ME-NOT WAY
2 PEARTREE CL
3 FIRS MDW
4 BLUEBELL CT
5 COLTSFOOT SQ
6 CELANDINE PL
7 SAGE WLK
8 POCHARD PL
9 CORIANDER WAY
10 BUTTERCUP SQ
11 BLACKSMITHS MDW
12 MARIGOLD CL
13 WOODPECKER GN
14 NORMAN SMITH RD
15 SWALLOW CL
16 JACK ARGENT CL
17 MOLE PL
18 CAMPION CL
19 SWIFT CL
20 PRIMROSE PL
21 JANE SEAMAN CT
A4
1 BUTTERWORT PL
2 REST HARROW
3 PERIWINKLE PL
4 STARWORT PATH
5 TIMOTHY WAY
Sandfordbrake Farm
Bushy Copse
OX4
OX44
Manor House
Toot Baldon
PH
41
4
3
2
1

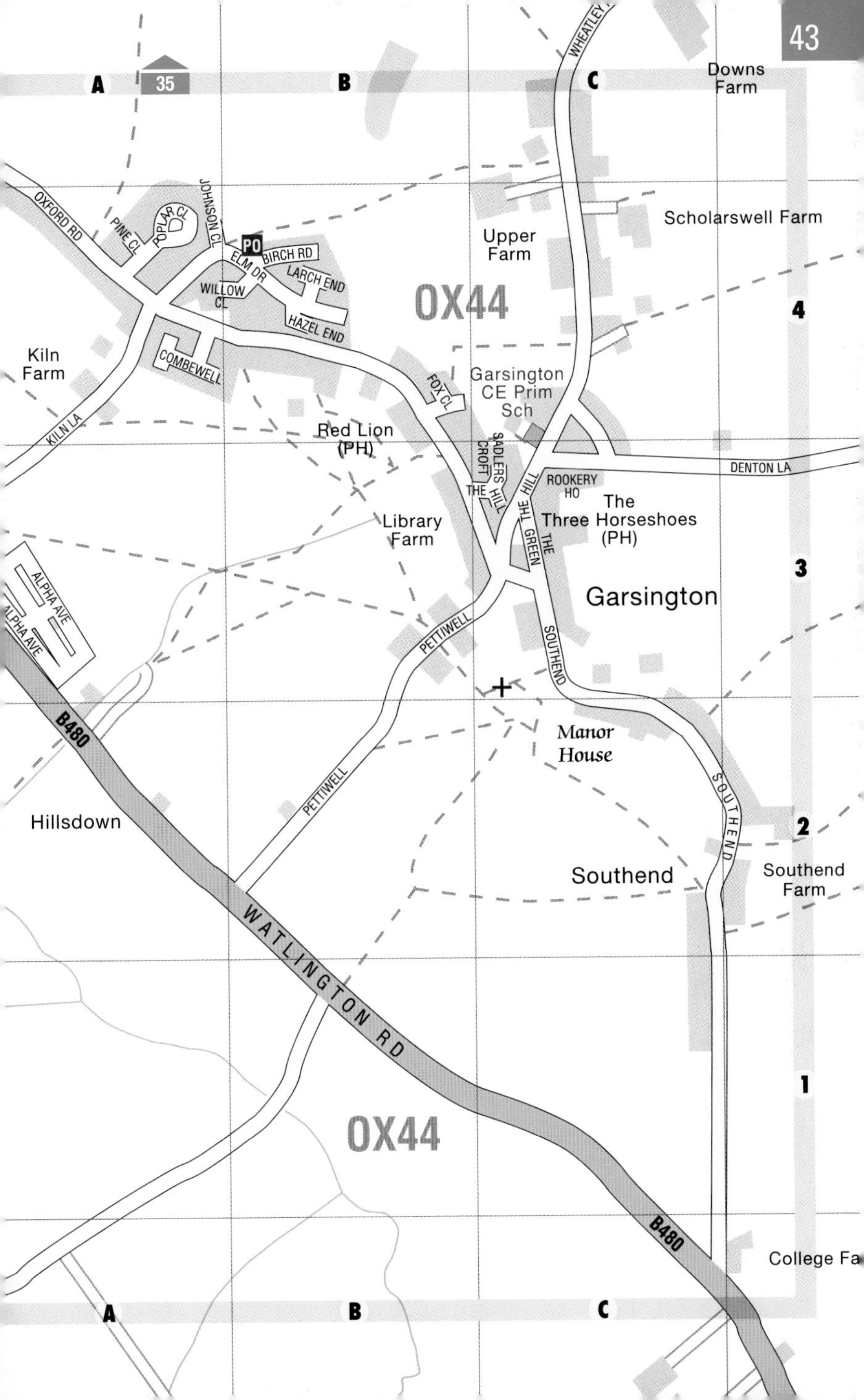

A
35
B
C
Downs Farm
WHEATLEY
Scholarswell Farm
Upper Farm
OXFORD RD
PINE CL
POPLAR CL
JOHNSON CL
PO
BIRCH RD
ELM DR
LARCH END
WILLOW CL
HAZEL END
OX44
Kiln Farm
COMBEWELL
FOX CL
Garsington CE Prim Sch
KILN LA
Red Lion (PH)
SADLERS CROFT
THE HILL
ROOKERY HO
DENTON LA
The Three Horseshoes (PH)
Library Farm
THE GREEN
Garsington
ALPHA AVE
ALPHA AVE
PETTIWELL
SOUTHEND
Manor House
B480
SOUTHEND
Hillsdown
PETTIWELL
Southend
Southend Farm
WATLINGTON RD
OX44
B480
College Fa
4
3
2
1
A
B
C

Manor Farm
36
37
A
B
C
Tommy Farm
OX1
PH
THE WILLOWS
BESSELSLEIGH RD
PO
WATSON CRES
MITCHELL CL
B4017
HOME CL
FOX LA
Broom Cops
Community Ctr
Wootton
LAMBOROUGH HILL
Copse View
Blagrove Copse
CANDY WAY
AMEY CRES
ARTHUR EVANS CL
MATHEWS WAY
HUXLEY CL
ST PETER'S CL
HAWKINS WAY
THE OLD POUND
4
Blagrove Farm
3
HONEYBOTTOM LA
Starveall Farm
WHITECROSS
OX13
2
LONG FURLONG RD
Airfield
SPEY RD
MEDWAY RD
MEDWAY CL
1
CHOLSWELL CT
Dalton Barracks
DART RD
AVON RD
CONWAY RD
TYNE RD
TYNE RD
SEVERN RD
WELLAND CL
DERWENT CL
NENE RD
LONG TOW
Dunmore Farm
B4017
CHOLSWELL RD
48
A34

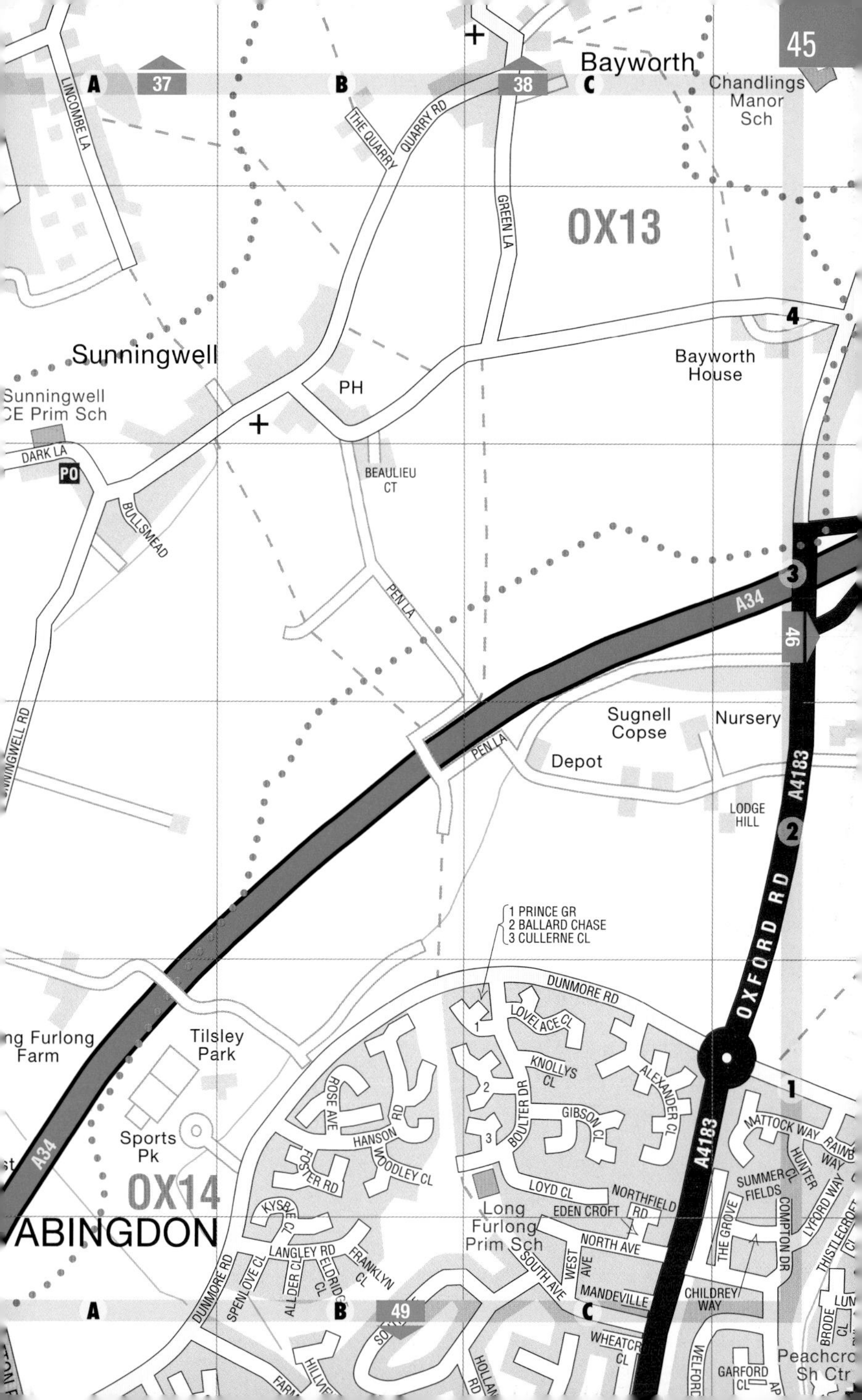

A
37
B
38
C
Bayworth
Chandlings
Manor
Sch
LINCOMBE LA
THE QUARRY
QUARRY RD
GREEN LA
OX13
4
Sunningwell
Bayworth
House
Sunningwell
CE Prim Sch
PH
DARK LA
PO
BEAULIEU
CT
BULLSMEAD
PEN LA
3
A34
46
SUNNINGWELL RD
Sugnell
Copse
Nursery
PEN LA
Depot
A4183
LODGE
HILL
2
OXFORD RD
1 PRINCE GR
2 BALLARD CHASE
3 CULLERNE CL
DUNMORE RD
LOVELACE CL
1
Long Furlong
Farm
Tilsley
Park
KNOLLYS
CL
ALEXANDER CL
1
ROSE AVE
HANSON RD
2
BOULTER DR
GIBSON CL
MATTOCK WAY
RAINBOW WAY
3
HUNTER CL
WOODLEY CL
Sports
Pk
A34
FOSTER RD
OX14
LOYD CL
SUMMERFIELDS
A4183
LYFORD WAY
NORTHFIELD RD
COMPTON DR
THISTLECROFT
ABINGDON
KYSBIE CL
Long
Furlong
Prim Sch
EDEN CROFT
THE GROVE
LANGLEY RD
FRANKLYN CL
NORTH AVE
DUNMORE RD
SPENLOVE CL
ALLDER CL
ELDRIDGE CL
SOUTH AVE
WEST AVE
MANDEVILLE
CHILDREY WAY
BRODE CL
A
B
49
C
WHEATCROFT CL
HOLLANDS RD
WELFORD
GARFORD CL
Peachcroft
Sh Ctr

Bayworth
Chandlings Manor Sch
A
38
Upper Sugworth Copse
B
Lower Sugworth Copse
39
C
OX1
OX14
OX13
4
Bayworth House
SUGWORTH LA
3
A34
45
LODGE HILL INTERCHANGE
Sugnell Copse
Nursery
A4183
LODGE HILL
2
Radley Park
Radley Coll
OXFORD RD
ABINGDON
OX14
1
ALEXANDER CL
MATTOCK WAY
HUNTER CL
RAINBOW WAY
1 SADLERS CT
2 BUCKLERS BURY RD
3 SHRIEVES CL
4 BARFLEUR CL
Peach Croft Farm
PYTENRY CL
COVENT CL
ETHELHELM CL
TWELVE ACRE DR
SUMMER FIELDS
LYFORD WAY
CARSE CL
NORTHFIELD RD
CROFT
NORTH AVE
THE GROVE
COMPTON DR
THISTLECROFT CL
OTWELL CL
BOREFORD RD
LYNGES CL
AMYCE CL
PENN CL
ELIZABETH AVE
BEAGLES CL
RUSHMEAD COPSE
MANDEVILLE
CHILDREY WAY
LUMBERD RD
A
PYKES CL
HEAN CL
50
B
C
WICK CL
STOCKEY END
CHARNEY AVE
GINGE CL
WHEATCROFT CL
WELFORD
GARFORD CL
Peachcroft Sh Ctr
PEACHCROFT RD
PAGISTERS

CRANBROOK DR
THE PADD
39
40
A
B
C
Lock
SANDFORD LA
SYCAMORE CRES
FIR TREES
WILLOW WAY
OAK AVE
SANDFORD
LA
Ind Est
OX1
OX4
LOWER FARM
4
Lower Farm
PEEBLE HILL MOBILE HOME PK
OX14
SUGWORTH CRES
KENNINGTON RD
BIGWOOD CVN PK
Towing Path
River Thames or Isis
adley Little Wood
3
North Close Copse
OX14
Thames Path
2
Park Farm
CHESTNUT AVE
WALLED GDNS
Radley CE Prim Sch
Radley
1
Pumping Station
CHURCH RD
SPINNEYS CL
PO
LITTLE HOWE CL
Lower Radley
FERNY CL
ST JAMES RD
CATHARINE CL
NEW RD
SHAW'S COPSE
LOWER RADLEY CVN PK
Bo Hou
Lower Farm
SELWYN CRES
ST JAMES TERR
PH
A
B
51
C
FOXBOROUGH RD
TURNERS CL
Radley
STONHOUSE CRES
BADGERS COPSE

44
A
B
C
Dalton Barracks
Dunmore Farm
CHOLSWELL CT
MEDWAY CL
DART RD
WELLAND CL
AVON RD
CONWAY RD
TYNE RD
SEVERN RD
DERWENT CL
NENE RD
LONG TOW
CHOLSWELL RD
Wildmoor Brook
MERLIN RD
HAWTHORNE AVE
SYCAMORE CL
CHERRY TREE DR
LABURNUM AVE
CHESTNUT TREE CL
WILLOW TREE CL
ROOKERY CL
ELM TREE WLK
WHITEHOUSE CL
FARINGDON RD
Stowford House
Shippon
The Manor Prep Sch
THE SPINNEY 1
LARKHILL RD 2
LARKHILL PL 3
COPENHAGEN DR
YPRES WAY
MONS WAY
INKERMAN CL
STEVENSON
RAWLINGS GR
HARDING RD
BARROW RD
Manor Farm
Church Farm
A34
Airfield
Sch
CURTYNE
C1
1 BUCKLES CL
2 SPRING TERR
3 BUCKLAND MEWS
4 JUNIPER CT
OX13
OX14
Larkmead Sch
Larkhill Stream
WYNDYKE FURLONG
FOXCOMBE CT
WESTFIELDS
Cemy
WINDRUSH CT
ANNA PAVLOVA CL
SPRING GDNS
SPRING RD
HITCHING CT
WILLOW BROOK
COLWELL DR
BLACKLANDS WAY
NUFFIELD WAY
Abingdon Bsns Pk
CEMETERY RD
EYSTON WAY
KIMBER RD
WINTERBORNE RD
EXBOURNE RD
PO
EDWARD ST
Abingdon
FAIRACRES
H
P
A415 Witney
A415 MARCHAM RD
MARCHAM RD
A415
OCK
OCK MILL CL
Ock Bridge
B4017
River Ock
52
JENYNS CT
POTENGER WAY
CHAUNTERELL WAY
Weir
LADYGROVE
RILEY
4
3
2
1

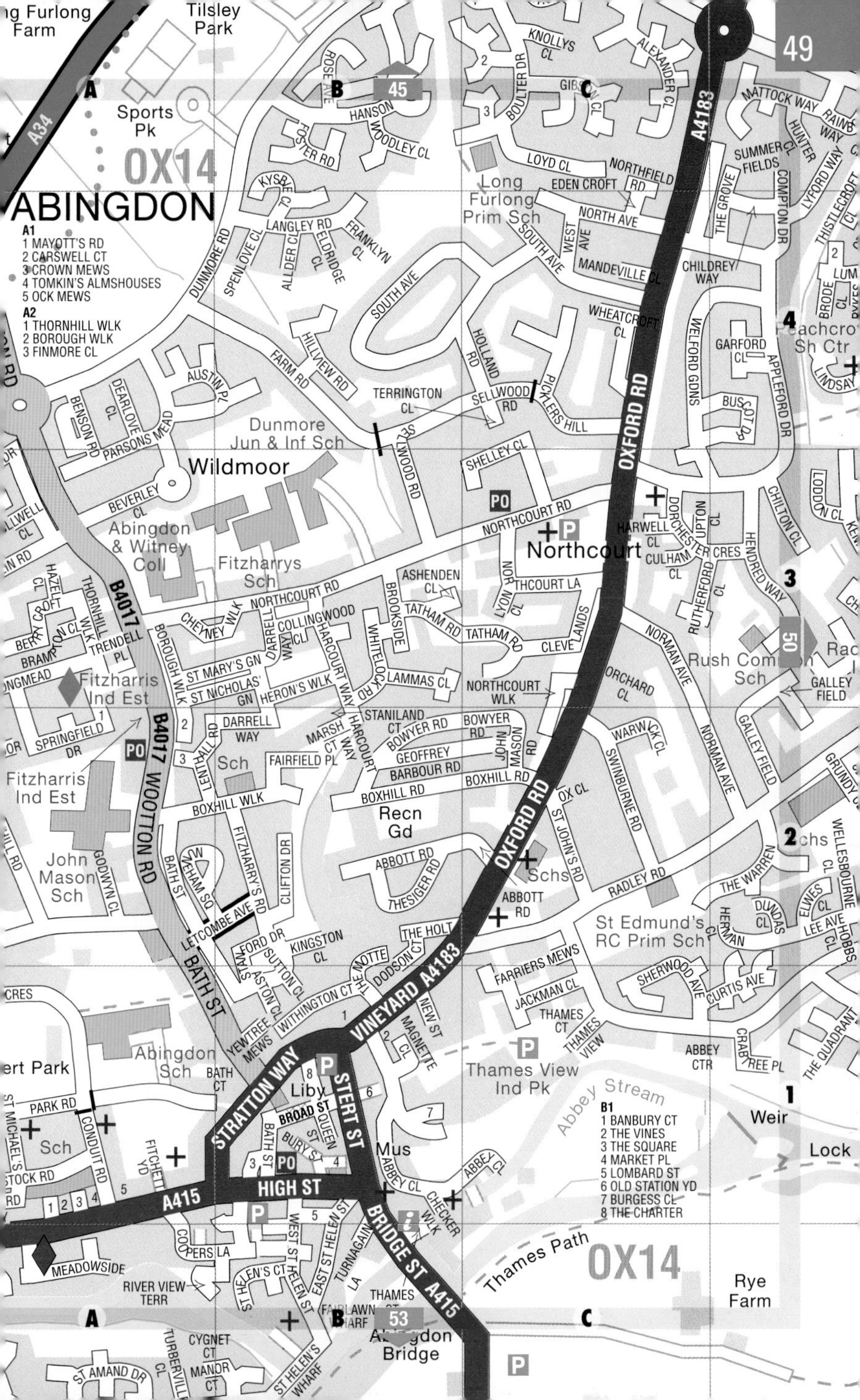
49
ABINGDON
OX14
A1
1 MAYOTT'S RD
2 CARSWELL CT
3 CROWN MEWS
4 TOMKIN'S ALMSHOUSES
5 OCK MEWS
A2
1 THORNHILL WLK
2 BOROUGH WLK
3 FINMORE CL
B1
1 BANBURY CT
2 THE VINES
3 THE SQUARE
4 MARKET PL
5 LOMBARD ST
6 OLD STATION YD
7 BURGESS CL
8 THE CHARTER
45
50
53
A
B
C
1
2
3
4
Tilsley Park
Sports Pk
A34
Long Furlong Prim Sch
Dunmore Jun & Inf Sch
Wildmoor
Abingdon & Witney Coll
Fitzharrys Sch
Northcourt
Fitzharris Ind Est
John Mason Sch
Recn Gd
Schs
St Edmund's RC Prim Sch
Rush Common Sch
Thames View Ind Pk
Abbey Stream
Weir
Lock
Thames Path
Rye Farm
Abingdon Sch
Liby
Mus
Abingdon Bridge
A4183
OXFORD RD
VINEYARD A4183
B4017
WOOTTON RD
A415
HIGH ST
BRIDGE ST A415
STRATTON WAY
STERT ST
BATH ST
BROAD ST
NORTHCOURT RD
BOXHILL RD
BOXHILL WLK
NORTHFIELD RD
NORTH AVE
SOUTH AVE
DUNMORE RD
FARM RD
SELLWOOD RD
RADLEY RD
NORMAN AVE

A
46
B
Peach Croft Farm
C
A4183
ALEXANDER CL
GIBSON CL
MATTOCK WAY
RAINBOW WAY
HUNTER CL
SUMMER FIELDS
LYFORD WAY
COMPTON DR
THE GROVE
NORTHFIELD RD
NORTH AVE
WEST AVE
MANDEVILLE CL
CHILDREY WAY
WHEATCROFT CL
PYTENRY CL
CARSE CL
COVENT CL
ETHELHELM CL
TWELVE ACRE DR
THISTLECROFT CL
BOREFORD RD
AMYCE CL
OTWELL CL
LYNGES CL
LUMBERD RD
BRODE CL
PYKES CL
HEAN CL
1 YELD HALL RD
2 BOXWELL CL
3 TRINITY CL
4 HENOR MILL CL
5 ST ANDREWS CL
6 SANDFORD CL
7 HOLYWELL CL
ELIZABETH AVE
PENN CL
BEAGLE CL
RUSHMEAD COPSE
WICK CL
GINGE CL
CHARNEY AVE
NORBROOK CL
STOCKEY END
OX14
PAGISTERS RD
HOUND CL
Peachcroft Sh Ctr
PEACHCROFT RD
LINDSAY DR
GARFORD CL
WELFORD GDNS
APPLEFORD DR
BUSCOT DR
ENEY CL
CHAMPS CL
BARROW HILL CL
NORRIS CL
DUFFIELD CL
WAXES CL
HEDGEMEAD AVE
CORN AVILL CL
Peachcroft
OXFORD RD
HILL
WINDRUSH WAY
LODDON CL
HAMBLE DR
ST PETER'S RD
CHANDLERS CL
BOWGRAVE COPSE
RADLEY RD
Barrow Hills
HARWELL CL
DORCHESTER CRES
UPTON CL
CHILTON CL
HENDRED WAY
GLYME CL
ISIS CL
EVENLODE PK
KENNET RD
RADLEY CT
CULHAM CL
RUTHERFORD CL
GORDON DR
THE COPSE
THE CHESTNUTS
AUDLETT DR
CHERWELL CL
CAMERON AVE
49
NORMAN AVE
Rush Common Sch
Radley Road Ind Est
EASON DR
HEATHCOTE PL
SEWELL CL
ORCHARD CL
GALLEY FIELD
CAMPION RD
WARWICK CL
SWINBURNE RD
EASON DR
ORCHID CT
WICK HALL
RAMSONS WAY
SAFFRON CT
GRUNDY CL
DAISY BANK
PURSLANE
FENNEL WAY
VILLEBOIS CL
HADLAND RD
MINCHINS CL
GARDINER CL
Schs
WELLESBOURNE CL
DENTON CL
LEVERY CL
GALL CL
RIVY CL
OLD FARM CL
THE WARREN
RADLEY RD
READE AVE
NYATT RD
FERGUSON PL
HART CL
DUNDAS CL
ELWES CL
LEE AVE
HOBBS CL
St Edmund's RC Prim Sch
HERMAN CL
AUDLETT DR
1 KEMPSTER CL
2 KENT CL
3 CLARENDON CL
4 MORTON CL
White Horse L Ctr
SHERWOOD AVE
CURTIS AVE
Abingdon Science Park
ABINGDON
THAMES VIEW
ABBEY CTR
CRABTREE PL
THE QUADRANT
BARTON LA
NAPIER CT
THE PENTAGON
Abbey Stream
Weir
Lock
Thrupp House
OX14
Rye Farm
Weirs
River Thames or Isis
1
2
3
4

Radley
CHURCH RD
SPINNEYS CL
PO
47
Pumping Station
Lower Radley
LITTLE HOWE CL
ST JAMES RD
FERNY CL
CATHARINE CL
NEW RD
SELWYN CRES
ST JAMES TERR
SHAW'S COPSE
LOWER RADLEY CVN PK
PH
Radley
TURNERS CL
FOXBOROUGH RD
BADGERS COPSE
STONHOUSE CRES
GOOSEACRE
Lower Farm
Boat House
Goose Acre Farm
OX14
OX44
Home Farm
Pumney Farm
Thames Path
Gravel Pit
Carfax Conduit
River Thames or Isis
Lock Wood
OX44
Reservoir
Lock Wood
A
B
C
1
2
3
4

A
B
C
48
Abingdon Bsns Pk
Cemy
Cemetery Rd
Acklands Way
Hitching Ct
Nuffield Way
Willow Brook
Colwell Dr
Kimber Rd
Eyston Way
Winterborne Rd
Exbourne Rd
Edward St
PO
Abingdon
H
Fairacres
P
A415 Witney
A415 Marcham Rd
Marcham Rd
A415
A34
Ock Mill Cl
Ock Bridge
B4017
Hotel
River Ock
Jenyns Ct
Potenger Way
Chaunterell Way
Weir
Orpwood Way
Nash Dr
Shepherd Gdns
Francis Little Dr
Suffolk Way
Ladygrove Paddock
Ladygrove Rd
Riley
Ely Cl
Medlicott Dr
Burton Cl
Abingdon Common
4
Byron Cl
Maberley Cl
Mill Rd
Caldecott Prim Sch
OX13
Tennyson Dr
Bridges Cl
Wordsworth Rd
New Cut Mill
Longfellow Dr
Coleridge Dr
Drayton Rd
Gainsborough
3
Weir
Masefield Cres
The Hyde
Turner Rd
Midget Cl
Hyde Pl
Lucca Dr
Argentan Cl
Bergen Ave
Schongau Cl
Sint Niklaas Cl
Coromandel
Virginia Way
2
A34
OX14
Stonehill House
Stonehill Farm
Stonehill La
A34 Newbury (A339)
1
B4017
Oday Hill
Abingdon Rd
Sutton Wick La
Sherwood Farm
Greenacres
Corneville Rd
Newman La
Sutton Wick

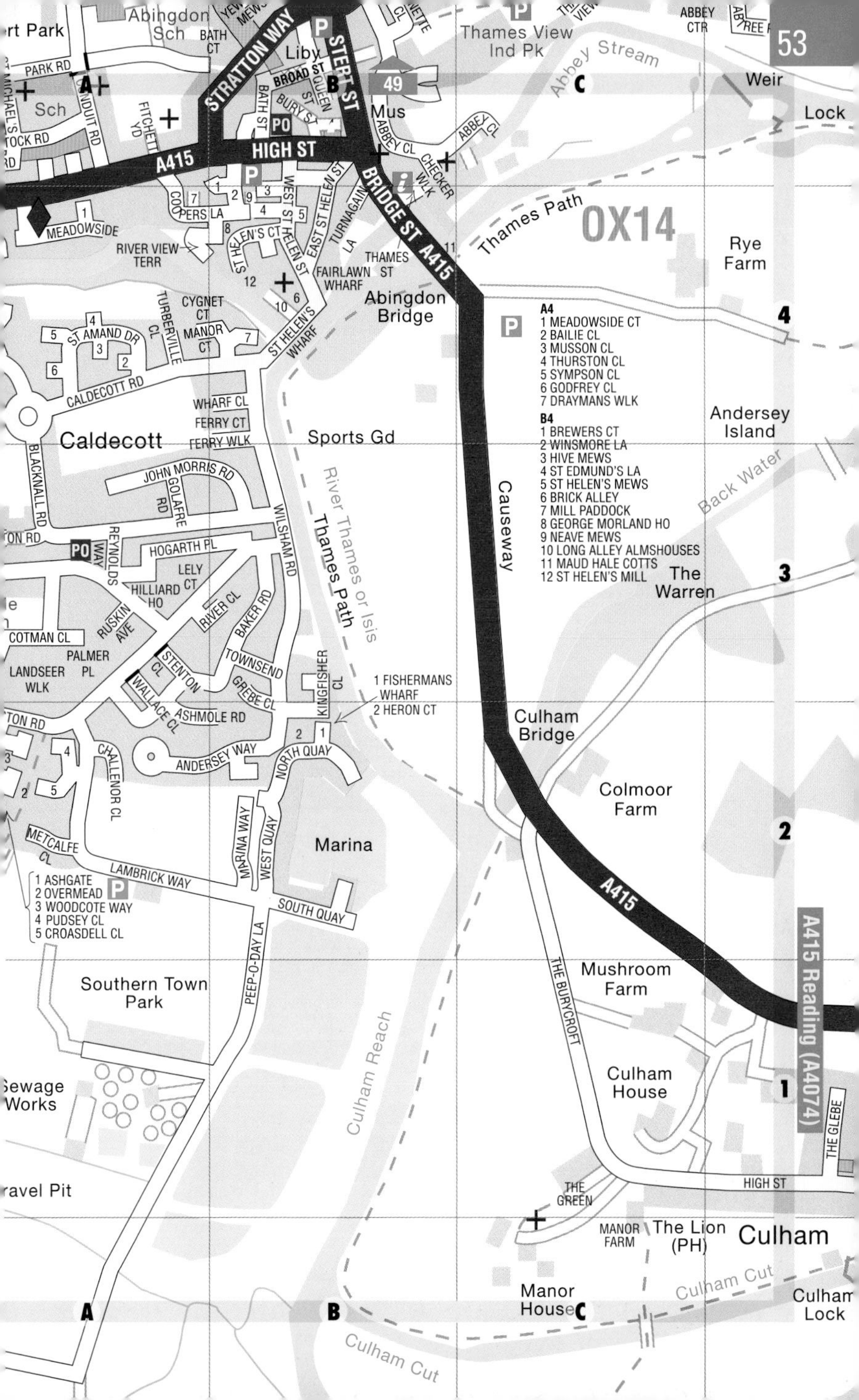

Abingdon Sch
Park Rd
Park
Sch
Bath Ct
Stratton Way
Liby
Broad St
Queen St
Bury St
Bath St
PO
Stert St
49
Mus
Abbey Cl
Checker Wlk
Thames View Ind Pk
Abbey Ctr
Abbey Stream
Weir
Lock
A415
High St
Fitchett Yd
Conduit Rd
Coopers La
Meadowside
River View Terr
St Helen's Ct
West St Helen St
East St Helen St
Turnagain La
Bridge St A415
Thames St
Fairlawn Wharf
Thames Path
OX14
Rye Farm
Abingdon Bridge
Cygnet Ct
Manor Ct
Turberville Cl
St Amand Dr
St Helen's Wharf
Caldecott Rd
Wharf Cl
Ferry Ct
Ferry Wlk
Caldecott
Sports Gd
A4
1 Meadowside Ct
2 Bailie Cl
3 Musson Cl
4 Thurston Cl
5 Sympson Cl
6 Godfrey Cl
7 Draymans Wlk
B4
1 Brewers Ct
2 Winsmore La
3 Hive Mews
4 St Edmund's La
5 St Helen's Mews
6 Brick Alley
7 Mill Paddock
8 George Morland Ho
9 Neave Mews
10 Long Alley Almshouses
11 Maud Hale Cotts
12 St Helen's Mill
Andersey Island
Back Water
Blacknall Rd
John Morris Rd
Golafre Rd
Wilsham Rd
River Thames or Isis
Thames Path
Causeway
Reynolds Way
Hogarth Pl
Lely Ct
Hilliard Ho
Ruskin Ave
River Cl
Baker Rd
Cotman Cl
Palmer Pl
Landseer Wlk
Stenton Cl
Wallace Cl
Townsend
Grebe Cl
Ashmole Rd
Kingfisher Cl
1 Fishermans Wharf
2 Heron Ct
The Warren
Culham Bridge
Andersey Way
North Quay
Challenor Cl
Colmoor Farm
Metcalfe Cl
Marina Way
West Quay
Marina
Lambrick Way
1 Ashgate
2 Overmead
3 Woodcote Way
4 Pudsey Cl
5 Croasdell Cl
South Quay
A415
Peep-O-Day La
Southern Town Park
The Burycroft
Mushroom Farm
A415 Reading (A4074)
Culham Reach
Culham House
Sewage Works
Gravel Pit
The Glebe
High St
The Green
Manor Farm
The Lion (PH)
Culham
Manor House
Culham Cut
Culham Lock
Culham Cut

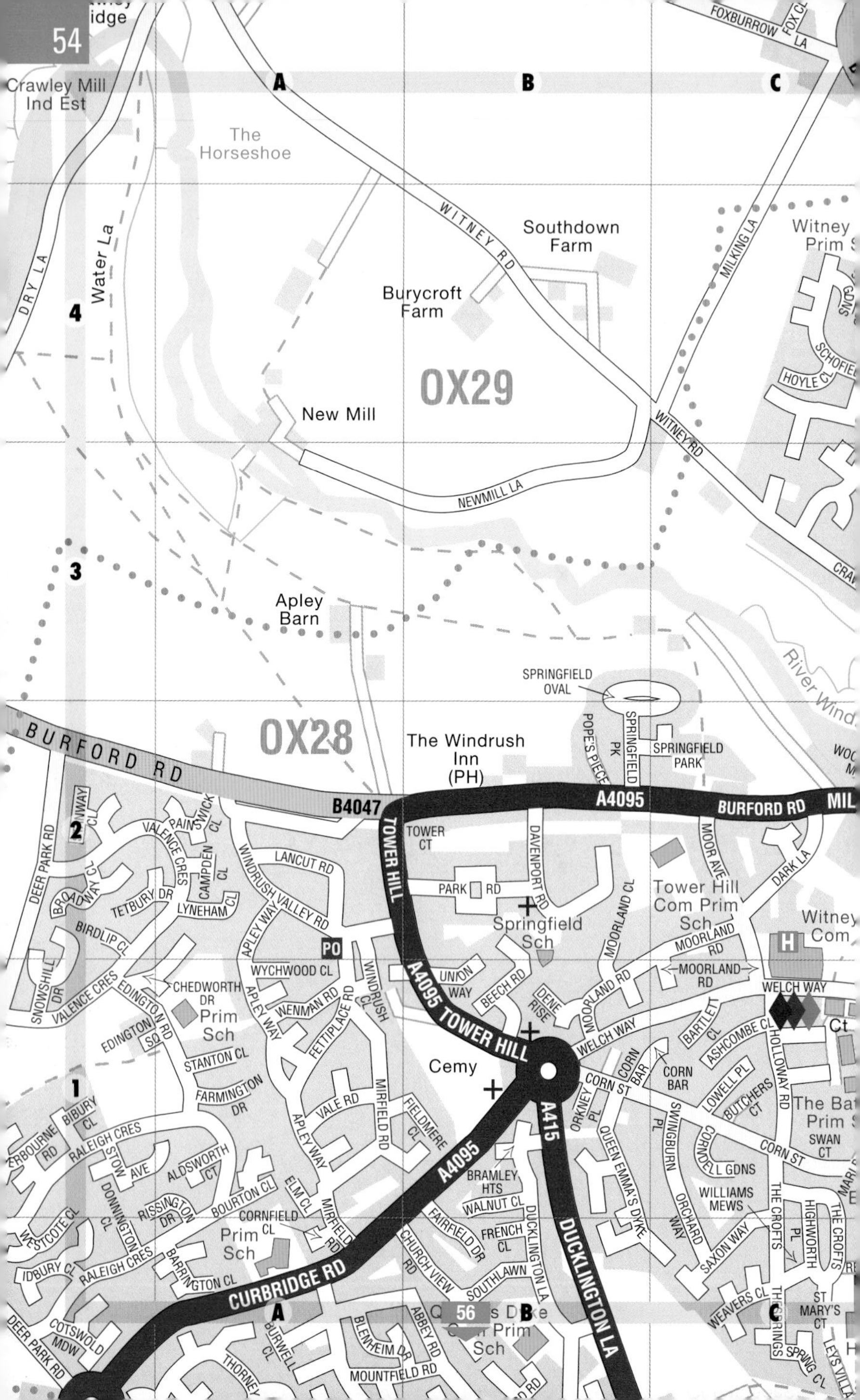
Crawley Mill
Ind Est
The Horseshoe
A
B
C
FOXBURROW
LA
WITNEY RD
Southdown Farm
Burycroft Farm
Water La
DRY LA
4
MILKING LA
Witney Prim Sch
SCHOFIELD
HOYLE CL
OX29
New Mill
WITNEY RD
NEWMILL LA
3
Apley Barn
River Windrush
SPRINGFIELD OVAL
POPE'S PIECE
PK
SPRINGFIELD
SPRINGFIELD PARK
OX28
The Windrush Inn (PH)
BURFORD RD
B4047
A4095
BURFORD RD
TOWER HILL
TOWER CT
2
DEER PARK RD
PAINSWICK CL
VALENCE CRES
CAMPDEN CL
LANCUT RD
WINDRUSH VALLEY RD
DAVENPORT RD
PARK RD
MOOR AVE
DARK LA
Tower Hill Com Prim Sch
BROADWAY CL
TETBURY DR
LYNEHAM CL
Springfield Sch
MOORLAND CL
Witney Com
BIRDLIP CL
APLEY WAY
PO
MOORLAND RD
H
SNOWSHILL DR
VALENCE CRES
EDINGTON RD
CHEDWORTH DR
WYCHWOOD CL
WINDRUSH CL
A4095
UNION WAY
BEECH RD
DENE RISE
MOORLAND RD
WELCH WAY
Prim Sch
WENMAN RD
FETTIPLACE RD
TOWER HILL
EDINGTON SQ
STANTON CL
Cemy
WELCH WAY
CORN BAR
BARTLETT CL
ASHCOMBE CL
HOLLOWAY RD
Ct
1
FARMINGTON DR
CORN ST
LOWELL PL
BUTCHERS CT
The Batt Prim Sch
SWAN CT
BIBURY CL
SHERBOURNE RD
RALEIGH CRES
STOW AVE
VALE RD
MIRFIELD RD
FIELDMERE CL
A415
ORKNEY PL
QUEEN EMMA'S DYKE
SWINGBURN PL
CORNDELL GDNS
CORN ST
ALDSWORTH CT
APLEY WAY
A4095
BRAMLEY HTS
WILLIAMS MEWS
WESTCOTE CL
DONNINGTON CL
RISSINGTON DR
BOURTON CL
ELM CL
MIRFIELD RD
WALNUT CL
DUCKLINGTON LA
ORCHARD WAY
THE CROFTS
HIGHWORTH PL
THE CROFTS
CORNFIELD CL
FAIRFIELD DR
FRENCH CL
SAXON WAY
Prim Sch
CHURCH VIEW RD
IDBURY CL
RALEIGH CRES
BARRINGTON CL
CURBRIDGE RD
SOUTHLAWN
DUCKLINGTON LA
WEAVERS CL
THE RINGS
ST MARY'S CT
A
B
C
COTSWOLD MDW
DEER PARK RD
BURWELL CL
BLENHEIM DR
ABBEY RD
Sch
THORNEY
MOUNTFIELD RD
SPRING CL
LEYS VILLA

56

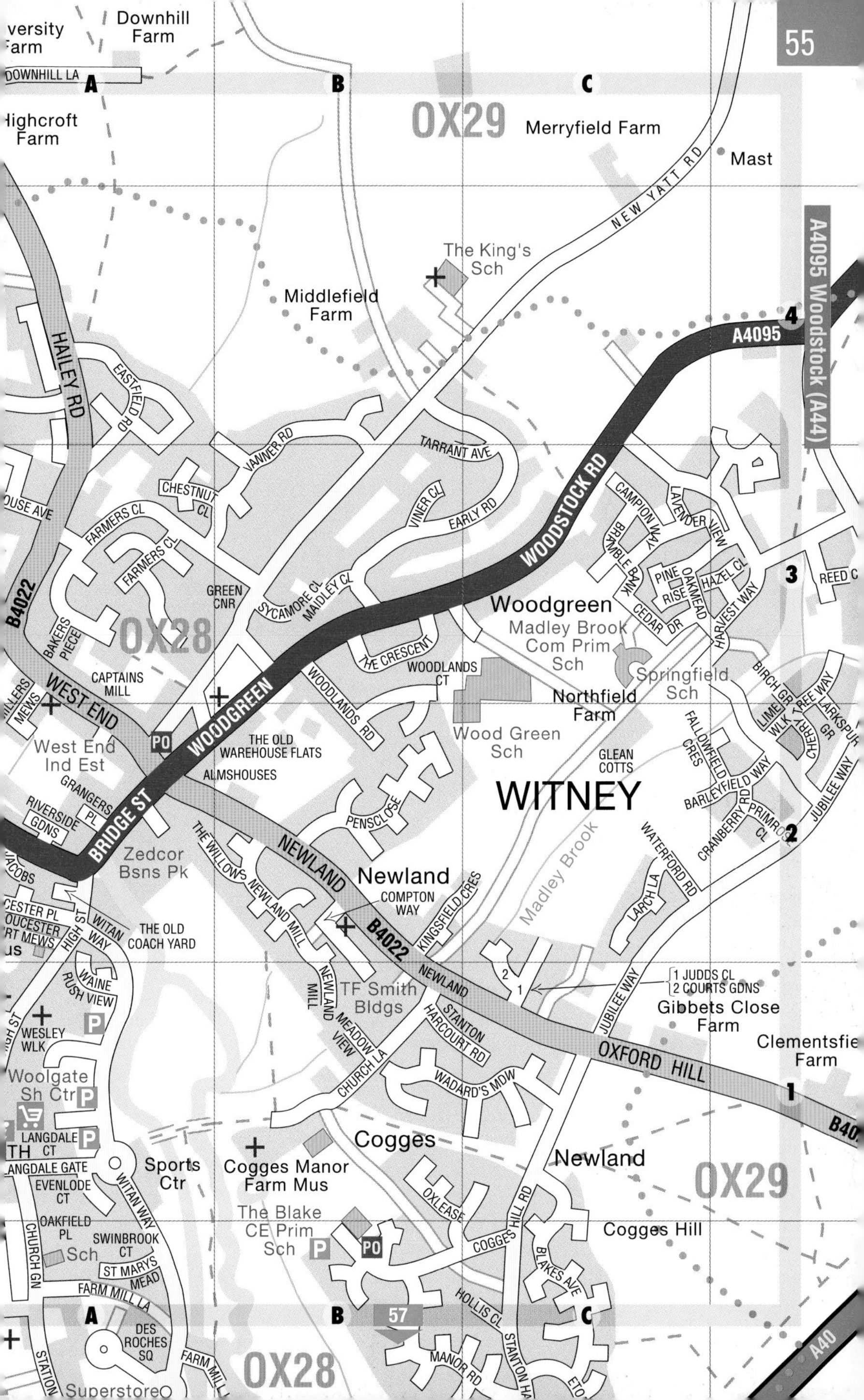
Downhill Farm
Highcroft Farm
OX29
Merryfield Farm
Mast
NEW YATT RD
A4095 Woodstock (A44)
The King's Sch
Middlefield Farm
A4095
HAILEY RD
EASTFIELD RD
VANNER RD
TARRANT AVE
WOODSTOCK RD
CAMPION WAY
LAVENDER VIEW
CHESTNUT CL
FARMERS CL
VINER CL
EARLY RD
BRAMBLE BANK
PINE RISE
OAKMEAD
HAZEL CL
REED CL
HARVEST WAY
B4022
GREEN CNR
SYCAMORE CL
MAIDLEY CL
Woodgreen
Madley Brook Com Prim Sch
CEDAR DR
OX28
BAKERS PIECE
THE CRESCENT
WOODLANDS CT
Springfield Sch
BIRCH GR
CHERRY TREE WAY
LARKSPUR GR
LIME WLK
CAPTAINS MILL
WEST END
MILLERS MEWS
WOODGREEN
WOODLANDS RD
Northfield Farm
FALLOWFIELD CRES
West End Ind Est
PO
THE OLD WAREHOUSE FLATS
Wood Green Sch
GLEAN COTTS
ALMSHOUSES
WITNEY
BARLEYFIELD WAY
JUBILEE WAY
GRANGERS PL
RIVERSIDE GDNS
BRIDGE ST
PENSCLOSE
BARLEYFIELD RD
PRIMROSE CL
CRANBERRY RD
Zedcor Bsns Pk
THE WILLOWS
NEWLAND
Newland
Madley Brook
WATERFORD RD
JACOBS
NEWLAND MILL
COMPTON WAY
KINGSFIELD CRES
LARCH LA
GLOUCESTER PL
GLOUCESTER CT MEWS
HIGH ST
WITAN WAY
THE OLD COACH YARD
1 JUDDS CL
2 COURTS GDNS
WAINE RUSH VIEW
NEWLAND MILL
TF Smith Bldgs
STANTON HARCOURT RD
Gibbets Close Farm
Clementsfield Farm
WESLEY WLK
MEADOW VIEW
OXFORD HILL
Woolgate Sh Ctr
CHURCH LA
WADARD'S MDW
LANGDALE CT
Coggès
LANGDALE GATE
Sports Ctr
Cogges Manor Farm Mus
Newland
OX29
EVENLODE CT
OXLEASE
The Blake CE Prim Sch
Cogges Hill
OAKFIELD PL
SWINBROOK CT
COGGES HILL RD
Sch
ST MARYS MEAD
BLAKES AVE
CHURCH GN
FARM MILL LA
HOLLIS CL
DES ROCHES SQ
STANTON HA
MANOR RD
OX28
FARM MILL
STATION
Superstore
A40
B4022

57

Cemy
54
STANTON CL
FARMINGTON DR
BIBURY CL
RALEIGH CRES
STOW AVE
ALDSWORTH CT
DONNINGTON CL
RISSINGTON DR
BOURTON CL
CORNFIELD CL
WESTCOTE CL
IDBURY CL
RALEIGH CRES
BARRINGTON CL
Prim Sch
VALE RD
APLEY WAY
MIRFIELD RD
FIELDMERE CL
ELM CL
A4095
CURBRIDGE RD
A415
BRAMLEY HTS
WALNUT CL
FAIRFIELD DR
FRENCH CL
CHURCH VIEW RD
SOUTHLAWN
DUCKLINGTON LA
Queen's Dyke Com Prim Sch
BURWELL CL
BLENHEIM DR
ABBEY RD
MOUNTFIELD RD
THORNEY LEYS
HOLFORD RD
PO
P
BURWELL CT
FARMHOUSE MDW
BURWELL DR
BURWELL MDW
WILMOT CL
COLWELL DR
OX28
A40
THORNEY LEYS
Thorney Leys Ind Pk
WELCH
CORN ST
CORN BAR
ORKNEY PL
QUEEN EMMA'S DYKE
SWINGBURN PL
ORCHARD WAY
LOWELL PL
BUTCHERS CT
CORNDELL GDNS
The Bat Prim S
SWAN CT
WILLIAMS MEWS
SAXON WAY
THE CROFTS
HIGHWORTH PL
WEAVERS CL
THE SPRINGS
ST MARY'S CT
SPRING CL
LEYS VILLAS
HENRY BOX CL
GORDON WAY
KINGFISHER DR
MALLARD DR
STONEGABLES
BEECHGATE
AVENUE ONE
Sewage Works
NEW CLOSE LA
Hotel
LAKESID
DALE WLK
MOORS CL
BEANHILL CL
BEANHILL RD
CHALCROFT
CURBRIDGE RD
OX29
Ducklingto
Coursehill Farm
Davis's Copse
Moulden's Wood
A40 Cheltenham
A4095 Faringdon
A
B
C
1
2
3
4

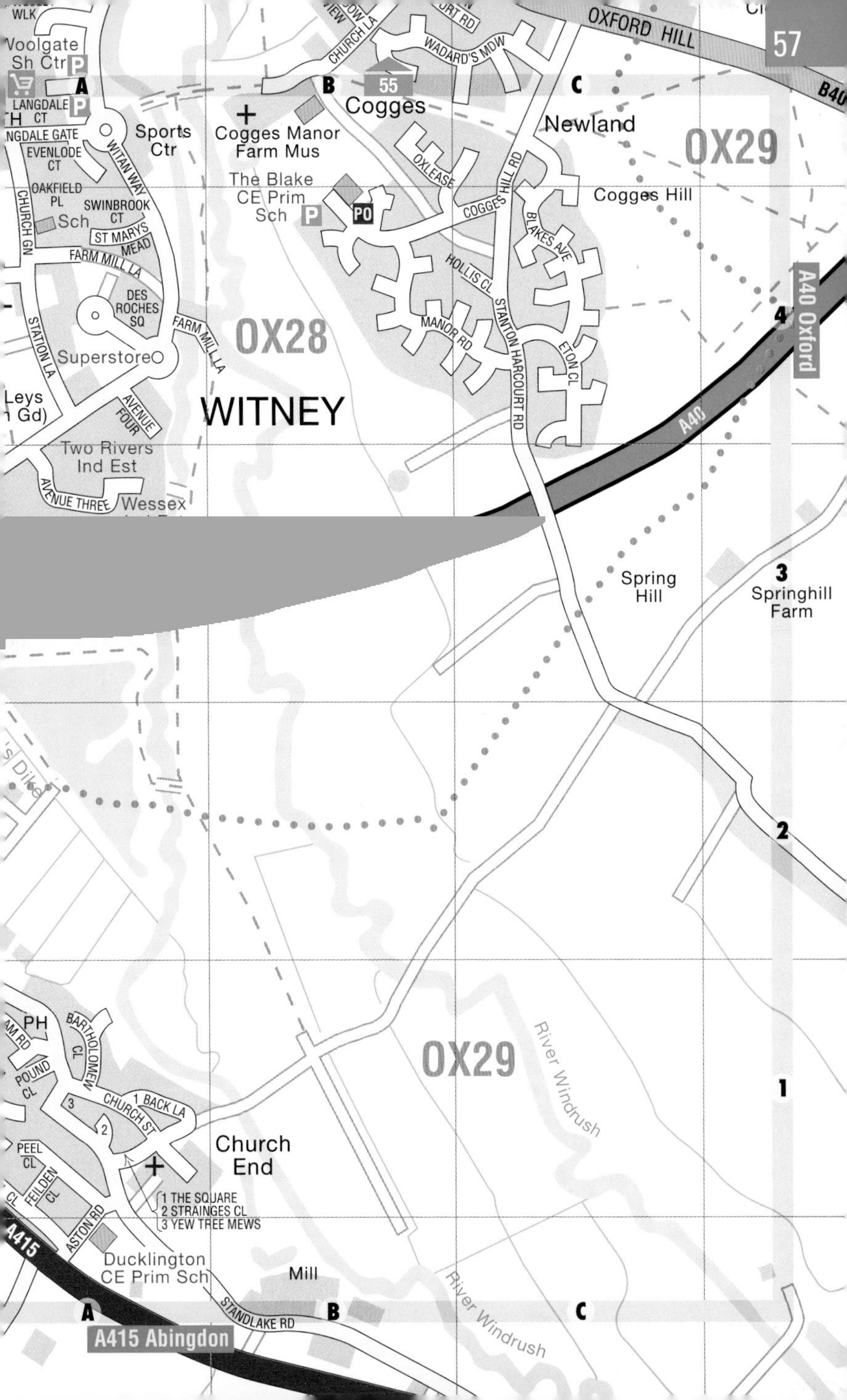
Woolgate Sh Ctr
LANGDALE CT
LANGDALE GATE
EVENLODE CT
OAKFIELD PL
SWINBROOK CT
CHURCH GN
Sch
ST MARYS MEAD
FARM MILL LA
DES ROCHES SQ
STATION LA
Superstore
WITAN WAY
Sports Ctr
Cogges Manor Farm Mus
The Blake CE Prim Sch
PO
CHURCH LA
WADARD'S MDW
Cogges
OXFORD HILL
Newland
OX29
OXLEASE
COGGES HILL RD
Cogges Hill
BLAKES AVE
HOLLIS CL
MANOR RD
STANTON HARCOURT RD
ETON CL
OX28
FARM MILL LA
AVENUE FOUR
WITNEY
Two Rivers Ind Est
AVENUE THREE
Wessex
A40 Oxford
A40
B40
Spring Hill
Springhill Farm
OX29
River Windrush
PH
BARTHOLOMEW CL
POUND CL
CHURCH ST
BACK LA
Church End
PEEL CL
FEILDEN CL
ASTON RD
1 THE SQUARE
2 STRAINGES CL
3 YEW TREE MEWS
A415
Ducklington CE Prim Sch
Mill
STANDLAKE RD
A415 Abingdon
River Windrush
A
B
C
1
2
3
4

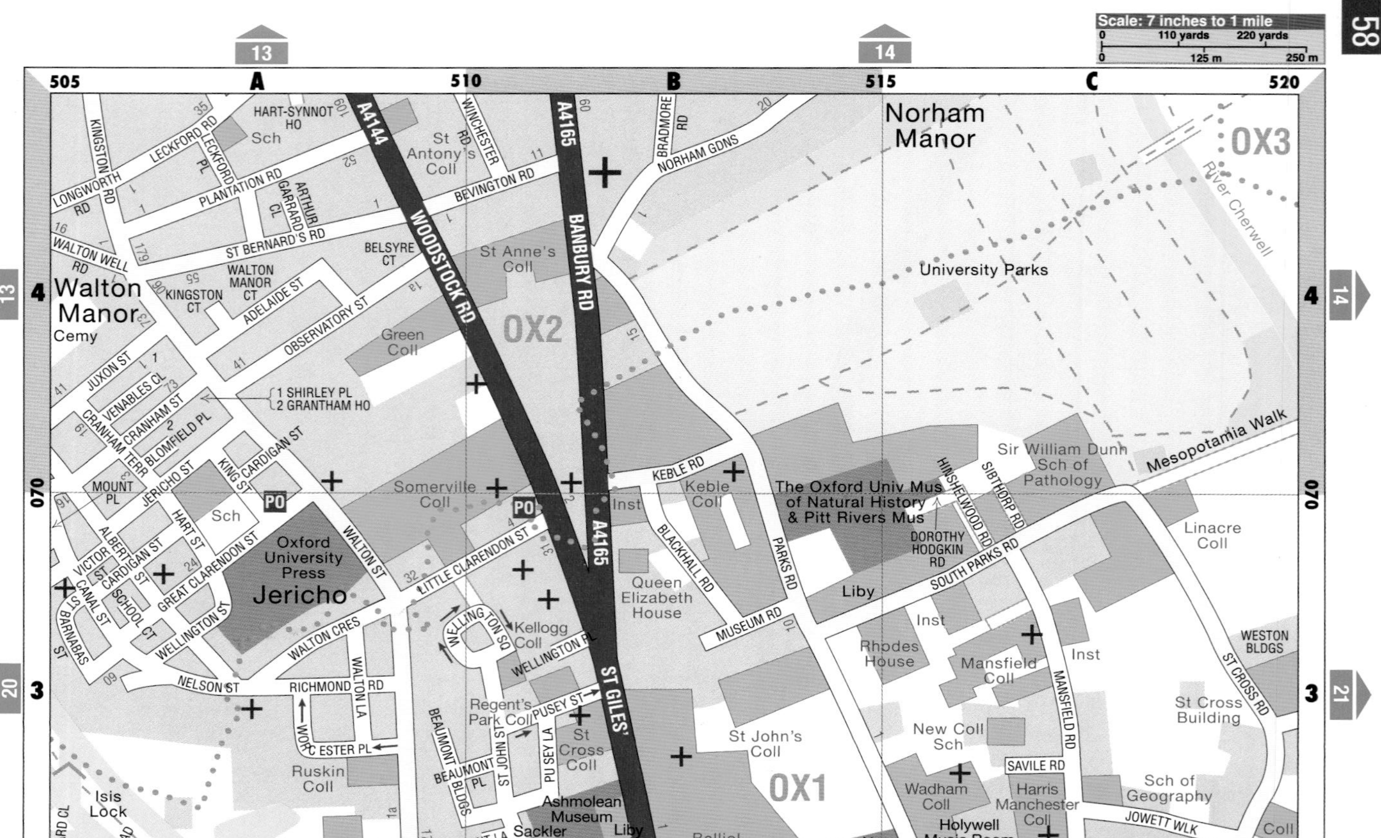
Scale: 7 inches to 1 mile
0
110 yards
220 yards
125 m
250 m
13
14
20
21
505
510
515
520
A
B
C
4
3
070
Norham Manor
OX3
River Cherwell
University Parks
Mesopotamia Walk
Sir William Dunn Sch of Pathology
Linacre Coll
WESTON BLDGS
ST CROSS RD
St Cross Building
Sch of Geography
JOWETT WLK
Coll
HINSHELWOOD RD
SIBTHORP RD
SOUTH PARKS RD
DOROTHY HODGKIN RD
The Oxford Univ Mus of Natural History & Pitt Rivers Mus
Liby
Inst
Rhodes House
Mansfield Coll
MANSFIELD RD
New Coll Sch
SAVILE RD
Wadham Coll
Harris Manchester Coll
Holywell Music Room
New
PARKS RD
MUSEUM RD
OX1
St John's Coll
Balliol
KEBLE RD
Keble Coll
BLACKHALL RD
Queen Elizabeth House
BRADMORE RD
NORHAM GDNS
A4165
BANBURY RD
ST GILES'
St Cross Coll
PUSEY ST
PUSEY LA
Ashmolean Museum
Sackler Library
Liby
Regent's Park Coll
ST JOHN ST
BEAUMONT PL
BEAUMONT BLDGS
WELLINGTON SQ
WELLINGTON PL
Kellogg Coll
LITTLE CLARENDON ST
PO
Somerville Coll
OX2
St Anne's Coll
A4144
WOODSTOCK RD
WINCHESTER RD
St Antony's Coll
BEVINGTON RD
BELSYRE CT
Green Coll
HART-SYNNOT HO
Sch
LECKFORD RD
LECKFORD PL
PLANTATION RD
ARTHUR GARRARD CL
ST BERNARD'S RD
KINGSTON RD
LONGWORTH RD
WALTON WELL RD
Walton Manor
Cemy
KINGSTON CT
WALTON MANOR CT
ADELAIDE ST
OBSERVATORY ST
1 SHIRLEY PL
2 GRANTHAM HO
JUXON ST
VENABLES CL
CRANHAM ST
CRANHAM TERR
BLOMFIELD PL
CARDIGAN ST
KING ST
JERICHO ST
MOUNT PL
HART ST
Sch
ALBERT ST
VICTOR ST
CARDIGAN ST
GREAT CLARENDON ST
CANAL ST
ST BARNABAS ST
SCHOOL CT
WELLINGTON ST
Oxford University Press
Jericho
WALTON ST
WALTON CRES
NELSON ST
RICHMOND RD
WALTON LA
WORCESTER PL
Ruskin Coll
Isis Lock

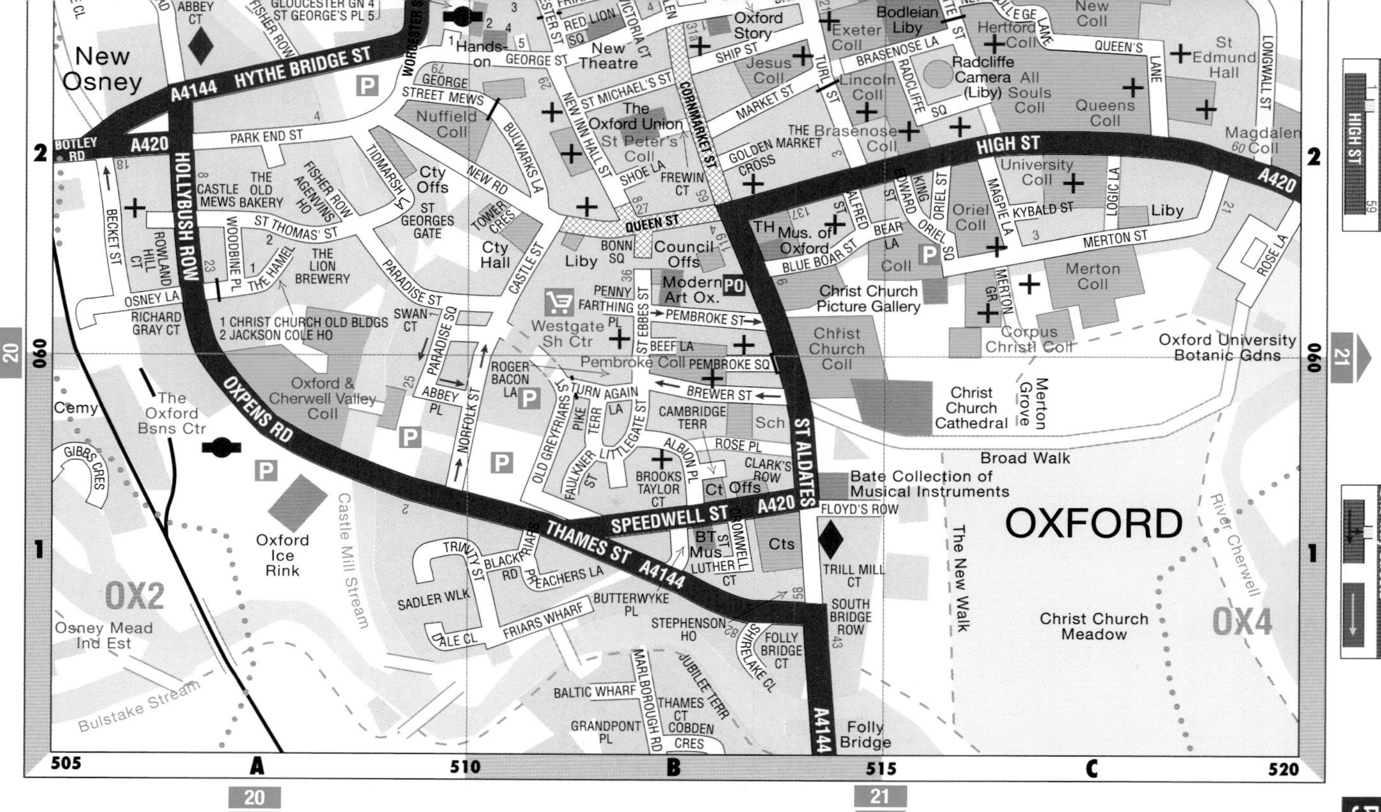
House numbers
1
59
HIGH ST
One-way streets
21
20
OXFORD
OX4
OX2
River Cherwell
Castle Mill Stream
Bulstake Stream
Christ Church Meadow
The New Walk
Broad Walk
Merton Grove
Oxford University Botanic Gdns
Christ Church Cathedral
Christ Church Coll
Christ Church Picture Gallery
Bate Collection of Musical Instruments
Folly Bridge
Oxford Ice Rink
The Oxford Bsns Ctr
Osney Mead Ind Est
New Osney
Cemy
HIGH ST
ST ALDATES
SPEEDWELL ST
THAMES ST
OXPENS RD
HOLLYBUSH ROW
HYTHE BRIDGE ST
CORNMARKET ST
QUEEN ST
A420
A4144
LONGWALL ST
ROSE LA
MERTON ST
LOGIC LA
KYBALD ST
MAGPIE LA
MERTON GR
ORIEL ST
ORIEL SQ
KING EDWARD ST
BEAR LA
ALFRED ST
BLUE BOAR ST
TURL ST
MARKET ST
GOLDEN MARKET
THE GOLDEN CROSS
SHIP ST
RADCLIFFE SQ
BRASENOSE LA
QUEEN'S LANE
Bodleian Liby
Radcliffe Camera (Liby)
All Souls Coll
Hertford Coll
New Coll
St Edmund Hall
Magdalen Coll
Queens Coll
University Coll
Oriel Coll
Merton Coll
Corpus Christi Coll
Exeter Coll
Lincoln Coll
Brasenose Coll
Jesus Coll
Mus. of Oxford
TH
Oxford Story
Modern Art Ox.
Council Offs
PENNY FARTHING PL
PEMBROKE ST
ST EBBES ST
BEEF LA
PEMBROKE SQ
BREWER ST
Pembroke Coll
Sch
ROSE PL
CLARK'S ROW
CAMBRIDGE TERR
ALBION PL
Ct Offs
Cts
CROMWELL CT
BT
ST LUTHER CT
Mus.
BROOKS TAYLOR CT
LITTLEGATE ST
TURN AGAIN LA
PIKE TERR
FAULKNER ST
OLD GREYFRIARS ST
ROGER BACON LA
FLOYD'S ROW
TRILL MILL CT
SOUTH BRIDGE ROW
FOLLY BRIDGE CT
SHIRELAKE CL
STEPHENSON HO
JUBILEE TERR
THAMES CT
COBDEN CRES
MARLBOROUGH RD
BUTTERWYKE PL
GRANDPONT PL
BALTIC WHARF
FRIARS WHARF
PREACHERS LA
BLACKFRIARS RD
TRINITY ST
SADLER WLK
DALE CL
Westgate Sh Ctr
Liby
BONN SQ
NEW INN HALL ST
SHOE LA
FREWIN CT
St Peter's Coll
The Oxford Union
ST MICHAEL'S ST
New Theatre
VICTORIA CT
RED LION SQ
GEORGE ST
GLOUCESTER GN 4
ST GEORGE'S PL 5
Hands-on
GEORGE STREET MEWS
Nuffield Coll
BULWARKS LA
NEW RD
TOWER CRES
Cty Hall
CASTLE ST
NORFOLK ST
PARADISE SQ
ABBEY PL
PARADISE ST
SWAN CT
ST GEORGES GATE
Cty Offs
TIDMARSH LA
FISHER ROW
AGENVINS HO
ST THOMAS' ST
THE LION BREWERY
THE HAMEL
1 CHRIST CHURCH OLD BLDGS
2 JACKSON COLE HO
Oxford & Cherwell Valley Coll
WOODBINE PL
THE OLD BAKERY
CASTLE MEWS
PARK END ST
ABBEY CT
ROWLAND HILL CT
OSNEY LA
RICHARD GRAY CT
BECKET ST
BOTLEY RD
GIBBS CRES
WORCESTER ST
A
B
C
1
2
505
510
515
520
060

Index

Street names are listed alphabetically and show the locality, the Postcode district, the page number and a reference to the square in which the name falls on the map page

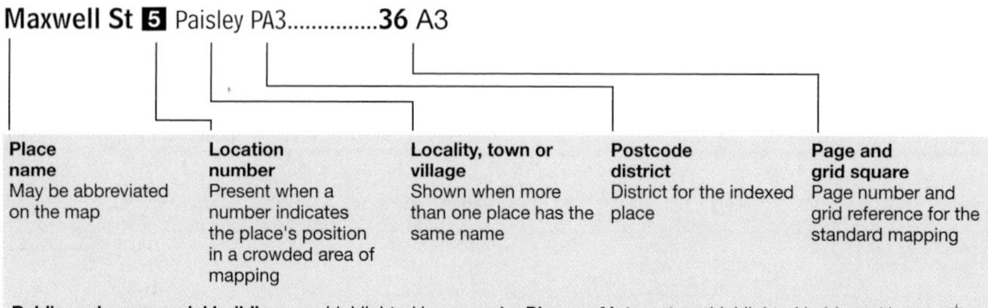

Public and commercial buildings are highlighted in **magenta. Places of interest** are highlighted in blue with a star★

Abbreviations used in the index

Acad	**Academy**	Ct	**Court**	Hts	**Heights**	Pl	**Place**
App	**Approach**	Ctr	**Centre**	Ind	**Industrial**	Prec	**Precinct**
Arc	**Arcade**	Ctry	**Country**	Inst	**Institute**	Prom	**Promenade**
Ave	**Avenue**	Cty	**County**	Int	**International**	Rd	**Road**
Bglw	**Bungalow**	Dr	**Drive**	Intc	**Interchange**	Recn	**Recreation**
Bldg	**Building**	Dro	**Drove**	Junc	**Junction**	Ret	**Retail**
Bsns, Bus	**Business**	Ed	**Education**	L	**Leisure**	Sh	**Shopping**
Bvd	**Boulevard**	Emb	**Embankment**	La	**Lane**	Sq	**Square**
Cath	**Cathedral**	Est	**Estate**	Liby	**Library**	St	**Street**
Cir	**Circus**	Ex	**Exhibition**	Mdw	**Meadow**	Sta	**Station**
Cl	**Close**	Gd	**Ground**	Meml	**Memorial**	Terr	**Terrace**
Cnr	**Corner**	Gdn	**Garden**	Mkt	**Market**	TH	**Town Hall**
Coll	**College**	Gn	**Green**	Mus	**Museum**	Univ	**University**
Com	**Community**	Gr	**Grove**	Orch	**Orchard**	Wk, Wlk	**Walk**
Comm	**Common**	H	**Hall**	Pal	**Palace**	Wr	**Water**
Cott	**Cottage**	Ho	**House**	Par	**Parade**	Yd	**Yard**
Cres	**Crescent**	Hospl	**Hospital**	Pas	**Passage**		
Cswy	**Causeway**	HQ	**Headquarters**	Pk	**Park**		

Index of localities, towns and villages

Abingdon.....49 A1
Barrow Hills.....50 C3
Barton.....16 C2
Bayworth.....38 B1
Begbroke.....2 C2
Binsey.....12 C2
Blackbird Leys.....42 A4
Blenheim.....25 A1
Boars Hill.....37 B3
Botley.....19 B2
Caldecott.....53 A4
Chawley.....28 C4
Church End.....57 B1
Cogges.....55 B1
Cold Harbour.....31 C3
Cowley.....34 A3
Cumnor Hill.....19 A1
Cutteslowe.....9 C4
Dean Court.....18 C2
Ducklington.....56 C1
Florence Park.....33 A3
Foxcombe Hill.....38 A2
Garden City.....6 C3
Garsington.....43 C3
Gosford.....4 A1
Grandpont.....21 B1
Harcourt Hill.....30 A4
Headington.....16 A2
Headington Hill.....22 B4
Headington Quarry.....23 C4
Henwood.....36 B3
Holton.....27 A4
Horspath.....35 C4
Iffley.....32 B2
Jericho.....58 A3
Kennington.....39 C1
Kidlington.....3 B1
Little Blenheim.....5 B3
Little London.....39 B2
Littlemore.....41 A3
Littleworth.....26 A1
Lower Radley.....47 C1
Lower Wolvercote.....8 B1
Marston.....14 C4
New Botley.....19 C3
New Headington.....23 A3
New Hinksey.....31 C4
Newland.....55 C1
New Marston.....15 A2
New Osney.....59 A2
Norham Manor.....58 C4
Northcourt.....49 C3
North Hinksey Village..19 C2
Old Boars Hill.....37 B2
Osney.....20 B3
Oxford.....59 C1
Park Town.....14 B2
Peachcroft.....50 B4
Radley.....47 A1
Risinghurst.....17 B1
Rose Hill.....32 C2
Sandford-on-Thames..40 C1
Sandhills.....17 C2
Shippon.....48 B3
Southend.....43 C2
South Hinksey.....31 B3
Summertown.....10 A1
Sunningwell.....45 A4
Sunnymead.....9 C2
Temple Cowley.....33 B3
The Moors.....56 C2
Upper Wolvercote.....9 A2
Walton Manor.....58 A4
Wheatley.....26 B2
Wildmoor.....49 B3
Witney.....57 B4
Wolvercote.....8 C2
Woodgreen.....55 C3
Wootton Village.....36 C2
Yarnton.....5 B4

A

Abberbury Ave OX4 . . . . . 32 C2
Abberbury Rd OX4. . . . . . 32 B2
Abbey Cl OX14. . . . . 49 B1
Abbey Ctr OX14. . . . . 49 C1
Abbey Pl OX1. . . . . 59 A1
Abbey Rd
  Oxford OX2. . . . . 20 B3
  Witney OX28. . . . . 56 B4
Abbey Wlk OX1. . . . . 20 B3
Abbots Wood OX3 . . . . . . 23 C2
Abbott Rd OX14 . . . . 49 B2
Abingdon Bsns Pk OX14 48 B1
Abingdon Hospl OX14 . . 48 B1
Abingdon Mus★ OX14 . . 49 B1
Abingdon Rd
  Cumnor OX2 . . . . 28 A2
  Kennington OX1 . . . . 31 C2
  Oxford OX1. . . . . 31 C4
Abingdon Sch OX14 . . . . 49 A1
Abingdon Science Pk
  OX14. . . . . 50 A1
Abingdon & Witney Coll
  OX14. . . . . 49 A3
Abingdon & Witney Coll
  Witney Campus OX28 . . 54 C1
Ablett Cl OX4. . . . . 22 B2
Acacia Ave OX4. . . . . 41 C3
Acland Cl OX3. . . . . 23 A3
Acre Cl OX3 . . . . 24 A1
Acremead Rd OX33 . . . . . 26 A2
Addison Cres OX4 . . . . . . 32 B4
Addison Dr OX4 . . . . 33 B1
Adelaide St OX2. . . . . 58 A4
Agenvins Ho OX1 . . . . 59 A2
Agnes Ct OX4 . . . . 33 B4
Alan Bullock Cl OX4 . . . . 21 C3
Albert St OX2. . . . . 58 A3
Albion Pl OX1 . . . . 59 B1
Aldbarton Dr OX3. . . . . . . 16 C2
Alden Cres OX3. . . . . 17 A2
Aldrich Rd OX2. . . . . 9 C2
Aldsworth Ct OX28. . . . . . 54 A1
Alec Issigonis Way OX4 . 33 C3
Alesworth Gr OX3 . . . . . . 15 C3
Alexander Cl OX14. . . . . . 45 C1
Alexandra Rd OX2 . . . . . . 20 A3
Alfred St OX1. . . . . 59 B2
Alice Smith Sq OX4. . . . . 41 A4
Alison Clay Ho OX3 . . . . . 23 A4
Allder Cl OX14. . . . . 49 B4
Allin Cl OX4 . . . . 34 A1
All Saints Rd OX3. . . . . . . 23 A4
All Soul's Coll OX1 . . . . . 59 C2
Alma Pl OX4. . . . . 22 A2
Almhouses OX28 . . . . 55 B2
Almond Ave OX5. . . . . 6 C4
Almshouses The OX5 . . . . 4 A4
Alpha Ave OX44. . . . . 43 A3
Ambassador Ave OX4 . . . 34 A2
Ambleside Dr OX3 . . . . . . 15 C2
Ambrose Rise OX33. . . . . 27 A2
Amey Cres OX13 . . . . 44 A4
Amory Cl OX4 . . . . 33 C1
Amyce Cl OX14. . . . . 50 A4
Andersey Way OX14 . . . . 53 B2
Andersons Cl OX5 . . . . 3 B2
Andover Ct 1 OX5. . . . . . . 4 A2
Andromeda Cl OX4 . . . . . 42 A3
Anemone Cl OX4 . . . . 41 C2
Angelica Cl OX4 . . . . 42 A3
Anna Pavlova Cl OX14. . . 48 C1
Anne Greenwood Cl
  OX4. . . . . 32 C2
Annesley Rd OX4 . . . . 32 C2
Anson Cl OX33. . . . . 27 A2
Apley Way OX28 . . . . 54 A1
Appleford Dr OX14. . . . . . 50 A4
Appletree Cl OX4 . . . . 42 A2
Apsley Rd OX2. . . . . 9 B2
Argentan Cl OX14. . . . . . . 52 C2
Argyle St OX4 . . . . 32 B4
Aristotle La OX2 . . . . 13 B2
Arlington Dr OX3 . . . . 14 C3
Armstrong Rd OX4. . . . . . 40 C3
Arnold's Way OX2 . . . . . . 19 A1
Arnold Rd OX4 . . . . 32 B4
Arthray Rd OX2. . . . . 19 B2
Arthur Garrard Cl OX2 . . 58 A4
Arthur St OX2 . . . . 20 B3
Ash Cl OX5 . . . . 3 C1
Ashcombe Cl OX28 . . . . . 54 C1
Ashcroft Cl OX2 . . . . 18 C3
Ashenden Cl OX14 . . . . . . 49 B3
Ashgate OX14 . . . . 53 A2
Ash Gr OX3. . . . . 16 B2
Ashlong Rd OX3 . . . . 15 B3
Ashmolean Mus★ OX1. . 58 B3
Ashmole Pl OX4 . . . . 34 B1
Ashmole Rd OX14 . . . . . . 53 A2
Ashurst Way OX4 . . . . 32 C1
Ashville Way OX4. . . . . . . 34 B1
Aspen Sq OX4 . . . . 41 C3
Asquith Rd OX4. . . . . 32 C1
Astley Ave OX5 . . . . 7 A4
Aston Cl OX14 . . . . 49 B1
Aston St OX4 . . . . 22 A1
Atkinson Cl OX3 . . . . 16 C3
Atkyns Rd OX3 . . . . 23 C2
Atwell Pl OX3 . . . . 23 B3
Aubrey Ct OX4. . . . . 32 C2
Audlett Dr OX14 . . . . 50 A2
Austin Pl OX14 . . . . 49 A4
Avens Way OX4. . . . . 41 C3
Avenue Four OX28 . . . . . . 57 A4
Avenue La OX4 . . . . 22 A2
Avenue One OX28. . . . . . . 56 C3
Avenue The
  Kennington OX1 . . . . 39 C2
  Wheatley OX33. . . . . 27 A1
Avenue Three OX28 . . . . . 57 A3
Avenue Two OX28. . . . . . . 57 A3
Avery Ct OX2 . . . . 9 C2
Avon Rd OX13 . . . . 48 B4
Awgar Stone Rd OX3. . . . 24 A1
Axtell Cl OX5 . . . . 3 B3
Aysgarth Rd OX5 . . . . 5 C4
Azalea Ave OX5. . . . . 6 C4
Azor's Ct OX4 . . . . 32 C2

B

Back La OX29. . . . . 57 A1
Badger La OX1 . . . . 31 A1
Badgers Copse OX14. . . . 51 A4
Bagley Cl OX1 . . . . 39 B4
Bagley Wood Rd OX1 . . . 39 B1
Bailey Rd OX4 . . . . 33 C2
Bailie Cl 2 OX14 . . . . 53 A4
Bainton Rd OX2 . . . . 13 B3
Baker Cl OX3 . . . . 24 A4
Baker Rd OX14 . . . . 53 B3
Bakers La OX4. . . . . 32 B2
Bakers Piece OX28. . . . . . 55 A3
Balfour Rd OX4. . . . . 34 A1
Ballard Chase OX14. . . . . 45 C1
Balliol Coll OX1 . . . . 58 B3
Balliol Ct OX2 . . . . 13 B2
Baltic Wharf OX1 . . . . 59 B1
Bampton Cl OX4 . . . . 33 C1
Banbury Ct 1 OX14. . . . . 49 B1
Banbury Rd
  Cutteslowe OX2 . . . . 9 B3
  Kidlington OX5 . . . . 3 B3
  Oxford OX2. . . . . 13 C4
Banbury Road Rdbt OX2 . 9 B3
Banjo Rd OX4 . . . . 33 B3
Bankside
  Kidlington OX5 . . . . 3 A4
  Oxford OX3. . . . . 16 C1
Bannister Cl OX4 . . . . 21 C1
Bardwell Ct OX2. . . . . 14 A2
Bardwell Rd OX2 . . . . 14 A2
Barfleur Cl OX14. . . . . 46 A1
Barleycott La OX1 . . . . . . 31 B2
Barlow Cl OX33. . . . . 26 A2
Barn's Rd OX4. . . . . 33 C2
Barn Cl
  Kidlington OX5 . . . . 3 B2
  Oxford OX2. . . . . 29 A4
Barnet St OX4 . . . . 22 B1
Barns Cl OX33 . . . . 26 C3
Barns Hay OX3 . . . . 15 A4
Barns Ho OX4 . . . . 33 B2
Barracks La
  Oxford OX4. . . . . 22 C1
  Oxford OX4. . . . . 33 C4
Barrett St OX2. . . . . 20 B3
Barrington Cl
  Oxford OX3. . . . . 23 A4
  Witney OX28. . . . . 56 A4
Barrow Hill Cl OX14. . . . . 50 B4
Barrow Rd OX13 . . . . 48 A2
Bartholomew Ave OX5 . . . 5 C3
Bartholomew Cl OX29 . . 57 A1
Bartholomew Rd OX4. . . 33 B2
Bartlemas Cl OX4. . . . . . . 22 B1
Bartlemas Rd OX4 . . . . . . 22 B2
Bartlett Cl OX28 . . . . 54 C1
Barton La
  Abingdon OX14. . . . . 50 A1
  Oxford OX3 . . . . 16 B2
Barton Rd OX3 . . . . 16 C2
Barton Village Rd OX3 . . 16 C3
Bassett Rd OX3. . . . . 17 A2
Basset Way OX5 . . . . 4 A2
Bate Collection of Musical
  Instruments★ OX1. . . . . 59 B1
Bateman St OX3. . . . . 23 B4
Bath Ct OX14 . . . . 49 B1
Bath Pl OX1 . . . . 59 C2
Bath St
  Abingdon OX14. . . . . 49 A2
  Abingdon OX14. . . . . 49 B1
  Oxford OX4. . . . . 22 A3
Batt CE Prim Sch The
  OX28. . . . . 54 C1
Batten Pl OX4 . . . . 40 B3
Bayard's Hill Prim Sch
  OX3. . . . . 17 A2
Bayswater Farm OX3 . . . 17 B2
Bayswater Farm Rd
  OX3. . . . . 17 B2
Bayswater Rd OX3 . . . . . . 17 A2
Bay Tree Cl OX4. . . . . 32 C2
Bayworth La OX1 . . . . 38 A2
Bayworth Pk OX13. . . . . . 38 A1
Beagle Cl OX14. . . . . 50 B4
Beagles Cl OX5. . . . . 4 B1
Beanhill Cl OX29. . . . . 56 C2
Beanhill Rd OX29. . . . . . . 56 C2
Bear La OX1. . . . . 59 C2
Bears Hedge OX4. . . . . . . 32 C2
Beauchamp La OX4. . . . . 33 A2
Beauchamp Pl OX4 . . . . . 33 A2
Beaulieu Ct OX13. . . . . . . 45 B3
Beaumont Bldgs OX1 . . . 58 A3
Beaumont Ct OX1 . . . . . . 39 C3
Beaumont La OX1 . . . . . . 58 B3
Beaumont Pl OX1. . . . . . . 58 B3
Beaumont Rd OX3 . . . . . . 17 A1
Beaumont St OX1. . . . . . . 58 B3
Becket St OX1 . . . . 59 A2
Bedford St OX4. . . . . 32 B4
Bedwells Heath OX1 . . . . 37 B3
Beech Cl OX13. . . . . 36 B1
Beech Cres OX5 . . . . 7 A4
Beech Croft Rd OX2 . . . . 13 C4
Beeches The OX3 . . . . 16 C2
Beechey Ave OX3 . . . . 15 A2
Beechgate OX28. . . . . 56 C3
Beeching Way OX33 . . . . 26 A2
Beech Lodge OX3 . . . . . . 16 A1
Beech Pl OX3. . . . . 15 C1
Beech Rd
  Oxford, Botley OX2. . . . . . . 19 B1
  Oxford, Headington OX3. . . 16 A1
  Wheatley OX33. . . . . 26 C1
  Witney OX28. . . . . 54 B1
Beechwood OX4. . . . . 32 C3
Beechwood Ho OX3 . . . . 16 C2
Beef La OX1 . . . . 59 B2
Begbroke Cres OX5. . . . . . 2 B3
Begbroke La
  Begbroke OX5. . . . . 2 B3
  Kidlington OX5 . . . . 3 A3
Begbroke Science Pk
  OX5. . . . . 2 C1
Belbroughton Rd OX2. . . 14 A3
Belgrove Cl OX5 . . . . 3 B2
Bellenger Way OX5 . . . . . . 3 B2
Bell La OX33. . . . . 26 C2
Belsyre Ct OX2 . . . . 58 A4
Belvedere Rd OX4 . . . . . . 22 B1
Ben Cl OX5. . . . . 3 C3
Benmead Rd OX5. . . . . 3 C3
Bennett Cres OX4. . . . . . . 33 C3
Benouville Cl OX4 . . . . . . 34 A4
Benson Pl OX2 . . . . 14 B2
Benson Rd
  Abingdon OX14. . . . . 49 A4
  Oxford OX3. . . . . 23 B2
Bergamont Pl 6 OX4 . . . 41 C3
Bergen Ave OX14 . . . . 52 C2
Berkeley Rd OX1. . . . . 37 C3
Bernard Cl OX5. . . . . 6 A3
Bernwood Rd OX3 . . . . . . 16 C2
Berry Cl OX4 . . . . 34 B1
Berry Croft OX14 . . . . 49 A3
Berrymere Rd OX13. . . . . 36 B1
Bertie Pl OX1. . . . . 31 C3
Bertie Rd OX2 . . . . 28 B3
Besselsleigh Rd OX13. . . 36 A2
Betty La OX1 . . . . 31 B1
Between Towns Rd OX4 33 B3
Beverley Cl OX14 . . . . 49 A3
Bevington Rd OX2 . . . . . . 58 B4
Bhandari Cl OX4. . . . . 33 A4
Bicester Rd OX5. . . . . 4 A1
Bickerton Rd OX3. . . . . . . 23 A4
Bigwood Cvn Pk OX14 . . 47 A4
Binsey La OX2 . . . . 19 C4

Binswood Ave OX3 23 C4
Birchfield Cl OX4 41 C4
Birch Rd OX44 43 B4
Biscoe Ct OX33 27 A2
Bishop Kirk Pl OX2 9 B1
Blackberry La OX4 42 B2
Blackbird Leys Rd
Oxford OX4 41 B4
Oxford OX4 41 C4
Blackfriars Rd OX1 59 B1
Blackhall Rd OX1 58 B3
Blacklands Way OX14 48 B1
Blackman Cl OX1 39 C4
Blacknall Rd OX14 53 A3
Blacksmiths Mdw 11
OX4 42 A3
Blackstock Cl OX3 23 C1
Blackthorn Cl OX3 16 C2
Bladon Cl OX2 9 A2
Blake CE Prim Sch The
OX28 57 B4
Blakes Ave OX28 57 C4
Blandford Ave OX2 9 B3
Blandford Rd OX5 3 B4
Blay Cl OX4 34 A1
Bleache Pl OX4 33 C3
Blenheim Ct
2 Kidlington OX5 4 A2
Oxford OX2 9 B2
Blenheim Dr
Oxford OX2 9 B1
Witney OX28 56 A4
Wolvercote OX2 9 A2
Blenheim La OX33 26 B2
Blenheim Rd
Horspath OX33 25 A1
Kidlington OX5 4 A2
Blenheim Way OX33 25 A1
Blewitt Ct OX4 40 C4
Blomfield Pl OX2 58 A4
Blossoms Glade OX14 47 A4
Bluebell Ct 4 OX4 42 A3
Bluebell Ride OX14 39 C1
Blue Boar St OX1 59 B2
Bobby Fryer Cl OX4 34 A2
Bodleian Liby★ OX1 59 C2
Bodleian (New Library)★
OX1 58 C3
Bodley Pl OX2 9 C2
Bodley Rd OX4 33 B1
Bonar Rd OX3 23 C3
Bonn Sq OX1 59 B2
Boreford Rd OX14 50 A4
Borough Wlk OX14 49 A3
Borrowmead Rd OX3 15 C3
Bostock Rd OX14 49 A1
Boswell Rd OX4 33 C2
Botley Intc OX2 19 B4
Botley Prim Sch OX2 19 B3
Botley Rd OX2 20 A3
Botley Works OX2 19 B3
Boulevard The OX5 2 C4
Boulter Dr OX14 45 C1
Boulter St OX4 22 A3
Boults Cl OX3 15 A3
Boults La OX3 15 A3
Boundary Brook Rd
OX4 32 C4
Bourlon Wood OX14 48 C3
Bourne Cl OX2 9 C3
Bourton Cl OX28 54 A1
Bowerman Cl OX5 3 B2
Bowgrave Copse OX14 50 B3
Bowness Ave OX3 15 B2
Bowyer Rd OX14 49 B2
Boxhill Rd OX14 49 B2
Boxhill Wlk OX14 49 B2
Boxwell Cl OX14 50 A4
Bracegirdle Rd OX3 23 C3
Bradlands OX3 10 C1
Bradmore Rd OX2 14 A2
Brake Hill OX4 42 B3
Bramble Bank OX28 55 C3
Brambling Way OX4 41 B4
Bramley Hts OX28 54 B1
Brampton Cl OX14 49 A3
Brampton Rd OX3 17 A2
Bramwell Pl OX4 22 A2
Brandon Cl OX5 3 B2
Brasenose Coll OX1 59 C2
Brasenose Dr OX5 4 A3
Brasenose Driftway
OX4 34 A4
Brasenose La OX1 59 C2
Brewers Ct 1 OX14 53 B4
Brewer St OX1 59 B1
Briar Cl OX5 3 A4
Briar End OX5 3 A4
Briar Way OX4 34 B1
Brick Alley 6 OX14 53 B4
Bridges Cl OX14 52 B3
Bridge St
Abingdon OX14 53 B4
Oxford OX2 20 B3
Witney OX28 55 A2
Brindley Cl OX2 13 B2
British Telecom Mus★
OX1 59 B1
Broad Cl
Kidlington OX5 3 B2
Oxford OX2 18 C3
Broad Field Rd OX5 2 C1
Broadfields OX4 41 B4
Broadhead Pl OX3 15 C3
Broadhurst Gdns OX4 40 B3
Broad Oak OX3 23 C2
Broad St
Abingdon OX14 49 B1
Oxford OX1 59 B2
Broadway The OX5 7 A4
Brocklesby Rd OX4 40 B4
Brode Cl OX14 50 A4
Brogden Cl OX2 19 C1
Brome Pl OX3 16 C2
Brookfield Cres OX3 15 B3
Brooklime Wlk 3 OX4 41 C3
Brookside
Abingdon OX14 49 B3
Oxford OX3 23 A4
Brook St OX1 21 A1
Brooks Taylor Ct OX1 59 B1
Brook View OX4 42 B4
Broughtons Cl OX3 15 A3
Browns Cl OX2 18 B2
Brumcombe La OX1,
OX13 38 A2
Bryony Cl OX4 42 B4
Buckingham St 1 OX1 21 A1
Buckland Ct OX5 4 A1
Buckland Mews 3
OX14 48 C1
Buckler Pl OX4 40 B3
Buckler Rd OX2 9 C2
Bucklers Bury Rd OX14 46 A1
Buckles Cl 1 OX14 48 C1
Bulan Rd OX3 23 C2
Bullingdon Rd OX4 22 A1
Bullsmead OX13 45 A3
Bullstake Cl OX2 20 A3
Bulrush Rd OX4 42 A3
Bulwarks La OX1 59 B2
Burbush Rd OX4 34 A3
Burchester Ave OX3 16 C2
Burdell Ave OX3 17 B2
Burford Lodge 4 OX1 21 A1
Burgan Cl OX4 33 C2
Burgess Cl 7 OX14 49 B1
Burgess Mead OX2 13 B3
Burlington Cres OX3 17 B1
Burra Cl OX4 40 B1
Burrows Cl OX3 16 B1
Bursill Cl OX3 17 B1
Burton Cl OX14 52 C4
Burton Pl OX4 34 A4
Burton Taylor Theatre★
OX1 59 B2
Burwell Cl OX28 56 A4
Burwell Ct OX28 56 B4
Burwell Dr OX28 56 B4
Burwell Mdw OX28 56 B3
Burycroft The OX14 53 C1
Buryhook Cnr OX33 27 A4
Bury St OX14 49 B1
Buscot Dr OX14 50 A4
Bushey Leys Cl OX3 16 C3
Bushnell Cl OX3 17 A1
Bushy Cl OX2 18 C3
Butchers Ct OX28 54 C1
Butler Cl
Horspath OX33 35 C4
Oxford OX2 13 C2
Butler Ho OX4 33 A1
Buttercup Sq 10 OX4 42 A3
Butterwort Pl 1 OX4 42 A4
Butterwyke Pl OX1 59 B1
Butts La OX3 11 A1
Butts Rd OX33 35 B4
Byron Cl OX14 52 B3

C

Calcot Cl OX3 23 C3
Caldecott Cl OX14 52 C4
Caldecott Prim Sch
OX14 52 C3
Caldecott Rd OX14 53 A4
Calves Cl OX5 3 B2
Cambridge Terr OX1 59 B1
Cameron Ave OX14 50 B3
Campbell Rd OX4 32 C3
Campden Cl OX28 54 A2
Campion Cl 18 OX4 42 A3
Campion Rd OX14 50 A2
Campion Way OX28 55 C3
Canal St OX2 58 A3
Candy Way OX13 44 A4
Canning Cres OX1 32 A3
Cannons Field OX3 15 A4
Canterbury Rd OX2 13 C2
Capel Cl OX2 9 C2
Captains Mill OX28 55 A3
Cardigan St
Oxford OX2 58 A3
Oxford OX2 58 A4
Cardinal Cl OX4 33 A1
Cardwell Cres OX3 22 C4
Carey Cl OX2 9 A3
Carlton Rd OX2 9 C3
Caroline St OX4 21 C3
Carpenter Cl OX4 41 A4
Carse Cl OX14 46 A1
Carswell Com Prim Sch
OX14 49 A1
Carswell Ct 2 OX14 49 A1
Carter Cl OX3 24 A4
Cassington Rd OX5 5 C2
Castle Mews OX1 59 A2
Castle Mill OX1 20 B4
Castle Mill Ho OX2 13 B1
Castle St OX1 59 B2
Catharine Cl OX14 47 B1
Catherine St OX4 22 B1
Catte St OX1 59 C2
Catwell Cl OX4 33 A4
Cavell Rd OX4 32 C3
Cavendish Dr OX3 14 C3
Cavendish Rd OX2 9 C2
Cave St OX4 22 A3
Cecil Sharpe Cl OX3 23 A4
Cedar Ct OX4 33 B3
Cedar Dr OX28 55 C3
Cedar Rd OX2 19 B1
Celandine Pl 6 OX4 42 A3
Cemetery Rd OX14 48 C1
Centaury Pl OX4 42 B4
Centremead OX2 20 B2
Centre Rise OX33 35 C4
Century Row OX2 9 C1
Chadlington Rd OX2 14 A3
Chaffinch Wlk OX4 42 A3
Chain Alley OX1 59 A2
Chalcroft Cl OX29 56 C2
Chalfont Rd OX2 13 C3
Challenor Cl OX14 53 A2
Chamberlain Pl OX5 3 A3
Champion Way OX4 33 A1
Champs Cl OX14 50 B4
Chancellor Ct OX4 33 C2
Chandlers Cl OX14 50 B3
Chandlings Manor Sch
OX1 38 C1
Chapel La OX4 40 C4
Chapel St OX4 22 A2
Chapel Way OX2 19 B3
Charlbury Cl OX5 3 B4
Charlbury Rd OX2 14 A3
Charles St OX4 32 B4
Charney Ave OX14 50 B4
Charter The 8 OX14 49 B1
Chatham Rd OX1 31 C3
Chaunterell Way OX14 52 C4
Chawley La OX2 28 C4
Checker Wlk OX14 49 B1
Chedworth Dr OX28 54 A1
Cheney La OX3 22 B3
Cheney Sch OX3 22 C3
Cheney Student Village
OX3 22 B3
Chequers Pl OX3 16 C1
Cherry Cl
Kidlington OX5 3 C1
Sandford-on-T OX4 42 A3
Cherry Tree Ct OX2 19 B1
Cherry Tree Dr OX13 48 B4
Cherwell Ave OX5 4 B2
Cherwell Bsns Ctr OX5 3 A4
Cherwell Cl OX14 50 A3
Cherwell Ct OX5 3 B3
Cherwell Dr OX3 15 A3
Cherwell Lodge OX2 10 A2
Cherwell Sch The OX2 14 A4
Cherwell St OX4 22 A3
Chester St OX4 22 A1

Chestnut Ave
Oxford OX3 16 B2
Radley OX14 47 A2
Chestnut Cl OX28 55 A3
Chestnut Ct OX4 33 B1
Chestnut Rd OX2 19 B1
Chestnuts The OX14 50 B3
Chestnut Tree Cl OX13 48 B3
Cheyney Wlk OX14 49 A3
Childrey Way OX14 50 A4
Chillingworth Cres OX3 23 C2
Chillingworth Ct OX3 23 C2
Chilswell La
Boars Hill OX1 30 B1
Sunningwell OX1 38 B4
Chilswell Rd OX1 21 A1
Chiltern Bsns Ctr OX4 34 A2
Chilterns The OX1 59 B2
Chilton Cl OX14 50 A3
Cholesbury Grange OX3 15 B2
Cholsey Cl OX4 33 B2
Cholswell Ct OX13 44 B1
Cholswell Rd OX13 48 B4
Chorefields OX5 3 B3
Choswell Spring OX4 41 C3
Christ Church Cath★ OX1 59 C1
Christ Church Cath Sch OX1 59 B1
Christ Church Coll OX1 59 B2
Christ Church Old Bldgs OX1 59 A2
Christ Church Picture Gallery★ OX1 59 C2
Church Cl OX1 31 A3
Church Cowley Rd OX4 33 A3
Church Cowley St James CE Prim Sch OX4 33 B2
Church Gn OX28 57 A4
Church Hill Rd OX4 33 A2
Churchill Dr OX3 23 A3
Churchill Hospl The OX3 23 A2
Churchill Pl OX2 9 A2
Churchill Rd OX5 3 C2
Church La
Marston OX3 15 A4
Witney OX28 55 B1
Wolvercote OX2 9 A2
Yarnton OX5 5 C2
Church Rd
Horspath OX33 35 B4
Radley OX14 47 A1
Sandford-on-T OX4 40 B2
Wheatley OX33 26 C2
Church St
Ducklington OX29 57 A1
Kidlington OX5 4 A4
Church View Rd OX28 56 B4
Church Way
Oxford, Dean Court OX2 19 B3
Oxford, Iffley OX4 32 B2
Church Wlk OX2 13 C2
Cinnaminta Rd OX3 23 C2
Circus St OX4 21 C2
Clarendon Cl OX14 50 A2
Clark's Row OX1 59 B1
Claymond Rd OX3 17 A2
Clays Cl OX3 15 B3
Cleavers Sq 4 OX4 41 C3
Clematis Pl OX4 42 A4
Clevedon Ct 3 OX5 4 A2
Cleveland Cl OX5 4 B1
Cleveland Dr OX4 33 B3
Clevelands OX14 49 C3
Clifford Pl OX2 8 B2
Clifton Dr OX14 49 B2
Clinton Cl OX4 32 B1
Clive Rd OX4 33 B3
Cloisters The 3 OX1 21 A1
Closes The OX5 3 C3
Clover Cl OX2 29 A4
Clover Pl OX4 42 A4
Cobden Cres OX1 21 A1
Cogges Hill Rd OX28 57 C4
Cogges Manor Farm Mus★ OX28 55 B1
Colegrove Down OX2 28 C4
Colemans Hill OX3 16 C1
Coleridge Cl OX4 33 C3
Coleridge Dr OX14 52 C3
Collcutt Cl OX33 25 A1
College Cl OX33 27 A3
College Flats OX4 40 C4
College La OX4 40 C4
College Way OX33 35 A4
Colley Wood OX1 39 B4
Collingwood Cl OX14 49 B3
Collins St 4 OX4 22 A2
Collinwood Cl OX3 17 A1
Collinwood Rd OX3 17 A1
Colterne Cl OX3 15 B3
Coltsfoot Sq 5 OX4 42 A3
Columbine Gdns OX4 42 B3
Colwell Dr
Abingdon OX14 48 C1
Oxford OX3 17 B2
Witney OX28 56 B3
Combe Rd OX2 20 B4
Combewell OX44 43 A4
Comfrey Rd OX4 34 B1
Compass Cl 4 OX4 33 B2
Complins Cl OX2 13 B4
Compton Dr OX14 50 A4
Compton Way OX28 55 B2
Conduit House★ OX2 20 A1
Conduit Rd OX14 49 A1
Conifer Cl OX2 19 A2
Coniston Ave OX3 15 B2
Conway Rd OX13 48 C4
Coolidge Cl OX3 23 B3
Cooper Pl OX3 17 A1
Coopers Cl OX33 26 A2
Coopers La OX14 53 A4
Copcot Pl OX33 35 C4
Cope Cl OX2 19 B2
Copenhagen Dr OX14 48 C3
Coppock Cl OX3 23 C4
Copse La OX3 15 B3
Copse The OX14 50 B3
Copthorne Rd OX5 3 C1
Cordrey Gn OX4 32 B2
Coriander Way 9 OX4 42 A3
Corn Avill Cl OX14 50 B4
Corn Bar OX28 54 B1
Corndell Gdns OX28 54 C1
Cornfield Cl OX28 56 A4
Cornmarket St OX1 59 B2
Corn St OX28 54 C1
Cornwallis Cl OX4 32 C3
Cornwallis Rd OX4 32 C3
Coromandel OX14 52 C2
Corpus Christi Coll OX1 59 C2
Corunna Cres OX4 34 A4
Cosin Cl OX4 22 B2
Costar Cl OX4 33 C1
Cot's Gn OX5 3 B3
Cotman Cl OX14 53 A3
Cotswold Cres OX3 15 A3
Cotswold Rd OX2 29 A4
Cottesmore Rd OX4 32 C1
Cotton Grass Cl OX4 41 C3
County Trad Est OX4 34 B2
Court Cl OX5 3 B2
Court Farm Rd OX4 32 B1
Courtland Rd OX4 32 C2
Court Place Gdns OX4 32 B1
Courts Gdns OX28 55 C1
Court The OX14 49 A3
Covent Cl OX14 46 A1
Coverley Rd OX3 23 B1
Cow La OX1 39 C3
Cowley Junc OX4 34 A2
Cowley Pl OX4 21 C2
Cowley Rd
Oxford, Littlemore OX4 40 C4
Oxford OX4 22 B1
Cox's Alley OX3 16 C1
Cox's Ground OX2 13 B3
Crabtree Pl OX14 50 A1
Crabtree Rd OX2 19 B2
Cranbrook Ct OX28 56 C3
Cranbrook Dr OX1 39 C1
Cranesbill Way 8 OX4 41 C3
Cranham St OX2 58 A4
Cranham Terr OX2 58 A4
Cranley Rd OX3 17 A2
Cranmer Rd OX4 34 A4
Cranston Ct 1 OX4 33 A1
Craufurd Rd OX4 34 A4
Crawley Rd OX28 54 C3
Crescent Cl OX4 33 C4
Crescent Ct OX4 33 C4
Crescent Rd OX4 33 C4
Crescent The
Oxford OX2 13 B1
Sandford-on-T OX4 41 A2
Witney OX29 55 B3
Cress Hill Pl OX3 17 A2
Cricket Rd OX4 33 A4
Crick Rd OX2 14 A2
Cripley Pl OX2 20 B3
Cripley Rd OX2 20 B3
Croasdell Cl OX14 53 A2
Croft Ave OX5 4 A2
Croft Cl OX3 15 A2
Croft Rd OX3 15 A2
Crofts The OX28 56 C4
Croft The OX3 16 A1
Cromwell Cl OX3 15 A2
Cromwell St OX1 59 B1
Cromwell Way OX5 4 B1
Crosslands Dr OX14 49 A3
Cross St OX4 22 A2
Crotch Cres OX3 15 B2
Crowberry Rd OX4 42 A4
Crowell Rd OX4 33 B2
Crown Mews 3 OX14 49 A1
Crown Rd
Kidlington OX5 3 B2
Wheatley OX33 26 C2
Crown Sq OX33 26 C2
Crown St OX4 22 A2
Croxford Gdns OX5 6 C4
Crozier Cl OX2 19 B2
Cuddesdon Way OX4 42 A4
Culham Cl OX14 49 C3
Cullerne Cl OX14 45 C1
Cullum Ho OX33 27 A2
Cullum Rd OX33 27 A1
Cumberland Rd OX4 22 C1
Cumberlege Cl OX3 10 C1
Cummings Cl OX3 23 C4
Cumnor CE Prim Sch OX2 28 A3
Cumnor Hill OX2 18 C1
Cumnor Rd OX1 36 B2
Cumnor Rise Rd OX2 19 A2
Cunliffe Cl OX2 14 A4
Curbridge Rd
Ducklington OX29 56 C1
Witney OX28 56 A4
Curtis Ave OX14 50 A1
Curtis Rd OX5 3 C3
Curtyn Cl OX14 48 C2
Cutteslowe Prim Sch OX2 10 A3
Cygnet Ct OX14 53 A4
Cyprus Terr OX2 9 A2

D

Daisy Bank OX14 50 A2
Dale Cl OX1 59 A1
Dale Pl OX5 3 C3
Dale The OX3 17 B2
Dale Wlk OX29 56 C2
Danvers Rd OX4 32 C1
Dark La
Sunningwell OX13 45 A3
Witney OX28 54 C2
Darrell Way OX14 49 B3
Dart Rd OX13 44 B1
Dashwood Ave OX5 5 C3
Dashwood Rd OX4 32 C1
Daubeny Rd OX4 32 B4
Davenant Ct OX2 9 B3
Davenant Rd OX2 9 B2
Davenport Rd OX28 54 B2
David Nicholls Cl OX4 40 C4
David Walter Cl OX2 9 C3
Dawson St 1 OX4 21 C2
Dean Court Rd OX2 18 C1
Deanfield Rd OX2 18 C3
Dearlove Cl OX14 49 A4
Deaufort Cl OX5 3 C3
Deer Wlk OX4 42 A3
Delamare Way OX2 18 C1
Delbush Ave OX3 17 C2
Dene Rd OX3 23 B2
Dene Rise OX28 54 B1
Denman's La OX2 28 A3
Denmark St OX4 22 A1
Denton Cl
Abingdon OX14 50 A2
Oxford OX2 18 B2
Dents Cl OX3 15 B3
Derwent Ave OX3 15 B2
Derwent Cl OX13 48 B4
Desborough Cres OX4 32 C1
Desmesne Furze OX3 23 A3
Des Roches Sq OX28 57 A4
Devereux Pl OX4 32 C1
Diamond Ct OX2 13 C4
Diamond Pl OX2 13 C4
Divinity Rd OX4 22 B2
Dodgson Rd OX4 33 B2
Dodson Ct OX14 49 B2
Don Boscoe Cl OX4 33 C4
Donnington Bridge Rd OX4 32 B4
Donnington Lodge OX4 32 B4
Don Stuart Pl OX4 22 C1
Dora Carr Cl OX3 15 B3

Dorchester Cl OX3 ...... 24 A3
Dorchester Cres OX14 .. 49 C3
Dorchester Ct
4 Kidlington OX5 .... 4 A2
Oxford OX2 .... 13 C4
Doris Field Cl OX3 ...... 15 B1
Dorothy Hodgkin Rd
OX1 .... 58 C3
Douglas Downes Cl
OX3 .... 23 C4
Dove House Cl OX2 ...... 9 A2
Downside End OX3 ..... 17 B1
Downside Rd OX3 ...... 17 B1
Doyley Rd OX2 .... 20 B2
Dragon Sch OX2 .... 14 A2
Draymans Wlk 7 OX14 . 53 A4
Drayton Rd OX14 .... 52 C3
Drewett Ct OX2 .... 8 C2
Drift Ctr OX4 .... 34 B4
Drove Acre Rd OX4 ..... 22 B1
Druce Way OX4 .... 34 B1
Drysdale Cl OX14 .... 51 A4
Ducklington La OX28 ... 56 B4
Dudgeon Dr OX4 .... 40 C4
Dudley Ct OX2 .... 9 C1
Dudley Gdns OX4 .... 22 A3
Duffield Cl OX14 .... 50 A4
Dukes Rd OX5 .... 4 A2
Duke St OX2 .... 20 A3
Dundas Cl OX14 .... 50 A2
Dunmore Jun & Inf Schs
OX14 .... 49 B3
Dunmore Rd OX14 ...... 49 A4
Dunnock Way OX4 ...... 42 A3
Dunstan Rd OX3 .... 16 A2
Dynham Pl OX3 .... 23 B3

E

Eagle Ind Est OX28 ..... 54 C1
Earl St OX2 .... 20 A3
Early Rd OX28 .... 55 C3
Eason Dr OX14 .... 50 B3
East Ave OX4 .... 22 B2
Eastchurch OX4 .... 32 B1
Eastern Ave OX4 .... 33 A1
Eastern By-Pass Rd OX3,
OX4 .... 34 A3
Eastern Ho OX4 .... 33 A1
East Field Cl OX3 .... 23 C1
Eastfield Pl OX4 .... 34 B4
Eastfield Rd OX8, OX28 .. 55 A4
East Oxford Prim Sch
OX4 .... 22 A2
East St Helen St OX14... 53 B4
East St OX2 .... 20 B3
Eaton Ct OX2 .... 10 A2
Eden Croft OX14 .... 49 C4
Eden Dr OX3 .... 15 C2
Eden Rd OX3 .... 15 B2
Edgecombe Rd OX3 .... 17 A2
Edgeway Rd OX3 .... 15 A1
Edinburgh Dr OX5 .... 4 B2
Edith Ct OX1 .... 39 B3
Edith Rd OX1 .... 21 A1
Edmund Halley Rd OX4 . 40 C3
Edmund Rd OX4 .... 33 B3
Edward Feild Prim Sch
OX5 .... 4 A1
Edward Rd OX1 .... 39 C4
Edward St OX14 .... 48 C1
Edwin Ct OX2 .... 20 A3
Egerton Rd OX4 .... 32 C2
Eighth Ave OX3 .... 24 A2
Elder Way OX4 .... 42 A3
Eldridge Cl OX14 .... 49 B4
Eleanor Cl OX4 .... 33 A2
Electric Ave OX2 .... 20 B2
Elizabeth Ave OX14 ..... 50 B4
Elizabeth Jennings Way
OX2 .... 13 B4
Ellesmere Rd OX4 ...... 32 C2
Elm Cl
Wheatley OX33 .... 27 A1
Witney OX28 .... 54 A1
Elm Dr OX44 .... 43 B4
Elm Gr OX5 .... 7 A4
Elms Dr OX3 .... 15 B3
Elms Par OX2 .... 19 B3
Elms Rd OX2 .... 19 B3
Elmthorpe Rd OX2 .... 8 C2
Elm Tree Cl OX4 .... 33 A1
Elm Tree Wlk OX13 ..... 48 B3
Elsfield Rd OX3 .... 15 A4
Elsfield Way OX2 .... 9 C3
Elton Cl OX3 .... 17 C2
Elton Cres OX33 .... 27 A1
Elwes Cl OX14 .... 50 A2
Ely Cl OX14 .... 52 B4
Emden Ho OX3 .... 16 B2
Emmanuel Christian Sch
OX4 .... 40 C4
Emperor Gdns OX4 ..... 41 C3
Eney Cl OX14 .... 50 B4
Erica Cl OX4 .... 34 B1
Essex St OX4 .... 22 B1
Ethelhelm Cl OX14 ..... 46 B1
Ethelred Ct OX3 .... 16 A2
Eton Cl OX28 .... 57 C4
Evans Ct OX5 .... 4 A2
Evans La OX5 .... 4 A2
Evelin Rd OX14 .... 49 A3
Evelyn Cl OX2 .... 18 C2
Evenlode Cres OX5 ...... 2 B4
Evenlode Ct OX28 ...... 55 A1
Evenlode Pk OX14 ...... 50 A3
Evenlode Twr OX4 ...... 41 C4
Everard Cl OX3 .... 23 B3
Ewert Pl OX2 .... 13 C4
Ewin Cl OX3 .... 15 A3
Ewin Ct OX3 .... 15 A3
Exbourne Rd OX14 ..... 48 C1
Exeter Coll OX1 .... 59 B2
Exeter Ct 5 OX5 .... 4 A2
Exeter Rd OX5 .... 3 C3
Eynsham Rd OX2 .... 18 C2
Eyot Pl OX4 .... 21 C1
Eyston Way OX14 ...... 48 B1

F

Faber Cl OX4 .... 41 A4
Fairacres OX14 .... 48 B1
Fairacres Rd OX4 .... 32 B4
Fairfax Ave OX3 .... 14 C2
Fairfax Ctr OX5 .... 7 A4
Fairfax Gate OX33 ...... 27 A2
Fairfax Rd
Kidlington OX5 .... 7 A4
Oxford OX4 .... 34 A4
Fairfield Dr OX28 .... 56 B4
Fairfield Pl OX14 .... 49 B2
Fairlawn End OX2 .... 9 A2
Fairlawn Flats OX2 ...... 9 A2
Fairlawn Wharf OX14 ... 53 B4
Fairlie Rd OX4 .... 33 A1
Fair View OX3 .... 23 B1
Falcon Cl OX4 .... 41 B4
Fallowfield Cres OX28 .. 55 C2
Fane Rd OX3 .... 14 C3
Fanshawe Pl OX4 .... 34 A3
Faringdon Rd OX14 ..... 48 C2
Farm Cl
Kidlington OX5 .... 4 A4
Sandford-on-T OX4 ...... 42 A3
Farm Close La OX33 .... 26 C2
Farm Close Rd OX33 .... 26 C2
Farmer Pl OX3 .... 15 A2
Farmers Cl OX28 .... 55 A3
Farmhouse Mdw OX28 .. 56 A4
Farmington Dr OX28 .... 54 A1
Farm Mill La OX28 ...... 57 A4
Farm Rd OX14 .... 49 B4
Farndon Rd OX2 .... 13 C2
Farnham Ct 6 OX5 ...... 4 A2
Farriers Mews OX14 .... 49 C1
Faulkner St OX1 .... 59 B1
Feilden Cl OX29 .... 57 A1
Feilden Gr OX3 .... 15 B1
Fennel Way OX14 .... 50 B2
Ferguson Pl OX14 ...... 50 B2
Fernhill Cl OX5 .... 3 B2
Fernhill Rd OX5 .... 2 B2
Fern Hill Rd OX4 .... 34 A3
Ferny Cl OX14 .... 47 A1
Ferry Ct OX14 .... 53 B4
Ferry Hinksey Rd OX2... 20 B3
Ferry Mills OX2 .... 20 B2
Ferry Pool Rd OX2 ...... 14 A4
Ferry Rd OX3 .... 15 A1
Ferry Wlk OX14 .... 53 B4
Fettiplace Rd
Oxford OX3 .... 16 C3
Witney OX28 .... 54 A1
Field Ave OX4 .... 42 A4
Field Cl
Kidlington OX5 .... 4 A2
Yarnton OX5 .... 5 C4
Fieldfare Rd OX4 .... 41 C2
Field Ho OX2 .... 19 A2
Field House Dr OX2 ...... 9 B2
Fieldmere Cl OX28 ..... 54 B1
Fieldside OX14 .... 48 C3
Fiennes Rd OX4 .... 32 C1
Finch Cl OX3 .... 23 A3
Finmore Cl 3 OX14 ..... 49 A2
Finmore Rd OX2 .... 19 B2
Firs Mdw OX4 .... 41 C2
First Ave OX3 .... 24 A2
Firs The OX2 .... 9 C2
First Turn OX2 .... 9 A2
Fir Trees OX14 .... 39 C1
Fishermans Wharf
OX14 .... 53 B2
Fisher Row OX1 .... 59 A2
Fitchett Yd OX14 .... 49 A1
Fitzharris Ind Est OX14 . 49 A2
Fitzharry's Rd OX14 .... 49 B2
Fitzharrys Sch OX14 .... 49 B3
Fitzherbert Cl OX4 ...... 32 B2
Five Mile Dr OX2 .... 9 B3
Flatford Pl OX5 .... 3 A4
Flaxfield Rd OX4 .... 42 A4
Fletcher Cl OX5 .... 5 C3
Fletcher Rd OX4 .... 34 A4
Flexney Pl OX3 .... 23 B3
Florence Cl OX5 .... 4 A2
Florence Park Rd OX4 .. 33 A3
Floyd's Row OX1 .... 59 B1
Fogwell Rd OX2 .... 18 C3
Follets Cl OX5 .... 5 C3
Folly Bridge Ct OX1 ..... 59 B1
Fords Cl OX33 .... 35 B4
Foresters Tower OX3 .... 23 C3
Forest Rd OX3 .... 17 A1
Forest Side OX1 .... 39 B4
Forget-me-not Way 1
OX4 .... 42 A3
Forster La OX2 .... 28 A2
Fortnam Cl OX3 .... 15 C1
Foster Rd OX14 .... 45 B1
Fountain Ct OX14 .... 49 B2
Fourth Ave OX3 .... 24 A2
Foxborough Rd OX14 ... 51 A4
Fox Cl OX44 .... 43 B4
Foxcombe Ct OX14 ..... 48 B2
Foxcombe La OX1 ...... 38 B3
Foxcombe Rd
Boars Hill OX1 .... 38 A3
Sunningwell OX1 .... 38 B4
Fox Cres OX1 .... 32 A3
Foxdown Cl OX5 .... 3 C3
Fox Furlong OX4 .... 40 B3
Foxglove Cl 7 OX4 ..... 41 C3
Foxglove Rd OX5 .... 2 C2
Fox La OX1 .... 37 B1
Foxton Cl OX2 .... 9 A3
Foxwell Dr OX3 .... 16 A3
Francis Little Dr OX14 .. 52 C4
Frank Cook Ct OX5 ...... 4 A3
Franklin Cl OX5 .... 4 A3
Franklin Rd OX3 .... 15 C1
Franklyn Cl OX14 .... 49 B4
Frederick Rd OX4 ...... 33 C2
Freeborn Cl OX5 .... 4 A4
Freelands Rd OX4 ...... 32 B3
Frenchay Rd OX2 .... 13 B3
French Cl OX28 .... 56 B4
Frewin Ct OX1 .... 59 B2
Friars' Entry OX1 .... 59 B2
Friars Wharf OX1 .... 59 B1
Friday La OX33 .... 26 C2
Frieze Way OX5 .... 7 A2
Frys Hill OX4 .... 41 C3
Fullwell Cl OX14 .... 49 A3
Furlong Cl OX4 .... 33 C1
Fyfield Rd OX2 .... 14 A2

G

Gainsborough Gn OX14 . 53 A3
Gaisford Rd OX4 .... 33 B2
Gall Cl OX14 .... 50 B2
Galley Field OX14 ...... 50 A2
Galpin Cl OX4 .... 22 B1
Gardiner Cl
Abingdon OX14 .... 50 B2
Wheatley OX33 .... 26 C2
Gardiner St OX3 .... 23 B4
Garford Cl OX14 .... 50 A4
Garford Rd OX2 .... 14 A3
Garsington CE Prim Sch
OX44 .... 43 C4
Garsington Rd OX4 ..... 34 A2
Garth The
Oxford OX2 .... 19 B2
Yarnton OX5 .... 5 C4
Gateley OX33 .... 35 C4
Gathorne Rd OX3 .... 23 B4
Gentian Rd OX4 .... 42 A4
Geoffrey Barbour Rd
OX14 .... 49 B2
George Moore Cl OX4... 32 C4

George Morland Ho [8] OX14 . . . . 53 B4
George St Mews OX1 . . . 59 A2
George St OX1 . . . . 59 B2
Gerard Pl OX4 . . . . 33 B3
Gibbs Cres OX2 . . . . 59 A1
Gibson Cl OX14 . . . . 45 C1
Gidley Way OX33 . . . . 25 B1
Giles Cl OX4 . . . . 40 C4
Giles Rd OX4 . . . . 41 A4
Gillians Way OX4 . . . . 33 A4
Ginge Cl OX14 . . . . 50 A4
Gipsy La OX3 . . . . 22 C3
Girdlestone Cl OX3 . . . . 23 B3
Girdlestone Rd OX3 . . . . 23 B3
Gladstone Ct OX3 . . . . 16 C1
Gladstone Rd OX3 . . . . 16 C1
Glanville Rd OX4 . . . . 22 C1
Glean Cotts OX28 . . . . 55 C2
Glebelands OX3 . . . . 23 B1
Glebe Rd OX2 . . . . 28 A3
Glebe St OX4 . . . . 22 A3
Glebe The
Cumnor OX2 . . . . 28 A3
Wheatley OX33 . . . . 26 C2
Gloucester Ct Mews OX28 . . . . 55 A2
Gloucester Gn OX1 . . . . 59 B2
Gloucester La OX1 . . . . 59 A2
Gloucester Pl OX28 . . . . 55 A2
Gloucester St OX1 . . . . 59 B2
Glyme Cl OX14 . . . . 50 A3
Godfrey Cl
[6] Abingdon OX14 . . . . 53 A4
Oxford OX3 . . . . 23 C3
Godstow Rd OX2 . . . . 8 B2
Godwyn Cl OX14 . . . . 49 A2
Golafre Rd OX14 . . . . 53 A3
Golden Cross OX1 . . . . 59 B2
Golden Rd OX4 . . . . 22 B1
Goodson Wlk OX3 . . . . 15 A1
Gooseacre OX14 . . . . 51 A4
Goose Green Cl OX2 . . . . 8 C2
Gordon Cl OX3 . . . . 15 A3
Gordon Dr OX14 . . . . 50 B3
Gordon St OX1 . . . . 31 C4
Gordon Way OX28 . . . . 56 C4
Gordon Woodward Way OX1 . . . . 31 C3
Goring Lodge [7] OX1 . . . 21 A1
Gorse Leas OX3 . . . . 15 C3
Gosford Cl OX5 . . . . 7 A4
Gosford Hill Ct OX5 . . . . 4 A1
Gosford Hill Sch OX5 . . . . 4 A1
Goslyn Cl OX3 . . . . 23 B3
Gouldland Gdns OX3 . . . . 15 C3
Grandpont Pl OX1 . . . . 59 B1
Grange Ct OX2 . . . . 18 C2
Grange Rd OX4 . . . . 40 C4
Grangers Pl OX28 . . . . 55 A2
Grantham Ho OX2 . . . . 58 A4
Grants Mews [2] OX4 . . . 22 A2
Granville Ct OX3 . . . . 22 B3
Grates The OX4 . . . . 33 B2
Gravel Pits La OX5 . . . . 5 C4
Grays Rd OX3 . . . . 22 C4
Great Clarendon St OX2 . . . . 58 A3
Great Close Rd OX5 . . . . 6 A3
Great Mead OX1 . . . . 58 A3
Grebe Cl
Abingdon OX14 . . . . 53 B3
Sandford-on-T OX4 . . . . 41 C3
Green Cnr OX28 . . . . 55 B3
Green Coll OX2 . . . . 58 A4
Greenfinch Cl OX4 . . . . 42 A3
Green Hill OX4 . . . . 42 B4
Green La
Oxford OX2 . . . . 18 B2
Sunningwell OX13 . . . . 45 C4
Green Pl OX1 . . . . 31 C4
Green Rd
Kidlington OX5 . . . . 3 C2
Oxford OX3 . . . . 17 A1
Green Ridges OX3 . . . . 17 B2
Green St OX4 . . . . 22 B1
Green The
Culham OX14 . . . . 53 C1
Garsington OX44 . . . . 43 C3
Horspath OX33 . . . . 35 B3
Grenoble Rd
Oxford OX4 . . . . 42 B3
Sandford-on-T OX4 . . . . 41 B3
Greystones Ct OX5 . . . . 3 B3
Grimbly Pl OX2 . . . . 9 C2
Grosvenor Rd OX2 . . . . 30 A4
Grove Ct OX4 . . . . 32 C3
Grovelands OX5 . . . . 3 B2
Grovelands Rd OX3 . . . . 24 B4
Grove St OX2 . . . . 9 C1
Grove The OX14 . . . . 50 A4
Grundy Cl OX14 . . . . 50 A2
Grundy Cres OX1 . . . . 39 C3
Grunsell Cl OX3 . . . . 16 A3
Guelder Rd OX4 . . . . 41 B3
Guildford Ct [7] OX5 . . . . 4 A2
Gurden Pl OX3 . . . . 16 C2
Gurl Cl OX3 . . . . 16 C2
Gwyneth Rd OX4 . . . . 40 B4

H

Hadland Rd OX14 . . . . 50 B2
Hadow Rd OX3 . . . . 15 B2
Hailey Rd OX8, OX28 . . . . 55 A4
Haldane Rd OX4 . . . . 41 C4
Halliday Hill OX3 . . . . 15 C3
Halls Cl OX2 . . . . 18 C1
Hamble Dr OX14 . . . . 50 A3
Hamels La OX1 . . . . 38 A3
Hamel The OX1 . . . . 59 A2
Hamilton Rd OX2 . . . . 9 C1
Hampden Dr OX5 . . . . 7 A4
Hampden Rd OX4 . . . . 33 B2
Handlo Pl OX3 . . . . 17 A2
Hands-on★ OX1 . . . . 59 B2
Hanson Rd OX14 . . . . 45 B1
Harberton Mead
Marston OX3 . . . . 15 A1
Oxford OX3 . . . . 15 B1
Harbord Rd OX2 . . . . 9 C4
Harcourt Hill OX2 . . . . 30 A4
Harcourt Terr OX3 . . . . 22 C4
Harcourt Way OX14 . . . . 49 B3
Harding Rd OX14 . . . . 48 C2
Hardings Cl OX4 . . . . 33 A1
Hardwick Ave OX5 . . . . 3 C1
Harebell Rd OX4 . . . . 42 A4
Harefields OX2 . . . . 9 C3
Harley Rd OX2 . . . . 20 A3
Harlow Way OX3 . . . . 11 A1
Harolde Cl OX3 . . . . 16 B2
Harold Hicks Pl OX4 . . . . 32 B4
Harold White Cl OX3 . . . . 24 A4
Harpes Rd OX2 . . . . 9 C2
Harpsichord Pl OX4 . . . . 22 A3
Harris Manchester Coll OX1 . . . . 58 C3
Harrow Rd OX4 . . . . 34 B1
Hart Cl OX14 . . . . 50 B2
Harts Cl OX5 . . . . 3 B2
Hart St OX2 . . . . 58 A3
Hart-synnot Ho OX2 . . . . 58 A4
Harwell Cl OX14 . . . . 49 C3
Haslemere Gdns OX2 . . . . 9 B4
Hastoe Grange OX3 . . . . 15 B2
Hathaways OX33 . . . . 26 C2
Havelock Rd OX4 . . . . 33 B3
Hawkins St [1] OX4 . . . . 22 A1
Hawkins Way OX13 . . . . 44 A4
Hawksmoor Rd OX2 . . . . 9 C3
Hawkswell Gdns OX2 . . . 10 A1
Hawkswell Ho OX2 . . . . 10 A1
Hawlings Row OX4 . . . . 42 B3
Hawthorn Ave OX3 . . . . 16 B1
Hawthorn Cl OX2 . . . . 19 B2
Hawthorne Ave OX13 . . . 48 B4
Hawthorn Way OX5 . . . . 3 C1
Hayes Cl OX3 . . . . 15 A1
Hayes The OX1 . . . . 59 B2
Hayfield Rd OX2 . . . . 13 C3
Haynes Rd OX3 . . . . 14 C3
Hayward Rd OX2 . . . . 9 C4
Hazel Cl OX14 . . . . 49 A3
Hazel Cres OX5 . . . . 7 A4
Hazel End OX44 . . . . 43 B4
Hazelnut Path OX14 . . . . 39 C1
Hazel Rd OX2 . . . . 19 A3
Hazel Wlk OX5 . . . . 7 A4
Headington Jun Sch OX3 . . . . 23 A4
Headington Rd OX3 . . . . 22 B4
Headington Rdbt OX3 . . . 17 A1
Headington Sch OX3 . . . 22 C4
Headley Ho OX3 . . . . 15 B2
Headley Way OX3 . . . . 15 C1
Healey Cl OX14 . . . . 53 A4
Hean Cl OX14 . . . . 50 A4
Heath Cl OX3 . . . . 23 B2
Heathcote Pl OX14 . . . . 50 B3
Heather Pl OX3 . . . . 15 A2
Hedgemead Ave OX14 . . 50 B4
Hedges Cl OX3 . . . . 16 C1
Helen Rd OX2 . . . . 20 A3
Helleborine Cl OX4 . . . . 42 A3
Helwys Pl OX5 . . . . 3 B4
Hendred Ho OX4 . . . . 33 A4
Hendred St OX4 . . . . 33 A4
Hendred Way OX14 . . . . 50 A3
Hengrove Cl OX3 . . . . 16 B3
Henley Ave OX4 . . . . 32 C3
Henley Rd OX4 . . . . 40 C2
Henley St OX4 . . . . 22 A1
Henor Mill Cl OX14 . . . . 50 A4
Henry Box Cl OX28 . . . . 56 C4
Henry Box Sch The OX28 . . . . 56 C4
Henry Rd OX2 . . . . 20 A3
Henry Taunt Cl OX3 . . . . 16 C3
Henwood Cotts OX1 . . . . 36 A3
Henwood Dr OX1 . . . . 36 B3
Herbert Cl OX4 . . . . 22 C1
Herman Cl OX14 . . . . 50 A2
Hermitage Rd OX14 . . . . 53 A4
Hernes Cl OX2 . . . . 9 C2
Hernes Cres OX2 . . . . 9 C2
Hernes Rd OX2 . . . . 9 C2
Heron's Wlk OX14 . . . . 49 B3
Heron Ct OX14 . . . . 53 B2
Herons Pl OX2 . . . . 9 C2
Herschel Cres OX4 . . . . 33 B1
Herschel Ct OX4 . . . . 33 B1
Hertford Coll OX1 . . . . 59 C2
Hertford Ct [8] OX5 . . . . 4 A2
Hertford St OX4 . . . . 22 B1
Heyford Hill La OX4 . . . . 40 A4
Heyford Hill Rdbt OX4 . . 40 A4
Heyford Mead OX5 . . . . 3 B3
Hid's Copse Rd OX2 . . . . 18 C1
High Cross Way OX3 . . . . 16 C3
Highfield Ave OX3 . . . . 23 A3
High St
Abingdon OX14 . . . . 49 B1
Kidlington OX5 . . . . 3 C3
Oxford OX1 . . . . 59 C2
Wheatley OX33 . . . . 26 C2
Witney OX28 . . . . 55 A1
Highworth Pl OX28 . . . . 56 C4
Hillary Way OX33 . . . . 27 A1
Hilliard Ho OX14 . . . . 53 A3
Hill Rise OX33 . . . . 35 C4
Hillsborough Cl [3] OX4 . 33 A1
Hillsborough Rd OX4 . . . 33 A2
Hillside OX2 . . . . 29 A4
Hill The OX44 . . . . 43 C3
Hilltop Ct OX4 . . . . 22 C2
Hill Top Rd OX4 . . . . 22 C2
Hill View OX3 . . . . 17 B2
Hill View La OX1 . . . . 36 B2
Hillview Rd
Abingdon OX14 . . . . 49 B4
Oxford OX2 . . . . 20 B3
Hinksey Bsns Ctr OX2 . . 19 B3
Hinksey Hill OX1 . . . . 31 A1
Hinksey Hill Interchange OX1 . . . . 31 B1
Hinshelwood Rd OX1 . . . 58 C3
Hitching Ct OX14 . . . . 48 B1
Hive Mews [3] OX14 . . . . 53 B4
Hobbs Cl OX14 . . . . 50 A2
Hobby Ct OX4 . . . . 42 A3
Hobson Rd OX2 . . . . 9 C1
Hockmore St OX4 . . . . 33 B2
Hodge Ct OX1 . . . . 21 A1
Hogarth Pl OX14 . . . . 53 A3
Holford Rd OX28 . . . . 56 B4
Holland Pl OX3 . . . . 23 C2
Holland Rd OX14 . . . . 49 C4
Holley Cres OX3 . . . . 16 C1
Hollis Cl OX28 . . . . 57 C4
Holloway Rd
Wheatley OX33 . . . . 26 C2
Witney OX28 . . . . 54 C1
Hollow Way OX3, OX4 . . . 33 C4
Hollybush Row OX1 . . . . 59 A2
Holly Cl OX5 . . . . 3 C1
Holly Ct OX4 . . . . 34 A1
Holt The OX14 . . . . 49 B2
Holt Weer Cl OX2 . . . . 9 C3
Holyoake Rd OX3 . . . . 16 B1
Holywell Bsns Ctr OX2 . . 20 B2
Holywell Cl OX14 . . . . 50 B4
Holywell Music Room★ OX1 . . . . 58 C3
Holywell St OX1 . . . . 58 C3
Home Cl
Kidlington OX5 . . . . 3 C3
Wolvercote OX2 . . . . 8 B2
Wootton OX13 . . . . 36 C1
Homestall Cl OX2 . . . . 18 C3
Homestead The OX5 . . . . 3 B2
Honeybottom La OX13 . . 44 A3
Honeysuckle Gr OX4 . . . . 42 B4
Honor Cl OX5 . . . . 4 A2

Hopkins Ct OX4 . . . . 33 C4
Hornbeam Dr OX4 . . . . . . 42 B4
Horseman Cl OX3 . . . . 15 B3
Horsepath Park Cvn Site
OX33 . . . . 35 C4
Horspath CE Prim Sch
OX33 . . . . 25 A1
Horspath Driftway OX3 . 23 C1
Horspath Rd OX4 . . . . 34 A4
Horspath Rd Ind Est
OX4 . . . . 34 B4
Horwood Cl OX3 . . . . 16 A1
Hosker Cl OX3 . . . . 17 B1
Hound Cl OX14 . . . . 50 B4
Howard St OX4 . . . . 32 C4
Howe Cl OX33 . . . . 26 B2
Hoyle Cl OX28 . . . . 54 C4
Hubble Cl OX3 . . . . 16 C3
Hugh Allen Cres OX3 . . . 15 A1
Hughes Ho OX4 . . . . 22 A2
Hugh Price Ho OX4 . . . . . 22 C1
Humfrey Rd OX3 . . . . 17 A2
Hunder Ct OX1 . . . . 39 B4
Hundred Acres Cl OX3 . . 23 C1
Hunsdon Rd OX4 . . . . 32 C2
Hunter Cl
Abingdon OX14 . . . . 46 A1
Oxford OX4 . . . . 34 A4
Hurst La OX2 . . . . 29 A4
Hurst Rise Rd OX2 . . . . . . 19 A2
Hurst St OX4 . . . . 22 A1
Hutchcombe Farm Cl
OX2 . . . . 19 A1
Hutchcomb Rd OX2 . . . . . 19 A2
Huxley Cl OX13 . . . . 44 A4
Hyacinth Wlk OX4 . . . . . . 41 C2
Hyde Pl
Abingdon OX14 . . . . 52 C3
Oxford OX2 . . . . 9 B1
Hyde The OX14 . . . . 52 C3
Hythe Bridge St OX1 . . . . 59 A2

I

Iffley Mead Sch OX4 . . . . 32 B3
Iffley Rd OX4 . . . . 22 A1
Iffley Turn OX4 . . . . 32 C3
Ilsley Rd OX3 . . . . 16 C2
Ingle Cl OX3 . . . . 15 C2
Inkerman Cl OX14 . . . . . . 48 C3
Inott Furze OX3 . . . . 23 B1
Inst of Virology &
Experimental
Microbiology OX1 . . . . . 58 C3
Isis Bsns Ctr OX4 . . . . 34 B4
Isis CE Mid Sch OX4 . . . . 32 A4
Isis Cl OX14 . . . . 50 A3
Islip Rd OX2 . . . . 9 C2
Ivy Cl OX4 . . . . 33 C3
Ivy La OX3 . . . . 16 A2

J

Jack Argent Cl 16 OX4 . . 42 A3
Jackdaw La OX4 . . . . 21 C1
Jackies La OX33 . . . . 27 A1
Jackman Cl OX14 . . . . 49 C1
Jackson Cole Ho OX1 . . . 59 A2
Jackson Dr OX1 . . . . 39 B4
Jackson Rd OX2 . . . . 9 C3
Jack Straw's La OX3 . . . . 15 B1
Jacobs Cl OX28 . . . . 55 A2
James St OX4 . . . . 22 A2
James Wolfe Rd OX4 . . . 23 C1
Janaway OX4 . . . . 40 B3
Jane Seaman Ct OX4 . . . 42 B3
Jarn Way OX1 . . . . 37 B3
Jasmine Cl OX4 . . . . 34 B1
Jenyns Ct OX14 . . . . 52 B4
Jericho St OX2 . . . . 58 A4
Jersey Rd OX4 . . . . 32 C1
Jessops Cl
Marston OX3 . . . . 14 C3
Oxford OX3 . . . . 15 B3
Jesus Coll OX1 . . . . 59 B2
Jeune Hall 1 OX4 . . . . . . 22 A2
Jeune St OX4 . . . . 22 A2
Joan Lawrence Pl OX3 . . 23 C3
John Allen Ctr OX4 . . . . . 33 B3
John Buchan Rd OX3 . . . 15 C3
John Garne Way OX3 . . . 22 B4
John Henry Newman CE
Prim Sch The OX4 . . . . . 40 C4
John Kallie Ho OX4 . . . . . 33 A4
John Mason Rd OX14 . . . 49 C2
John Mason Sch OX14 . . 49 A2
John Morris Rd OX14 . . . 53 A3
John Piers La OX1 . . . . . . 31 B3
John Radcliffe Hospl
OX3 . . . . 15 C2
John Smith Dr OX4 . . . . . 33 C2
John Snow Pl OX3 . . . . . . 16 C1
Johnson Cl OX44 . . . . 43 B4
John Towle Cl OX1 . . . . . . 31 C3
John Watson Sch OX33 . 26 C3
Jordan Hill OX2 . . . . 9 B4
Jourdain Rd OX4 . . . . 34 B1
Jowett Wlk OX1 . . . . 58 C3
Jubilee Terr OX1 . . . . 59 B1
Judds Cl OX28 . . . . 55 C1
Judges Cl OX5 . . . . 3 B2
Junction Rd OX4 . . . . 33 C4
Juniper Ct 4 OX14 . . . . . 48 C1
Juniper Dr OX4 . . . . 42 A4
Juxon St OX2 . . . . 58 A4

K

Kames Cl OX4 . . . . 33 A3
Kassam Stad (Oxford Utd
FC) OX4 . . . . 41 B3
Keble Coll OX1 . . . . 58 B4
Keble Rd OX1 . . . . 58 B4
Keene Cl OX4 . . . . 40 C2
Kelburne Rd OX4 . . . . 33 A2
Kelham Hall Dr OX33 . . . 26 C1
Kellog Coll OX1 . . . . 58 B3
Kelly's Rd OX33 . . . . 26 A2
Kempson Cres OX4 . . . . . 40 B4
Kempster Cl OX14 . . . . . . 50 A2
Kendall Cres OX2 . . . . 9 C3
Kenilworth Ave OX4 . . . . 22 C1
Kenilworth Ct OX4 . . . . . . 22 B1
Kenilworth Rd OX2 . . . . . 28 A2
Kennedy Cl OX4 . . . . 23 C1
Kennet Rd OX14 . . . . 50 A3
Kennett Rd OX3 . . . . 23 B4
Kennington Rd
Kennington OX1 . . . . 31 C2
Kennington OX1 . . . . 39 C4
Kennington OX1, OX14 . . . . 47 A4
Kennington Rdbt OX1 . . . 31 C1
Kensington Cl OX14 . . . . . 53 A2
Kent Cl
Abingdon OX14 . . . . 50 A2
Oxford OX4 . . . . 34 A1
Kenville Rd OX1 . . . . 39 B4
Kersington Cres OX4 . . . . 33 C1
Kestrel Cres OX4 . . . . 41 B4
Keydale Rd OX33 . . . . 26 A2
Kidlington Ctr The OX5 . . 3 C3
Kiln Cl OX4 . . . . 41 A2
Kiln La
Garsington OX44 . . . . 43 A4
Oxford OX3 . . . . 24 A4
Wheatley OX33 . . . . 26 B2
Kimber Cl OX33 . . . . 26 C2
Kimber Rd OX14 . . . . 48 B1
Kineton Rd OX1 . . . . 21 A1
King's Cross Rd OX2 . . . . . 9 C1
King's Mill La OX3 . . . . . . 22 A4
King's Sch The OX29 . . . . 55 C4
King Edward St OX1 . . . . 59 C2
Kingfisher Cl OX14 . . . . . . 53 B3
Kingfisher Dr OX28 . . . . . 56 C3
Kingfisher Gn OX4 . . . . . . 42 A3
Kingfisher Specl Sch
OX14 . . . . 50 A2
Kingsfield Cres OX28 . . . 55 B2
Kingsgate OX4 . . . . 33 C2
Kings Meadow Ind Est
OX2 . . . . 20 A2
King St OX2 . . . . 58 A4
Kingston Cl OX14 . . . . 49 B2
Kingston Ct OX2 . . . . 58 A4
Kingston Rd OX2 . . . . 13 C2
Kingsway Dr OX5 . . . . 4 B2
Kirby Pl OX4 . . . . 33 C3
Kirk Cl
Cutteslowe OX2 . . . . 9 B3
Kennington OX1 . . . . 39 C2
Knapp Cl OX14 . . . . 48 C2
Knights Ho OX3 . . . . 24 A4
Knights Rd OX4 . . . . 41 C4
Knolles Rd OX4 . . . . 33 B3
Knollys Cl OX14 . . . . 45 C1
Kybald St OX1 . . . . 59 C2
Kysbie Cl OX14 . . . . 45 B1

L

Laburnum Ave OX13 . . . . 48 B3
Laburnum Cres OX5 . . . . . 6 C4
Laburnum Rd OX2 . . . . . . 19 B1
Ladder Hill OX33 . . . . 26 B1
Ladenham Rd OX4 . . . . . . 34 A1
Ladygrove Paddock
OX14 . . . . 52 C4
Ladygrove Rd OX14 . . . . . 52 C4
Lady Margaret Hall Coll
OX2 . . . . 14 B2
Lakefield Rd OX4 . . . . 40 C3
Lakeside
Cutteslowe OX2 . . . . 9 A4
Witney OX28 . . . . 56 C3
Lakesmere Cl OX5 . . . . 3 A4
Lake St OX1 . . . . 31 C4
Lamarsh Rd OX2 . . . . 19 C3
Lamborough Hill OX13 . . 44 A4
Lambourn Rd OX4 . . . . . 32 C1
Lambrick Way OX14 . . . . 53 A2
Lambs Cl OX5 . . . . 3 C4
Lambton Cl OX4 . . . . 23 C1
Lammas Cl OX14 . . . . 49 B3
Lancut Rd OX28 . . . . 54 A2
Landseer Wlk OX14 . . . . . 53 A3
Lane Cl OX5 . . . . 3 B2
Langdale Ct OX28 . . . . 55 A1
Langdale Gate OX28 . . . . 55 A1
Langford Bsns Pk OX5 . . . 2 C4
Langford La OX5 . . . . 2 B4
Langford Locks OX5 . . . . . 3 A4
Langley Cl OX3 . . . . 23 B4
Langley Rd OX14 . . . . 49 B4
Lanham Way OX4 . . . . 40 C4
Larch Cl OX2 . . . . 19 B2
Larch End OX44 . . . . 43 B4
Larches The OX3 . . . . 17 B1
Larch La OX28 . . . . 55 C2
Larkfields OX3 . . . . 23 C4
Lark Hill OX2 . . . . 13 B4
Larkhill Pl OX14 . . . . 48 C3
Larkhill Rd OX14 . . . . 49 A2
Larkins La OX3 . . . . 16 B2
Larkmead Sch OX14 . . . . 48 B2
Larkrise Prim Sch OX4 . 32 C4
Lashford La OX13 . . . . 36 A1
Lathbury Rd OX2 . . . . 13 C3
Latimer Grange OX3 . . . . 23 A4
Latimer Rd OX3 . . . . 23 A4
Laurel Ct OX4 . . . . 22 B2
Laurel Farm Cl OX3 . . . . . 16 A2
Lavender View OX28 . . . . 55 C3
Lawrence Rd OX4 . . . . 33 B3
Leafield Rd OX4 . . . . 33 B4
Leckford Pl OX2 . . . . 58 A4
Leckford Rd OX2 . . . . 58 A4
Ledgers Cl OX4 . . . . 41 A4
Lee Ave OX14 . . . . 50 A2
Lee Cl OX5 . . . . 3 B4
Leiden Rd OX3 . . . . 23 C2
Leigh Croft OX13 . . . . 36 B1
Lely Ct OX14 . . . . 53 A3
Lenthall Rd
Abingdon OX14 . . . . 49 B2
Oxford OX4 . . . . 32 B1
Leoline Jenkins Ho
OX4 . . . . 22 C1
Leon Cl OX4 . . . . 22 A2
Leopold St OX4 . . . . 22 B1
Letcombe Ave OX14 . . . . 49 B2
Levery Cl OX14 . . . . 50 B2
Lewell Ave OX3 . . . . 15 A2
Lewin Cl 1 OX4 . . . . 33 B2
Lewis Cl OX3 . . . . 24 B4
Leyshon Rd OX33 . . . . 27 A1
Leys Pl OX4 . . . . 22 B1
Leys Villas OX28 . . . . 56 C4
Liddell Rd OX4 . . . . 33 B2
Liddiard Cl OX1 . . . . 39 C2
Lime Rd OX2 . . . . 19 B1
Lime Wlk OX3 . . . . 23 A4
Linacre Coll OX1 . . . . 58 C3
Linacre Ct OX3 . . . . 24 A4
Lincoln Coll OX1 . . . . 59 B2
Lincoln Rd OX1 . . . . 31 C3
Lincombe La OX1 . . . . 37 C1
Lincraft Cl OX5 . . . . 3 C1
Linden Ct OX3 . . . . 16 B1
Lindsay Dr OX14 . . . . 50 A4
Linkside Ave OX2 . . . . 9 A4
Links Rd OX1 . . . . 39 C2
Link The
Marston OX3 . . . . 14 C2
Oxford OX3 . . . . 17 A1
Linnet Cl OX4 . . . . 41 B4
Linton Rd OX2 . . . . 14 A3
Lion Brewery The OX1 . . 59 A2
Little Acreage OX3 . . . . . . 15 A4
Little Blenheim OX5 . . . . . 5 C3
Little Brewery St OX4 . . . 22 A3
Little Bury OX4 . . . . 42 B4
Little Clarendon St OX1 58 B3
Littlefields OX4 . . . . 33 C1

Littlegate St OX1 . . . . 59 B1
Littlehay Rd OX4. . . . . 33 A3
Little Howe Cl OX14. . . . . 47 A1
Littlemore Rd OX4 . . . . . . 33 B2
Littlemore Rdbt OX4. . . . 33 A1
Littleworth Bsns Ctr
OX33. . . . . 26 A1
Littleworth Ind Est
OX33. . . . . 26 A1
Littleworth Pk OX33 . . . . 26 A2
Littleworth Rd OX33 . . . . 26 B2
Livingstone Cl OX5 . . . . . . 2 C1
Lobelia Rd OX4. . . . . 42 A4
Lock Cres OX5. . . . . 6 C4
Lockheart Cres OX4 . . . . 33 C2
Loddon Cl OX14 . . . . 50 A3
Lodge Cl OX3. . . . . 11 A1
Lodge Hill OX14 . . . . 46 A2
Lodge Hill Intc OX14. . . . 46 A3
Logic La OX1 . . . . 59 C2
Lombard St 5 OX14 . . . . 49 B1
London Ct OX3 . . . . 23 A4
London Pl OX4 . . . . 22 A3
London Rd
Oxford OX3. . . . . 16 B1
Wheatley OX33. . . . . 27 B1
Long Alley Almshouses 10
OX14. . . . . 53 B4
Long Cl
Oxford, Dean Court OX2. . . 18 C3
Oxford, New Headington
OX3 . . . . 23 C2
Longfellow Dr OX14 . . . . 52 B3
Long Ford Cl OX1. . . . . . . 21 A1
Long Furlong Prim Sch
OX14. . . . . 45 C1
Long Furlong Rd OX13 . . 44 C2
Long Ground OX4. . . . . . . 41 C3
Long La OX4. . . . . 33 B1
Longlands Rd OX4 . . . . . 34 A1
Longmead OX14. . . . . 49 A3
Long Tow OX13 . . . . 48 C4
Longwall OX4 . . . . 33 A1
Longwall St OX1. . . . . 59 C2
Longworth Rd OX2 . . . . . 58 A4
Lonsdale Rd OX2 . . . . 9 C1
Lovelace Cl OX14 . . . . 45 C1
Lovelace Dr OX5. . . . . 4 B2
Lovelace Rd OX2 . . . . 9 B3
Lovelace Sq OX2 . . . . 9 B3
Lovell Cl OX29. . . . . 57 A1
Lowell Pl OX28 . . . . 54 C1
Lower Radley Cvn Pk
OX14. . . . . 51 B4
Loyd Cl OX14 . . . . 45 C1
Lucas Pl OX4 . . . . 32 B3
Lucca Dr OX14. . . . . 52 C2
Lucerne Rd OX2 . . . . 10 A2
Lumberd Rd OX14 . . . . . . 50 A4
Luther Ct OX1 . . . . 59 B1
Lydia Cl OX3 . . . . 17 A2
Lye Valley OX3 . . . . 23 B1
Lyford Way OX14 . . . . 50 A4
Lyndworth Cl OX3 . . . . . . 16 C2
Lyndworth Mews OX3. . . 16 C1
Lyneham Cl OX28. . . . . . . 54 A2
Lyne Rd OX5 . . . . 3 B3
Lynges Cl OX14. . . . . 50 A4
Lynn Cl OX3 . . . . 15 A2
Lyon Cl OX14 . . . . 49 C3
Lytton Rd OX4 . . . . 33 A3

M

Mabel Prichard Sch
OX4 . . . . 40 C4
Maberley Cl OX14. . . . . . . 52 B4
Macray Rd OX29 . . . . 57 A1
Madley Brook Com Prim
Sch OX28. . . . . 55 C3
Magdalen Coll OX1 . . . . . 21 C3
Magdalen Coll Sch OX4 21 C2
Magdalen Rd OX4 . . . . . . 22 A1
Magdalen St OX1 . . . . 59 B2
Magnette Cl OX14 . . . . . . 49 B1
Magnolia Cl OX5 . . . . 3 C1
Magpie La OX1 . . . . 59 C2
Maidcroft Rd OX4 . . . . . . 33 B3
Maidley Cl OX28 . . . . 55 B3
Main Ave OX4 . . . . 41 A2
Malford Rd OX3 . . . . 17 A2
Mallard Cl OX4 . . . . 41 B4
Mallard Dr OX28. . . . . 56 C3
Mallinson Ct OX2. . . . . . . 20 B3
Maltfield Rd OX3 . . . . 15 C3
Mandeville Cl OX14. . . . . 49 C4
Mandlebrote Dr OX4. . . . 40 C3
Manor Ct OX14 . . . . 53 A4
Manor Dr OX33. . . . . 35 B4
Manor Farm Rd OX33 . . . 35 B4
Manor Gr OX1. . . . . 39 C1
Manor Ho★ OX5 . . . . 5 C2
Manor Hospl The OX3 . . 16 A1
Manor Pk OX3. . . . . 16 A1
Manor Pl OX1 . . . . 21 C4
Manor Prep Sch The
OX13. . . . . 48 B3
Manor Rd
Ducklington OX29. . . . . 56 C1
Oxford OX1. . . . . 21 C4
South Hinksey OX1. . . . . . . 31 A3
Witney OX28. . . . . 57 B4
Wootton OX13 . . . . 36 B1
Manor Way OX5 . . . . 4 A4
Mansfield Coll OX1. . . . . 58 C3
Mansfield Rd OX1 . . . . . . 58 C3
Manzil Way OX4 . . . . 22 B2
Maple Ave OX5 . . . . 4 A1
Maple Cl OX2. . . . . 19 B2
Maple Ct OX5 . . . . 4 A1
Marcham Rd OX14. . . . . . 52 B4
Margaret Rd OX3 . . . . 23 C4
Marigold Cl 12 OX4 . . . . . 42 A3
Marina Way OX14. . . . . . . 53 B2
Marjoram Cl OX4 . . . . 42 B4
Market Pl 4 OX14 . . . . . . 49 B1
Market Sq OX28 . . . . 55 A1
Market St OX1. . . . . 59 B2
Market The OX1 . . . . 59 B2
Mark Rd OX3 . . . . 23 C4
Marlborough Ave OX5 . . . 3 B4
Marlborough Cl
Kidlington OX5 . . . . 3 B4
Oxford OX4. . . . . 40 C4
Marlborough Ct OX2. . . . 20 A3
Marlborough La OX28. . . 54 C1
Marlborough Rd OX1 . . . 21 A1
Marriott Cl OX2. . . . . 9 C3
Marshall Rd OX4 . . . . 33 C4
Marsh Cl OX5. . . . . 6 A3
Marsh Ct OX14 . . . . 49 B2
Marsh La OX3 . . . . 15 B3
Marsh Rd OX4. . . . . 33 B4
Marston Ferry Ct OX2. . . 14 A4
Marston Ferry Rd OX2 . . 14 B4
Marston Rd OX3, OX4. . . . 15 A1
Marston St OX4 . . . . 22 A2
Martin Ct OX2 . . . . 9 C1
Mascall Ave OX3. . . . . 23 C1
Masefield Cres OX14. . . . 52 B3
Masey Cl OX3 . . . . 23 B3
Masons Rd OX3. . . . . 23 C3
Mather Rd OX3 . . . . 17 A2
Mathews Way OX13. . . . . 44 A4
Matthew Arnold Sch
OX2. . . . . 19 A1
Mattock Cl OX3. . . . . 23 B4
Mattock Way OX14. . . . . . 46 A1
Maud Hale Cotts 11
OX14. . . . . 53 B4
Mayfair Rd OX4. . . . . 33 A2
Mayfield Rd OX2. . . . . 9 C1
Mayott's Rd 1 OX14 . . . 49 A1
Meaden Hill OX3 . . . . 15 C3
Meadow La
Oxford OX4. . . . . 21 C1
Oxford OX4. . . . . 32 B3
Meadow Prospect OX2. . . 8 B2
Meadowside OX14. . . . . . 53 A4
Meadowside Ct 1
OX14. . . . . 53 A4
Meadow View
Kidlington OX5 . . . . 3 C4
Oxford OX2. . . . . 10 A2
Witney OX28. . . . . 55 B1
Meadow View Rd OX1. . . 40 A2
Meadow Way OX5 . . . . 6 A3
Mead Rd OX5. . . . . 6 A2
Mead Way OX5 . . . . 3 C4
Medlicott Dr OX14. . . . . . 52 B4
Medway Cl OX13. . . . . 44 B1
Medway Rd OX13. . . . . . . 44 B1
Mercury Rd OX4. . . . . 42 B4
Mere Rd OX2. . . . . 9 A2
Merewood Ave OX3. . . . . 17 B2
Merlin Rd
Abingdon OX13. . . . . 48 A4
Oxford OX4. . . . . 41 C4
Merrivale Sq OX2. . . . . . . 13 B2
Merton Coll OX1 . . . . 59 C2
Merton Ct OX2 . . . . 13 B2
Merton Gr OX1 . . . . 59 C2
Merton St OX1 . . . . 59 C2
Merton Way OX5 . . . . 5 C3
Metcalfe Cl OX14. . . . . . . 53 A2
Meyseys Rd OX3. . . . . 23 C1
Middle Way OX2. . . . . 9 C1
Midget Cl OX14. . . . . 52 C3
Mileway Gdns OX3. . . . . . 23 A3
Milking La OX28, OX29. . . 54 C4
Millbank OX2. . . . . 20 B2
Millbuck Ind Est OX28 . . 57 A3
Mill End OX5 . . . . 4 B3
Miller's Acre 1 OX2 . . . . . 9 C3
Miller Rd OX33 . . . . 27 A1
Millers Mews OX28 . . . . . 55 A2
Mill La
Marston OX3. . . . . 10 C2
Marston OX3. . . . . 11 A1
Oxford OX4. . . . . 32 B2
Mill Paddock 7 OX14. . . 53 B4
Mill Rd
Abingdon OX14. . . . . 52 B3
Wolvercote OX2 . . . . 8 B2
Mill St
Kidlington OX5 . . . . 4 A3
Oxford OX2. . . . . 20 B3
Witney OX28. . . . . 54 C2
Millstream Ct OX2 . . . . 8 B2
Millway Cl OX2 . . . . 9 A2
Milne Pl OX3 . . . . 15 C3
Milton Rd OX4. . . . . 33 A4
Milvery Way OX4 . . . . 33 A1
Minchery Farm Cotts
OX4. . . . . 41 A3
Minchery Rd OX4 . . . . 41 A3
Minchins Cl OX14. . . . . . . 50 B2
Minster Rd OX4 . . . . 22 B2
Mirfield Rd OX28 . . . . 54 A1
Mistletoe Gn OX4. . . . . . . 41 C3
Mitchell Cl OX13. . . . . 36 B1
Moberly Cl OX4. . . . . 22 A2
Modern Art Oxford★
OX1. . . . . 59 B2
Mole Pl
Oxford OX4. . . . . 42 B3
17 Sandford-on-T OX4 . . . . 42 A3
Monard Terr 2 OX4. . . . . 22 A1
Monks Cl OX4 . . . . 41 B4
Monmouth Rd OX1 . . . . . 31 C3
Mons Way OX14 . . . . 48 C3
Montagu Rd OX2 . . . . 19 B2
Moody Rd OX3 . . . . 15 A1
Moor Ave OX28. . . . . 54 C2
Moorbank OX4 . . . . 41 C4
Moorhen Wlk OX4 . . . . . . 41 C3
Moorland Cl OX28 . . . . . . 54 B2
Moorland Rd OX28. . . . . . 54 B1
Moorlands The OX5. . . . . . 3 C4
Moors Cl OX29 . . . . 56 C2
Moors The OX5 . . . . 3 B4
Moreton Rd OX2. . . . . 13 C4
Morland Cl OX33 . . . . 26 C2
Morrell Ave OX4. . . . . 22 B2
Morrell Cl OX5 . . . . 3 B2
Morrell Cres OX4 . . . . 40 B4
Morris Cres OX4. . . . . 33 A4
Morris Ho OX4 . . . . 33 B2
Mortimer Dr OX3 . . . . 15 A2
Mortimer Rd OX4. . . . . . . 32 B1
Morton Ave OX5 . . . . 3 C1
Morton Cl
Abingdon OX14. . . . . 50 B2
Kidlington OX5 . . . . 3 C2
Motte The OX14 . . . . 49 B1
Mountfield Rd OX28 . . . . 56 B4
Mount Pl OX2 . . . . 58 A3
Mount St OX2 . . . . 20 B4
Mulberry Ct OX2. . . . . 9 B2
Mulberry Dr OX33 . . . . . . 26 C2
Mulcaster Ave OX5 . . . . . . 4 A2
Mullard Way OX14 . . . . . . 49 A1
Murray Ct OX2 . . . . 14 A2
Museum Rd OX1. . . . . 58 B3
Mus of Oxford★ OX1 . . . 59 B2
Musson Cl 3 OX14 . . . . . 53 A4

N

Napier Ct OX14. . . . . 50 A1
Napier Rd OX4 . . . . 33 C3
Nash Ct OX4. . . . . 33 C2
Nash Dr OX14 . . . . 52 B4
Navigation Way OX2 . . . . 13 B3
Neave Mews 9 OX14 . . . 53 B4
Nelson St OX2. . . . . 58 A3
Nene Rd OX13 . . . . 48 B4
Nether Durnford Cl
OX3. . . . . 24 A1
Netherwoods Rd OX3 . . . 24 A4
Nettlebed Mead OX4. . . . 41 C3
New Close La OX28 . . . . . 56 B2

New Coll OX1 . . . . 59 C2
New College La OX1 . . . . 59 C2
New Coll Sch OX1 . . . . . . 58 C3
Newcombe Ct OX2. . . . . . . 9 B1
New Cross Rd OX3 . . . . . . 16 C1
New High St OX3 . . . . 23 A4
New Hinksey CE Prim Sch OX1 . . . . 31 B4
New Inn Hall St OX1 . . . . 59 B2
Newland OX28. . . . . 55 B2
Newland Mill OX28 . . . . . 55 B2
Newlin Cl OX4. . . . . 32 B1
Newman Ct OX4 . . . . 22 A3
Newman Rd OX4 . . . . 33 A1
New Marston Prim Sch OX3 . . . . 15 B3
Newmill La OX28 . . . . 54 B3
Newport Cl OX5 . . . . 3 B1
New Rd
Oxford OX1. . . . . 59 B2
Radley OX14 . . . . 51 A4
New St OX14 . . . . 49 B1
Newtec Pl OX4 . . . . 22 A1
New Theatre★ OX1. . . . . 59 B2
Newton Rd OX1 . . . . 21 A1
Nicholas Ave OX3. . . . . . . 15 A2
Nicholson Rd OX3 . . . . . . 15 A1
Nightingale Ave OX4. . . . 42 A3
Ninth Ave OX3, OX4. . . . . . 24 A1
Nixon Rd OX4 . . . . 32 B3
Nobles Cl OX2. . . . . 18 B2
Nobles La OX2. . . . . 18 B2
Nor Brook Cl OX14. . . . . . 50 B4
Norfolk Cl OX14 . . . . 51 A4
Norfolk St OX1 . . . . 59 B1
Norham End OX2 . . . . 14 A2
Norham Gdns OX2. . . . . . 58 B4
Norham Rd OX2 . . . . 14 A2
Norman Ave OX14 . . . . . . 49 C3
Normandy Cres OX4 . . . . 34 A3
Norman Smith Rd 14 OX4. . . . . 42 A3
Norreys Ave OX1. . . . . 31 C4
Norreys Rd OX2 . . . . 28 B3
Norris Cl OX14. . . . . 50 A4
Northampton Rd OX1 . . . 31 C3
North Ave OX14. . . . . 49 C4
Northbrook Ho 1 OX4. . 41 C4
Northcourt La OX14. . . . . 49 C3
Northcourt Rd OX14 . . . . 49 B3
Northcourt Wlk OX14 . . . 49 C2
Northern By-Pass Rd
Cutteslowe OX2 . . . . 8 C3
Oxford OX3. . . . . 16 A3
Northfield Cl OX4. . . . . . . 41 A4
Northfield Rd
Abingdon OX14. . . . . 45 C1
Oxford OX3. . . . . 16 C2
Northfield Sch OX4 . . . . . 41 B3
North Hinksey CE Prim Sch OX2. . . . . 19 C2
North Hinksey La OX2. . . 19 C2
North Hinksey Village OX2. . . . . 20 A1
North Kidlington Prim Sch OX5 . . . . 3 B3
North Lodge OX2 . . . . 19 B3
North Manor Estate The OX44 . . . . 43 C4
Northmoor Pl OX2. . . . . . 14 A3
Northmoor Rd OX2 . . . . . 14 A3
North Parade Ave OX2 . . 14 A2
North Pl OX3 . . . . 16 B1
North Quay OX14 . . . . 53 B2
North St OX2 . . . . 20 B3
North Way
Cutteslowe OX2 . . . . 9 B3
Oxford OX3. . . . . 16 C2
Norton Cl OX3. . . . . 23 B4
Nowell Rd OX4 . . . . 32 C1
Nuffield Coll OX1. . . . . . . 59 A2
Nuffield Ind Est OX4. . . . 41 A4
Nuffield Orthopaedic Ctr OX3 . . . . 23 B3
Nuffield Rd OX3 . . . . 24 A3
Nuffield Way OX14. . . . . . 48 B1
Nuneham Sq OX14. . . . . . 49 B2
Nunnery Cl OX4 . . . . 41 B4
Nurseries Rd OX5. . . . . 3 B2
Nursery Cl OX3. . . . . 23 A3
Nuthatch Cl 1 OX4. . . . . 41 C3
Nyatt Rd OX14. . . . . 50 B2
Nye Bevan Cl OX4 . . . . . . 22 B2

O

Oak Ave OX14 . . . . 47 A4
Oak Dr OX5 . . . . 4 A3
Oakfield Pl OX28 . . . . 57 A4
Oakmead OX28. . . . . 55 C3
Oakthorpe Pl OX2 . . . . . . 13 C4
Oakthorpe Rd OX2. . . . . . 13 C4
Oatlands Rd OX2 . . . . 20 A3
Observatory St OX2. . . . . 58 A4
Ockham Ct OX2 . . . . 14 A2
Ock Mews 5 OX14 . . . . . 49 A1
Ock Mill Cl OX14. . . . . 52 C4
Ock St OX14. . . . . 52 C4
Old Bakery The OX1. . . . . 59 A2
Old Barn Ground OX3. . . 24 A1
Old Boars Hill
Boars Hill OX1 . . . . 37 B3
Wootton OX1 . . . . 37 A2
Old Chapel Cl OX5. . . . . . . 3 C3
Old Coach Yard The OX28. . . . . 55 A2
Old Farm Cl OX14. . . . . . . 50 B2
Old Greyfriars St OX1 . . . 59 B1
Old High St OX3 . . . . 16 B1
Old London Rd OX33. . . . 27 B2
Old Marston Rd OX3 . . . . 15 A2
Old Nursery View OX1. . . 31 C1
Old Pound The OX13 . . . . 44 A4
Old Rd
Littleworth OX33. . . . . 25 C2
Oxford OX3. . . . . 23 C3
Old Rectory Mews OX28. . . . . 56 C4
Old School The OX4. . . . . 33 B4
Old Stables The OX3 . . . . 16 A2
Old Station Yd 6 OX14. . 49 B1
Old Warehouse Flats The OX28. . . . . 55 B2
Oliver Rd OX4 . . . . 34 A3
Onley Ct 8 OX1 . . . . 21 A1
Orchard Cl
Abingdon OX14. . . . . 49 C3
Wheatley OX33. . . . . 26 C1
Orchard Ct OX4. . . . . 33 A2
Orchard La OX1 . . . . 37 A3
Orchard Meadow Fst Sch OX4. . . . . 41 C4
Orchard Rd OX2 . . . . 18 B2
Orchard Way
Kidlington OX5 . . . . 4 A2
Oxford OX4. . . . . 33 B1
Orchard Way *continued*
Witney OX28. . . . . 54 C1
Oriel Coll OX1. . . . . 59 C2
Oriel Sq OX1 . . . . 59 C2
Oriel St OX1. . . . . 59 C2
Orkney Pl OX28. . . . . 54 B1
Ormerod Sch OX3 . . . . . . 17 B1
Orpwood Way OX14. . . . . 52 B4
Osberton Rd OX2 . . . . 9 B1
Osborne Cl
Kidlington OX5 . . . . 3 B1
Wolvercote OX2 . . . . 9 A2
Osler Rd OX3. . . . . 16 A1
Osney La
Oxford OX1. . . . . 20 B3
Oxford OX1. . . . . 59 A2
Osney Mead OX2 . . . . 20 B2
Osney Mead Ind Est OX2. . . . . 20 B2
Osney Mews OX2 . . . . 20 B3
Oswestry Rd OX1 . . . . 31 C3
Otters Reach OX1. . . . . . . 39 C3
Otwell Cl OX14 . . . . 50 A4
Our Lady's Convent Jun & Senior Sch OX14. . . . . . . 49 C2
Our Lady's RC Prim Sch OX4. . . . . 33 C3
Our Lady of Lourdes RC Prim Sch OX28 . . . . 56 A4
Ouseley Cl OX3 . . . . 15 A2
Outram Rd OX4. . . . . 33 A3
Oval The OX4 . . . . 32 C1
Overbrooke Gdns OX4 . . 42 B4
Overdale Cl OX3 . . . . 16 C2
Overmead OX14 . . . . 53 A2
Overmead Gn OX4 . . . . . . 41 C4
Owlington Cl OX2. . . . . . . 19 A3
Ox Cl OX14 . . . . 49 C2
Oxeye Ct OX4. . . . . 41 C2
Oxford Brookes Univ OX3 . . . . 22 C4
Oxford Brookes Univ, Sch of Occupational Therapy OX3 . . . . 23 A4
Oxford Bsns Ctr The OX1 . . . . 59 A1
Oxford Bsns Pk OX2 . . . . . 9 B4
Oxford Bsns Pk N OX4 . . 33 C3
Oxford Bsns Pk S OX4 . . 33 C2
Oxford Com Sch OX4 . . . 22 C1
Oxford High Sch For Girls OX2. . . . . 14 A4
Oxford Hill OX28, OX29 . . 55 C1
Oxford Ice Rink★ OX1 . . 59 A1
Oxford Motor Pk OX5. . . . 2 C4
Oxford Playhouse★ OX1 . . . . 58 B3
Oxford Rd
Abingdon OX1, OX13, OX14 . . . . 46 A3
Cumnor OX2 . . . . 28 B3
Cutteslowe OX2 . . . . 7 B1
Garsington OX44 . . . . 43 A4
Horspath OX33 . . . . 35 A4
Kidlington OX5 . . . . 4 A1
Marston OX3. . . . . 15 A3
Marston OX3. . . . . 15 A4
Oxford, Littlemore OX4. . . . 33 A1
Oxford, Temple Cowley OX4 . . . . 33 B3
South Hinksey OX1 . . . . . . 38 C4
Oxford Retail Pk OX4 . . . 34 A2
Oxford Science Pk The OX4. . . . . 41 A3
Oxfordshire Hospital Sch OX3. . . . . 23 B3
Oxford Sta OX2. . . . . 20 B3
Oxford Story (Mus) The★ OX1. . . . . 59 B2
Oxford Union The★ OX1. . . . . 59 B2
Oxford Univ Botanic Gdns★ OX1. . . . . 59 C2
Oxford University Press★ OX2. . . . . 58 A3
Oxford Univ Inst of Experimental Psychology OX1. . . . . 58 C3
Oxford Univ Mus of Natural History The★ OX1 . . . . 58 B3
Oxlease OX28. . . . . 55 B1
Oxpens Rd OX1. . . . . 59 A1
Ozone Leisure Park OX4. . . . . 41 B3

P

Paddocks The OX5. . . . . . . 5 C3
Paddock The OX1. . . . . . . 39 C1
Paddox Cl OX2 . . . . 9 B2
Paddox The OX2. . . . . 9 B2
Paget Rd OX4 . . . . 34 A4
Pagisters Rd OX14. . . . . . 50 B4
Painswick Cl OX28. . . . . . 54 A2
Palladian Ct OX4 . . . . 33 A4
Palmer Pl OX14. . . . . 53 A3
Palmer Rd OX3. . . . . 23 C3
Parade The
Kidlington OX5 . . . . 7 A4
Oxford OX3. . . . . 16 B1
Paradise Sq OX1. . . . . 59 A1
Paradise St OX1 . . . . 59 A2
Park Ave OX5. . . . . 3 B4
Park Cl
Cutteslowe OX2 . . . . 9 C4
Yarnton OX5 . . . . 5 C2
Park Cres OX14. . . . . 49 A1
Park End Pl OX1. . . . . 59 A2
Park End St OX1. . . . . 59 A2
Parker St OX4 . . . . 32 B4
Park Hill OX33. . . . . 26 C3
Park Hospl For Children OX3. . . . . 23 A3
Parklands OX3 . . . . 23 C3
Park Rd
Abingdon OX14. . . . . 49 A1
Ducklington OX29. . . . . . . 56 C1
Witney OX28. . . . . 54 B2
Parkside OX28. . . . . 57 A3
Parks Rd OX1 . . . . 58 B3
Park The OX2. . . . . 28 A2
Park Town OX2 . . . . 14 A2
Park Way OX3 . . . . 11 A1
Parkway Ct OX4 . . . . 33 C2
Parma Ho OX2 . . . . 9 C1
Parry Cl OX3 . . . . 15 A1
Parsons Mead OX14 . . . . 49 A4
Parsons Pl OX4. . . . . 22 B2
Partridge Pl OX5 . . . . 3 A3
Partridge Wlk OX4. . . . . . 42 B3
Pattison Pl OX4. . . . . 32 C1
Pauling Rd OX3. . . . . 23 C3
Peachcroft Rd OX14 . . . . 50 A4
Peachcroft Sh Ctr OX14 50 A4
Peacock Rd OX3. . . . . 15 A1
Peartree Cl 2 OX4 . . . . . 42 A3
Peartree Interchange OX2. . . . . 8 C4

Peat Moors OX3 23 B2
Peeble Hill Mobile Home Pk OX14 47 A4
Peel Cl OX29 57 A1
Peel Pl OX1 31 C3
Peep-O-Day La OX14 53 B1
Peers Sch OX4 41 A4
Pegasus Ct 5 OX1 21 A1
Pegasus Rd OX4 42 A4
Pegasus Sch OX4 42 A4
Pembroke Coll OX1 59 B1
Pembroke Ct 3 OX4 22 A2
Pembroke Sq OX1 59 B1
Pembroke St OX1 59 B2
Penfold Ct OX3 15 C3
Pen La OX13, OX14 45 B3
Penn Cl OX14 50 B4
Pennycress Rd OX4 42 B4
Pennyfarthing Pl OX1 59 B2
Pennywell Dr OX2 9 C3
Pensclose OX28 55 B2
Penson's Gdns OX4 21 C3
Pentagon The OX14 50 A1
Peppercorn Ave OX3 23 C2
Percy St OX4 32 B4
Peregrine Rd OX4 41 B4
Periwinkle Pl 3 OX4 42 A4
Perkins OX1 39 B4
Perrin St OX3 23 A4
Peter's Way OX4 33 B1
Peterley Rd OX4 34 B4
Pether Rd OX3 23 C3
Petre Pl OX5 4 A3
Pettiwell OX44 43 B2
Pheasant Wlk OX4 40 B3
Phelps Pl OX4 22 A3
Phelps The OX5 3 B2
Phipps Rd OX4 33 C2
Phoebe Ct OX2 13 B3
Pickett Ave OX3 23 C1
Picklers Hill OX14 49 C4
Pike Terr OX1 59 B1
Pilcher Ct OX4 22 A3
Pimpernel Cl OX4 42 B4
Pine Cl
Garsington OX44 43 A4
Oxford OX4 34 B1
Pine Rise OX28 55 C3
Pinnocks Way OX2 18 C2
Piper St OX3 23 B4
Pipit Cl OX4 41 C3
Pipkin Way OX4 32 C4
Pipley Furlong OX4 40 C4
Pitt Rivers Mus★ OX1 58 B3
Pitts Rd OX3 16 C1
Pixey Pl OX2 9 A2
Plain The OX4 21 C2
Plantation Rd OX2 58 A4
Plater Coll OX3 22 B4
Plater Dr OX2 13 B2
Playfield Rd OX1 39 C1
Plough Cl OX2 9 A2
Ploughley Cl OX5 3 B2
Plover Dr OX4 41 C3
Pochard Pl 8 OX4 42 A3
Polstead Rd OX2 13 C2
Pond Cl OX3 17 B1
Ponds La OX3 15 A4
Pony Rd OX4 34 B4
Pope's Piece OX28 54 B2
Poplar Cl
Garsington OX44 43 A4
Kidlington OX5 4 A1
Poplar Gr OX1 39 C2
Poplar Rd OX2 19 A3
Portland Rd OX2 9 C1
Potenger Way OX14 52 C4
Pottery Piece OX4 41 C3
Pottle Cl OX2 18 C3
Poulton Pl OX4 34 B1
Pound Cl
Ducklington OX29 57 A1
Yarnton OX5 5 C3
Pound Field Cl OX3 16 C3
Pound Way OX4 33 B2
Preachers La OX1 59 B1
Prestidge Pl OX5 4 A2
Preston Rd OX14 53 A2
Prestwich Pl OX2 20 A3
Prichard Rd OX3 15 B1
Primrose Pl 20 OX4 42 A3
Prince Gr OX14 45 C1
Princes St OX4 22 A2
Prior's Forge OX2 9 C3
Priory Ct OX2 9 C3
Priory Rd OX4 41 A4
Prospect Pk OX33 25 A1
Prunus Cl OX4 34 B1
Puck La OX28 55 A2
Pudsey Cl OX14 53 A2
Pulker Cl OX4 33 B2
Pullens Field OX3 22 B4
Pullens La OX3 22 B4
Purcell Rd OX3 15 A1
Purland Cl OX4 33 B4
Purslane OX14 50 A2
Pusey La OX1 58 B3
Pusey St OX1 58 B3
Pykes Cl OX14 50 A4
Pytenry Cl OX14 46 A1

Q

Quadrangle The OX2 9 A2
Quadrant The OX14 50 A1
Quarry End OX5 2 C2
Quarry High St OX3 16 C1
Quarry Hollow OX3 23 C4
Quarry Rd
Oxford OX3 23 C4
Sunningwell OX13 38 A1
Witney OX28 54 C3
Quarry School Pl OX3 23 C4
Quarry The OX13 38 A1
Quartermain Cl OX4 32 C4
Queen's Dyke Com Prim Sch OX28 56 B4
Queen's La OX1 59 C2
Queen Elizabeth Ho OX1 58 B3
Queen Emma's Dyke OX28 54 B1
Queens Ave OX5 4 B2
Queens Cl OX2 18 C2
Queens Coll OX1 59 C2
Queen St
Abingdon OX14 49 B1
Oxford OX1 59 B2
Quercus Ct OX2 13 C4

R

Radcliffe Camera★ OX1 59 C2
Radcliffe Infmy The OX2 58 A4
Radcliffe Rd OX4 32 B3
Radcliffe Science Liby OX1 58 B3
Radcliffe Sq OX1 59 C2
Radford Cl OX4 32 B1
Radley CE Prim Sch OX14 47 A1
Radley Coll OX14 46 C2
Radley Ct OX14 50 A3
Radley Ho OX2 14 A4
Radley Rd OX14 50 B3
Radley Road Ind Est OX14 50 A3
Radley Sta OX14 51 B4
Rahere Rd OX4 33 B2
Railway La OX4 40 C4
Rainbow Way OX14 46 A1
Raleigh Park Rd OX2 19 C1
Rampion Cl OX4 42 B4
Ramsey Rd OX3 16 C1
Ramsons Way OX14 50 B2
Randolph St 7 OX4 22 A2
Rawlings Gr OX14 48 C2
Rawlinson Rd OX2 13 C3
Rawson Cl OX2 9 A3
Raymund Rd OX3 15 A3
Rayson Ho OX3 15 C2
Reade Ave OX14 50 A2
Rectory Rd OX4 22 A2
Red Bridge Hollow OX1 31 B2
Red Copse La
Boars Hill OX1 38 A4
Sunningwell OX1 38 B4
Rede Cl OX3 23 C3
Redland Rd OX3 15 C3
Red Lion Sq OX1 59 B2
Redmoor Cl OX4 41 A4
Redwood Cl OX4 42 B4
Reedmace Cl OX4 42 B4
Regents Park Coll OX1 58 B3
Regent St OX4 22 A2
Reliance Way OX4 22 C1
Remy Pl OX4 32 B3
Renault Ho OX4 32 B4
Rest Harrow 2 OX4 42 A4
Rewley Abbey Ct OX1 59 A2
Rewley Rd OX1 59 A2
Reynolds Way OX14 53 A3
Rhodes Ho OX1 58 C3
Richard Gray Ct OX1 59 A2
Richards La OX2 9 B1
Richardson Ct OX4 22 A3
Richards Way OX3 24 A4
Richmond Rd OX1 58 A3
Rickyard Cl OX1 58 A3
Riddell Pl OX2 9 B3
Ridgefield Rd OX4 22 B1
Ridgemont Cl OX2 9 B1
Ridgeway OX1 37 B3
Ridgeway Rd OX3 17 A1
Ridings The
Kidlington OX5 3 A3
Oxford OX3 24 A2
Ridley Rd OX4 34 A4
Riley Cl OX14 52 C4
Riley Ho OX4 33 B2
Rimmer Cl OX3 15 A3
Ringwood Rd OX3 17 B1
Rippington Dr OX3 15 A2
Rissington Dr OX28 54 A1
River Cl OX14 53 A3
Rivermead Rd OX4 32 B1
Riverside Ct OX1 21 A1
Riverside Gdns OX28 55 A2
Riverside Rd OX2 20 A3
River View
Kennington OX1 39 C3
Sandford-on-T OX4 40 B1
River View Terr OX14 53 A4
Rivy Cl OX14 50 B2
Robert Robinson Ave OX4 41 A3
Roberts Cl OX3 17 B2
Robin Pl OX4 41 C3
Robsart Pl OX2 28 A2
Rock Edge OX3 23 B4
Rock Farm La OX4 40 C2
Roger Bacon La OX1 59 B1
Roger Dudman Way OX1, OX2 20 B4
Rogers St OX2 9 C1
Rolfe Pl OX3 15 B1
Roman Rd OX33 27 A1
Roman Way OX4 34 B3
Rookery Cl OX13 48 A3
Rookery Ho OX44 43 C3
Rookery The OX5 3 B3
Roosevelt Dr OX3 23 A3
Rosamund Rd OX2 8 C2
Rose Ave OX14 45 B1
Rose Ct 2 OX4 33 A1
Rose Gdns OX2 19 A2
Rose Hill OX4 33 A2
Rose Hill Prim Sch OX4 32 C1
Rose La OX1 59 C2
Rosemary Ct OX4 22 A1
Rose Pl OX1 59 B1
Ross Ct OX1 39 C3
Rotha Field Rd OX2 9 B3
Roundham Cl OX5 3 B3
Roundway The OX3 17 A1
Routh Rd OX3 17 A2
Rowan Cl OX5 3 C1
Rowan Gr OX4 42 B3
Rowel Dr OX5 2 C3
Rowland Cl OX2 8 B2
Rowland Hill Ct OX1 59 A2
Rowlands Ho OX3 17 B1
Rowles Cl OX1 39 C3
Rowney Pl OX4 32 C2
Rupert Rd OX4 34 A4
Rush Common Sch OX14 50 A3
Rushmead Copse OX14 50 B4
Ruskin Ave OX14 53 A3
Ruskin Coll
Oxford, Headington OX3 16 A2
Oxford OX1 58 A3
Russell Ct OX2 13 C2
Russell St OX2 20 B3
Rutherford Cl OX14 49 C3
Rutherway OX2 13 B1
Rutten La OX5 5 B4
Rutters Cl OX5 3 B2
Ryder Cl OX5 5 C4
Rye St Antony Sch OX3 15 C1
Rymers La OX4 33 A3

S

Sackler Liby The OX1 58 B3
Sadlers Croft OX44 43 C3
Sadlers Ct OX14 46 A1
Sadler Wlk OX1 59 A1
Saffron Ct OX14 50 A2
Sage Wlk 7 OX4 42 A3

St Aldate's OX1 59 B1
St Aloysius RC Prim Sch OX2 13 C2
St Amand Dr OX14 53 A4
St Andrew's CE Prim Sch OX3 16 B1
St Andrew's La OX3 16 B2
St Andrew's Rd OX3 16 A2
St Andrews Cl OX14 50 B4
St Anne's Coll OX2 58 B4
St Anne's Rd OX3 23 B4
St Antony's Coll OX2 58 A4
St Barnabas CE Prim Sch OX2 58 A3
St Barnabas St OX2 58 A3
St Bernard's Rd OX2 58 A4
St Catherine's Coll OX1 21 C4
St Catherines Ho OX4 21 C3
St Christopher's CE Sch OX4 33 B4
St Christopher's Pl OX4 33 B4
St Clement's St OX4 22 A3
St Cross Bldg OX1 58 C3
St Cross Coll OX1 58 B3
St Cross Coll (Annexe) OX1 58 C3
St Cross Rd OX1 58 C3
St Ebbe's CE Fst Sch OX1 21 A1
St Ebbes St OX1 59 B2
St Edmund's La 4 OX14 53 B4
St Edmund's RC Prim Sch OX14 49 C2
St Edmund Hall OX1 59 C2
St Edward's Ave OX2 9 B1
St Edwards Ct OX2 13 C4
St Edwards Sch
Oxford OX2 9 B1
Oxford OX2 13 C4
SS Philip & James Prim Sch OX2 58 A4
St Francis CE Prim Sch OX4 34 A4
St Francis Ct OX3 23 C1
St George's Pl OX1 59 B2
St Georges Gate OX1 59 A2
St Giles' OX1 58 B3
St Gregory the Great RC Sec Sch OX4 32 C4
St Helen's Ct OX14 53 B4
St Helen's Mews 5 OX14 53 B4
St Helen's Pas OX1 59 C2
St Helen's Wharf OX14 53 B4
St Helen's Mill 12 OX14 53 B4
St Hilda's Coll OX4 21 C2
St Hugh's Coll OX2 13 C2
St James Rd OX14 47 A1
St James Terr OX14 51 A4
St John's Rd OX14 49 C2
St John Fisher RC Prim Sch OX4 33 C1
St John's Coll OX1 58 B3
St Johns Dr OX5 4 A3
St John St OX1 58 B3
St Joseph's RC Prim Sch OX3 15 B2
St Lawrence Rd OX1 31 A3
St Leonard's Rd OX3 16 B1
St Luke's Rd OX4 33 C3
St Margaret's Rd OX2 13 C2
St Martin's Rd OX4 32 C1
St Mary's CE Inf Sch OX28 57 A4
St Mary's Cl
Kidlington OX5 3 C4
Oxford OX4 40 C4
Wheatley OX33 26 C2
St Mary's Ct OX28 56 C4
St Mary's Gn OX14 49 B3
St Mary's Rd OX4 22 A1
St Mary and John CE Prim Sch OX4 22 B1
St Mary's Ho OX33 26 C2
St Marys Mead OX28 57 A4
St Michael's Ave OX14 49 A1
St Michael's La OX5 2 A2
St Michael's St OX1 59 B2
St Michaels CE Prim Sch OX3 22 A4
St Nicholas' Gn OX14 49 B3
St Nicholas Pk (Cvn Pk) OX3 11 A1
St Nicholas Prim Sch OX3 15 A3
St Nicholas Rd OX4 41 A4
St Nicolas CE Prim Sch OX14 49 B2
St Omer Rd OX4 33 B3
St Paul's Cres OX2 19 B2
St Peter's Cl OX13 44 A4
St Peter's Coll OX1 59 B2
St Peter's Rd
Abingdon OX14 50 B3
Wolvercote OX2 9 A2
St Swithun's Rd OX1 39 C2
St Swithun's CE Prim Sch OX1 39 C2
St Thomas' St OX1 59 A2
St Thomas More RC Prim Sch OX5 3 C1
Salegate La OX4 33 C3
Salesian Gdns OX4 33 C4
Salesian Ho OX4 33 C4
Salford Rd OX3 14 C2
Salisbury Cres OX2 9 C2
Salter Cl OX1 21 A1
Samphire Rd OX4 42 A4
Sandfield Rd OX3 15 C1
Sandford Cl OX14 50 A4
Sandford La OX1 40 A1
Sandford Rd OX4 40 B3
Sandhill Rd OX5 2 B2
Sandhills Com Prim Sch OX3 17 C2
Sandleigh Rd OX13 36 B1
Sands Cl OX2 28 A3
Sandy La
Boars Hill OX1 37 A4
Oxford OX4 34 A1
Yarnton OX5 3 A1
Sandy La W OX4 33 C1
Saunders Rd OX4 33 A4
Savile Rd OX1 58 C3
Sawpit Rd OX4 34 A1
Saxifrage Sq 5 OX4 41 C3
Saxon Ct OX3 16 A1
Saxon Way
Oxford OX3 15 C2
Witney OX28 56 C4
Saxton Rd OX14 53 A3
Sch of Geography OX1 58 C3
Schofield Ave OX28 54 C4
Schofield Gdns OX28 54 C4
Scholar Pl OX2 19 A1
Scholar's Mews OX2 13 C4
Schongau Cl OX14 52 C2
School Ct OX2 58 A3
School of St Helen & St Katherine OX14 48 C2
School Pl OX1 31 C4
School Rd OX5 3 C3
Scott Cl OX5 3 B2
Scott Rd OX2 9 C2
Scrutton Cl OX3 16 C1
Seacourt Rd OX2 19 A3
Sealham Rd OX29 57 A1
Sefton Rd OX3 16 C1
Sellwood Rd OX14 49 B3
Selwyn Cres OX14 51 A4
Sermon Cl OX3 24 A4
Seventh Ave OX3 24 A2
Severn Rd OX13 48 C4
Sewell Cl OX14 50 B3
Shaftesbury Rd OX3 16 C3
Shaw's Copse OX14 51 B4
Sheepway Ct OX4 32 C2
Sheldonian Theatre★ OX1 59 C2
Sheldon Way OX4 33 B1
Shelford Pl OX3 23 B3
Shelley Cl
Abingdon OX14 49 C3
Oxford OX3 24 A4
Shelley Rd OX4 33 A4
Shepherd Gdns OX14 52 B4
Shepherds Hill OX4 42 A3
Sheriff's Dr OX2 9 A2
Sherwood Ave OX14 49 C1
Ship St OX1 59 B2
Shire Lake Cl OX1 59 B1
Shirley Pl OX2 58 A4
Shoe La OX1 59 B2
Shorte Cl OX3 23 C1
Shotover Ctry Pk★ OX3 24 B3
Shotover Kilns OX3 24 A3
Shotover Trad Est OX3 24 A3
Shrieves Cl OX14 50 A4
Sibthorp Rd OX1 58 C3
Sidney St OX4 22 A1
Silkdale Cl OX4 33 C3
Silver Rd OX4 22 B1
Simon's Cl OX33 26 B2
Simon Ho OX3 16 B1
Simpsons Way OX1 39 C2
Singletree OX4 33 A2
Sinnet Ct OX4 22 B2
Sint Niklaas Cl OX14 52 C2
Sir William Dunn Sch of Pathology OX1 58 C4
Skelton Ct OX4 22 A3
Skene Cl OX3 23 A3
Skylark Pl OX4 41 B4
Slade Cl OX3 23 B3
Slade The OX3 23 C2
Slaymaker Cl OX3 24 A4
Snowdon Mede OX3 15 B2
Sollershott OX2 9 A4
Somerville Coll OX2 58 A3
Songers Cl OX2 18 C2
Sorrel Rd OX4 42 B4
South Ave
Abingdon OX14 49 B4
Kidlington OX5 7 A4
South Bridge Row OX1 59 B1
South Cl OX5 7 A3
Southcroft OX3 15 A4
Southdale Rd OX2 9 C2
Southend OX44 43 C2
Southern By-pass Rd
Kennington OX1 31 C2
Oxford, Botley OX2 19 C2
Southfield Pk OX4 22 C2
Southfield Rd OX4 22 B2
Southlawn OX28 56 B4
Southmoor Pl OX2 13 C2
Southmoor Rd OX2 13 B2
Southmoor Way OX14 49 A2
South Par OX2 9 C1
South Park Ct 5 OX4 22 A2
South Parks Rd OX1 58 C3
South Quay OX14 53 B2
South St OX2 20 B2
Sparrow Way OX4 42 A3
Sparsey Pl OX2 9 C3
Spears The OX5 5 C4
Speedwell St OX1 59 B1
Spencer Ave OX5 5 C3
Spencer Cres OX4 33 A2
Spenlove Cl OX14 49 B4
Spey Rd OX13 44 B1
Spindleberry Cl OX4 41 C4
Spindlers OX5 4 A4
Spinney Field OX4 41 C3
Spinneys Cl OX14 47 B1
Spinney The OX14 48 C3
Spooner Cl OX3 16 C1
Spring Cl OX28 56 C4
Spring Copse OX1 31 B1
Springfield Dr OX14 49 A2
Springfield Oval OX28 54 B3
Springfield Pk OX28 54 B2
Springfield Rd
Kidlington OX5 4 A2
Oxford OX2 19 A2
Springfield Sch
Witney OX28 54 B2
Witney, Woodgreen OX28 55 C3
Spring Gdns OX14 48 C1
Spring Hill Rd OX5 2 A2
Spring La
Horspath OX33 25 A1
Oxford, Headington Quarry OX3 24 A4
Oxford OX4 41 B4
Spring Rd OX14 48 C1
Springs The OX28 56 C4
Spring Terr 2 OX14 48 C1
Spruce Gdns OX4 41 C2
Spruce Rd OX5 3 C1
Square The
3 Abingdon OX14 49 B1
Ducklington OX29 57 A1
Oxford, Botley OX2 19 B3
2 Oxford OX4 33 B2
Squitchey La OX2 9 B2
Stable Cl OX1 59 A2
Stainer Pl OX3 15 A2
Stainfield Rd OX3 15 C3
Standon Ct OX3 23 A4
Stanford Dr OX14 49 B2
Staniland Ct OX14 49 B2
Stanley Cl
Oxford OX2 19 B2
Yarnton OX5 2 C1
Stanley Rd OX4 22 A1
Stansfeld Pl OX3 23 C3
Stansfield Cl OX3 24 A3
Stanton Cl OX28 54 A1
Stanton Harcourt Rd
Witney, Cogges OX28 55 B1
Witney OX28 57 C4
Stanton Rd OX2 30 A4

Stanville Rd OX2 18 C1
Stanway Rd OX3 17 B1
Stapleton Rd OX3 23 A4
Starnham Rd OX29 56 C1
Starwort Path [4] OX4 42 A4
Station App OX5 3 A4
Station Field Ind Est OX5 3 A4
Station La OX28 57 A3
Station Rd OX33 26 C2
Staunton Rd OX3 15 C1
Staverton Rd OX2 13 C3
Steep Rise OX3 16 A3
Stenton Cl OX14 53 A3
Stephen Ct OX3 16 A1
Stephen Rd OX3 16 A1
Stephenson Ho OX1 59 B1
Sterling Cl OX5 3 C2
Sterling Rd OX5 3 C2
Sterling Road App OX5 3 C3
Stert St OX14 49 B1
Stevens Cl OX2 13 C2
Stevenson Dr OX14 48 C2
Stewart St OX1 31 B4
Stile Rd OX3 16 B1
Stimpsons Cl OX2 18 C3
Stockey End OX14 50 B4
Stockleys Rd OX3 15 B3
Stockmore St OX4 22 A2
Stocks Tree Cl OX5 5 C3
Stoke Pl OX3 16 A2
Stone Cl OX2 18 C3
Stonegables OX28 56 C3
Stonehill La OX14 52 C1
Stonehill Wlk OX14 52 C2
Stone Mdw OX2 13 B3
Stone Quarry La OX4 32 C2
Stone St OX4 22 B2
Stonhouse Cres OX14 51 A4
Stonor Pl OX3 22 C4
Stoutsfield Cl OX5 5 B3
Stowford Ct OX3 17 A3
Stowford Rd OX3 17 A2
Stowood Cl OX3 16 C2
Strainges Cl OX29 57 A1
Stratfield Rd
Kidlington OX5 6 C4
Oxford OX2 13 C4
Stratford St OX4 22 A1
Stratton Way OX14 49 B1
Strawberry Path OX4 42 A4
Streatley Lodge [6] OX1 21 A1
Stubble Cl OX2 18 B2
Stubbs Ave OX3 23 C1
Sturges Cl OX3 16 B3
Suffolk Way OX14 52 C4
Sugworth Cres OX14 47 A4
Sugworth La OX14 46 C4
Summerfield OX1 31 C4
Summerfield Rd OX2 9 C1
Summer Fields OX14 46 A1
Summerhill Rd OX2 9 C1
Summertown Ct OX2 9 B1
Summertown Ho OX2 9 B2
Sunderland Ave OX2 9 B3
Sundew Cl OX4 42 B4
Sunningwell CE Prim Sch OX13 45 A4
Sunningwell Rd
Oxford OX1 31 C4
Sunningwell OX13 45 A2
Sunnymeade Ct [2] OX2 9 C3
Sunny Rise OX33 35 C4
Sunnyside
Oxford OX4 33 C4
Sunnyside *continued*
Wheatley OX33 27 A2
Sutton Cl OX14 49 B1
Sutton Rd OX3 15 C3
Swain Ct OX28 56 C3
Swallow Cl [15] OX4 42 A3
Swan Ct
Oxford OX1 59 A2
Witney OX28 54 C1
Swan St OX2 20 B3
Sweet Green Cl OX3 17 C2
Sweetmans Rd OX2 19 C1
Swift Cl
Oxford OX4 42 B3
[19] Sandford-on-T OX4 42 A3
Swinbourne Rd OX4 40 C4
Swinbrook Ct OX28 57 A4
Swinburne Rd
Abingdon OX14 49 C2
Oxford OX4 32 B4
Swingburn Pl OX28 54 C1
Sycamore Cl
Abingdon OX13 48 B3
Witney OX28 55 B3
Sycamore Cres OX14 39 C1
Sycamore Rd OX2 19 B1
Sycamores The OX3 16 C2
Sympson Cl [5] OX14 53 A4

T

Tackley Pl OX2 13 C2
Taggs Gate OX3 17 A3
Talbot Rd OX2 9 B4
Taphouse Ave OX28 55 A3
Tarragon Dr OX4 42 A3
Tarrant Ave OX28 55 C3
Tatham Rd OX14 49 B3
Taverner Pl OX3 15 A2
Tawney St OX4 22 B2
Taylor Inst Main Liby OX1 58 B3
Teal Cl OX4 42 A3
Templar Ho OX4 33 B3
Templar Rd OX2 9 C3
Templars Cl OX33 26 B2
Templars Sq [5] OX4 33 B2
Temple Cloisters OX4 33 C4
Temple Rd OX4 33 B4
Temple St OX4 21 C2
Templeton Coll OX1 31 C1
Tennyson Dr OX14 52 B3
Tern Wlk OX4 41 C3
Terrett Ave OX3 17 C2
Terrington Cl OX14 49 C4
TF Smith Bldgs OX28 55 B1
Thackley End OX2 13 C3
Thames Ct
Abingdon OX14 49 C1
Oxford OX1 59 B1
Thameside Prim Sch OX14 52 C3
Thames St
Abingdon OX14 53 B4
Oxford OX1 59 B1
Thames View OX14 49 C1
Thames View Ind Pk OX14 49 C1
Thames View Rd OX4 32 B1
Thelwell Ho OX4 22 C1
Thesiger Rd OX14 49 B2
Third Acre Rise OX2 18 C2
Thistlecroft Cl OX14 50 A4
Thistle Down Cl OX4 41 C2
Thistle Dr OX4 42 B4
Thomas Mews OX4 22 A3
Thomas Reade Prim Sch OX14 50 A2
Thomson Terr OX4 40 B4
Thorncliffe Rd OX2 13 C4
Thorne Cl OX5 3 A3
Thorney Leys OX28 56 A3
Thorney Leys Ind Pk OX28 56 B3
Thornhill Wlk OX14 49 A3
Three Corners Rd OX4 42 B4
Three Fields Rd OX3 23 C2
Thrift Pl OX4 42 A4
Thrupp La OX14 50 C3
Thurston Cl [4] OX14 53 A4
Tidmarsh La OX1 59 A2
Tilbury La OX2 19 A3
Tilehouse Cl OX3 16 C1
Timothy Way [5] OX4 42 A4
Titup Hall Dr OX3 23 C3
Tomkin's Almshouses [4] OX14 49 A1
Toot Hill Butts OX3 17 A1
Tower Cl OX14 52 C4
Tower Cres OX1 59 B2
Tower Ct OX28 54 B2
Tower Hill OX28 54 B1
Tower Hill Com Prim Sch OX28 54 C2
Town Furze OX3 23 B1
Town Gn The OX5 4 A3
Townsend OX14 53 B3
Townsend Sq OX4 32 B4
Toynbee Cl OX2 19 B2
Trafford Rd OX3 16 C1
Tree Close Bay OX4 32 C2
Treeground Pl OX5 3 C2
Tree La OX4 32 C2
Trefoil Pl OX4 42 B4
Trendell Pl OX14 49 A3
Trevor Pl OX4 33 A3
Trill Mill Ct OX1 59 B1
Trinity Cl OX14 50 A4
Trinity Coll OX1 58 B3
Trinity Rd OX3 24 A4
Trinity St OX1 59 B1
Tristram Rd OX29 57 A1
Troy Cl OX3 23 C1
Tucker Rd OX4 34 A1
Tudor Cl OX4 32 B2
Tudor Ct OX2 18 B2
Tumbling Bay Ct OX2 20 B3
Turberville Cl OX14 53 A4
Turl St OX1 59 B2
Turnagain La OX14 53 B4
Turn Again La OX1 59 B1
Turner Cl OX4 33 C4
Turner Ct OX5 4 A1
Turner Rd OX14 52 C3
Turners Cl OX14 51 B4
Turnpike Rd OX2 29 A4
Turret Ho OX3 16 A1
Twelve Acre Dr OX14 46 B1
Two Rivers Ind Est OX28 57 A3
Tyndale Pl OX33 27 A2
Tyndale Rd OX4 21 C2
Tyne Rd OX13 48 B4

U

Ulfgar Rd OX2 9 A2
Underhill Cir OX3 17 A2
Union St OX4 22 A2
Union Way OX28 54 B1
Univ Coll Oxford (Annexe) OX2 13 C3
University Coll OX1 59 C2
Univ of Oxford Mathematical Inst OX1 58 B3
Upland Park Rd OX2 9 B2
Upper Barr [3] OX4 33 B2
Upper Fisher Row OX1 59 A2
Upper Rd OX1 39 C4
Upton Cl
Abingdon OX14 49 C3
Oxford OX4 41 A4
Upway Rd OX3 15 C3

V

Valence Cres OX28 54 A2
Valentia Rd OX3 23 A4
Vale Rd OX28 54 A1
Van-Dieman's La OX4 33 B1
Vanner Rd OX28 55 B3
Venables Cl OX2 58 A4
Venneit Cl OX1 20 B4
Verbena Way [2] OX4 41 C3
Vernon Ave OX2 30 A4
Vetch Pl OX4 42 A4
Vicarage Cl OX4 40 C4
Vicarage Ct OX1 31 C4
Vicarage La OX1 31 B4
Vicarage Rd
Kidlington OX5 4 A3
Oxford OX1 31 C4
Victoria Ct
Oxford, Headington OX3 22 C4
Oxford OX1 59 B2
Victoria Gate OX2 9 C2
Victoria Rd
Abingdon OX14 48 C1
Oxford OX2 9 C2
Victor St OX2 58 A3
Villeboys Cl OX14 50 B2
Villiers Ct OX4 33 A2
Villiers La OX4 33 A2
Viner Cl OX28 55 B3
Vines The [2] OX14 49 B1
Vineyard OX14 49 B1
Violet Way OX4 41 C2
Virginia Way OX14 52 C2
Vivienne Ct OX3 23 B3

W

Wadard's Mdw OX28 55 C1
Wadham Coll OX1 58 C3
Waine Rush View OX28 55 A1
Wallace Cl OX14 53 A3
Wallbrook Ct OX2 19 B3
Walled Gdns OX14 47 A1
Walnut Cl OX28 54 B1
Walter's Row OX4 22 A3
Walton Cres OX1 58 A3
Walton La OX1 58 A3
Walton Manor Ct OX2 58 A4
Walton St OX1, OX2 58 A3
Walton Well Rd OX2 13 B1
Warbler Wlk OX4 41 C3
Warburg Cres OX4 34 B1
Warnborough Rd OX2 13 C2

Warneford Hospl OX3, OX4 . . . 22 C3
Warneford La OX3, OX4 . . 22 C3
Warneford Rd OX4 . . . 22 B2
Warren The OX14 . . . 50 A2
Warwick Cl OX14 . . . 49 C2
Warwick St OX4 . . . 22 A1
Water Eaton La OX5 . . . 4 B1
Water Eaton Rd OX2 . . . 10 A2
Waterford Rd OX28 . . . 55 C2
Watermans Reach [2] OX1 . . . 21 A1
Watermead OX5 . . . 4 B2
Watermill Way OX3 . . . 17 B2
Watlington Rd
Garsington OX44 . . . 43 B1
Oxford OX4, OX44 . . . 42 C4
Watson Cres OX13 . . . 36 B1
Watts Way OX5 . . . 3 C3
Waverley Ave OX5 . . . 4 B2
Waxes Cl OX14 . . . 50 B4
Wayfaring Cl OX4 . . . 41 C2
Waynflete Rd OX3 . . . 17 B2
Weavers Cl OX28 . . . 56 C4
Webb's Cl OX2 . . . 8 B2
Webb's Way OX5 . . . 4 A3
Weirs La OX1 . . . 31 C3
Welch Way OX28 . . . 54 C1
Weldon Rd OX3 . . . 15 A1
Welford Gdns OX14 . . . 49 C4
Welland Cl OX13 . . . 48 B4
Wellesbourne Cl OX14 . . 50 A2
Wellington Pl OX1 . . . 58 B3
Wellington Sq OX1 . . . 58 B3
Wellington St OX2 . . . 58 A3
Wenman Rd OX28 . . . 54 A1
Wentworth Rd OX2 . . . 9 C2
Wesley Cl OX4 . . . 34 A1
Wesley Wlk OX28 . . . 55 A1
Wessex Ind Est OX28 . . . 57 A3
West Ave OX14 . . . 49 C4
Westbury Cres OX4 . . . 33 A2
West End OX28 . . . 55 A3
West End Ind Est OX28 . . 55 A2
Western By-Pass Rd
Cutteslowe OX2 . . . 8 C3
Wytham OX2 . . . 12 A3
Western Rd OX1 . . . 21 A1
Westfield Cl OX4 . . . 33 A4
Westfield Rd
Wheatley OX33 . . . 26 B3
Witney OX28 . . . 55 A3
Westfields OX14 . . . 48 C1
Westgate Sh Ctr OX1 . . . 59 B2
West Gr OX2 . . . 9 C2
West Kidlington Prim Sch OX5 . . . 3 C1
Westlands Dr OX3 . . . 15 C3
Westminster Inst of Ed (Harcourt Hill Campus) OX2 . . . 29 C4
Westminster Way OX2 . . 19 C2
Weston Bldgs OX1 . . . 59 B2
West Oxford Com Prim Sch OX2 . . . 20 B3
West Quay OX14 . . . 53 B2
Westrup Cl OX3 . . . 15 A1
West St Helen St OX14 . . 53 B4
West St OX2 . . . 20 B3
West View OX4 . . . 32 C2
West Way OX2 . . . 19 B3
West Witney Prim Sch OX28 . . . 54 A1
Weyland Rd OX3 . . . 23 C4
Wharf Cl OX14 . . . 53 B4
Wharton Rd OX3 . . . 16 B1
Wheatcroft Cl OX14 . . . 49 C4
Wheatley Bsns Ctr OX33 . . . 27 A2
Wheatley Campus (Brookes Univ)
Holton OX33 . . . 27 A3
Wheatley OX33 . . . 27 A2
Wheatley CE Prim Sch OX33 . . . 26 B2
Wheatley Park Sch OX33 . . . 26 C4
White's La OX14 . . . 46 C1
White Barn OX1 . . . 37 A4
Whitecross OX13 . . . 44 C2
White Hart OX3 . . . 15 A4
White Hill La OX1 . . . 36 B3
Whitehouse Cl OX13 . . . 48 B3
Whitehouse Rd OX1 . . . 21 A1
Whitelock Rd OX14 . . . 49 B3
White Rd OX4 . . . 34 A4
Whitethorn Way [2] OX4 . . . 41 C4
White Way OX5 . . . 3 C2
Whitson Pl OX4 . . . 22 B1
Whitworth Pl OX2 . . . 20 B4
Wick Cl
Abingdon OX14 . . . 50 B4
Oxford OX3 . . . 16 C2
Wick Farm Pk OX3 . . . 16 C3
Wick Hall OX14 . . . 50 C2
Wilberforce St OX3 . . . 23 B4
Wilcote Rd OX3 . . . 17 A2
Wildmoor Gate OX14 . . . 49 A3
Wilkins Rd OX4 . . . 34 A4
William Fletcher Prim Sch OX5 . . . 5 B3
William Kimber Cres OX3 . . . 16 C1
William Orchard Cl OX3 16 A2
Williams Mews OX28 . . . 56 C4
Williamson Way OX4 . . . 32 C1
William St OX3 . . . 15 A1
Willow Brook OX14 . . . 48 C1
Willow Cl
Garsington OX44 . . . 43 B4
Yarnton OX5 . . . 5 C4
Willows The
Witney OX28 . . . 55 B2
Wootton OX1 . . . 36 B1
Willow Tree Cl OX13 . . . 48 B3
Willow Way
Begbroke OX5 . . . 2 B3
Kennington OX14 . . . 39 C1
Oxford OX4 . . . 41 C4
Wilmot Cl OX28 . . . 56 B3
Wilsdon Way OX5 . . . 3 B3
Wilsham Rd OX14 . . . 53 B3
Winchester Rd OX2 . . . 13 C2
Windale Ave OX4 . . . 41 C3
Windale Com Prim Sch OX4 . . . 41 C3
Windale Ho [3] OX4 . . . 41 C4
Windmill La OX33 . . . 26 A1
Windmill Prim Sch The OX3 . . . 23 B4
Windmill Rd OX3 . . . 23 B4
Windows Ct OX33 . . . 27 A1
Windrush Cl OX28 . . . 54 A1
Windrush Ct OX14 . . . 48 B1
Windrush Twr OX4 . . . 41 C4
Windrush Valley Rd OX28 . . . 54 A2
Windrush Way OX14 . . . 50 A3
Windsor Cres OX3 . . . 14 C3
Windsor St OX3 . . . 23 B4
Wingate Cl OX4 . . . 34 A1
Wingfield Ct OX4 . . . 22 A3
Winnyards The OX2 . . . 28 A2
Winsmore La [2] OX14 . . . 53 B4
Winston Cl OX5 . . . 3 C1
Winterborne Rd OX14 . . . 48 C1
Wise Ave OX5 . . . 3 B3
Witan Pk OX28 . . . 57 A3
Witan Way OX28 . . . 55 A1
Withington Ct OX14 . . . 49 B1
Witney Com Hospl OX28 . . . 54 C1
Witney Com Prim Sch OX28 . . . 55 A4
Witney & District Mus★ OX28 . . . 55 A2
Witney Rd
Crawley OX29 . . . 54 B4
Ducklington OX29 . . . 56 C2
Wolfson Coll OX2 . . . 14 A3
Wolsely Ho OX4 . . . 33 B2
Wolsey Rd OX2 . . . 9 C3
Wolvercote Gn OX2 . . . 9 A2
Wolvercote Prim Sch OX2 . . . 9 A2
Wolvercote Rdbt OX2 . . . 9 A3
Woodbine Pl OX1 . . . 59 A2
Woodcote Way OX14 . . . 53 A2
Woodcroft OX1 . . . 39 C3
Wood Farm Prim Sch OX3 . . . 23 C3
Wood Farm Rd OX3 . . . 23 C3
Woodford Mill OX28 . . . 54 C2
Woodgreen OX28 . . . 55 B2
Wood Green Sch OX28 . . 55 C2
Woodhouse Way OX4 . . . 32 C2
Woodland Pk Cvn Site The OX14 . . . 39 C1
Woodlands OX5 . . . 4 B2
Woodlands Cl OX3 . . . 15 C1
Woodlands Ct OX28 . . . 55 B3
Woodlands Rd
Oxford OX3 . . . 15 C1
Witney OX28 . . . 55 B2
Woodland Wlk OX1 . . . 38 A3
Woodley Cl OX14 . . . 45 B1
Woodman Ct OX4 . . . 22 A3
Woodman Villas OX3 . . . 23 A4
Woodpecker Gn [13] OX4 42 A3
Woodruff Cl OX4 . . . 42 A4
Woodstock Cl OX2 . . . 9 B2
Woodstock Close Flats OX2 . . . 9 B2
Woodstock Ct OX2 . . . 9 B1
Woodstock Rd
Oxford OX2 . . . 13 C3
Witney OX28 . . . 55 C3
Wolvercote OX2 . . . 6 B2
Woodstock Rd E OX5 . . . 2 A3
Woodstock Rd W OX20 . . . 2 A3
Woolgate Sh Ctr OX28 . . 55 A1
Wootten Dr OX4 . . . 32 C2
Wootton Bsns Pk OX13 . 36 A1
Wootton Rd
Abingdon OX13, OX14 . . . 49 A4
Abingdon OX14 . . . 49 A2
Wootton St Peter CE Prim Sch OX1 . . . 36 C2
Worcester Coll OX1 . . . 58 A3
Worcester Pl OX1 . . . 58 A3
Worcester St OX1 . . . 59 A2
Wordsworth Rd OX14 . . . 52 C3
Wren Cl OX33 . . . 26 C2
Wren Rd OX2 . . . 10 A3
Wrightson Cl OX33 . . . 35 B4
Wyatt Rd OX2 . . . 9 C3
Wychwood Cl OX28 . . . 54 A1
Wychwood La OX3 . . . 24 B4
Wychwood Sch OX2 . . . 14 A2
Wykeham Cres OX4 . . . 33 A2
Wylie Cl OX3 . . . 23 B3
Wynbush Rd OX4 . . . 32 C1
Wyndham Way OX2 . . . 9 B2
Wyndyke Furlong OX14 . 48 B2
Wytham St OX1 . . . 31 C3

Y

Yarnell's Hill OX2 . . . 19 B1
Yarnell's Rd
Oxford OX2 . . . 19 C2
Oxford OX2 . . . 19 C2
Yarnton Ct OX5 . . . 3 C2
Yarnton La OX5 . . . 6 B4
Yarnton Rd OX5 . . . 3 C2
Yarrow Cl OX4 . . . 41 C3
Yeats Cl OX4 . . . 34 A4
Yeftly Dr OX4 . . . 40 B3
Yeld Hall Rd OX14 . . . 50 A4
Yew Cl OX4 . . . 42 B4
Yewtree Mews OX14 . . . 49 B1
Yew Tree Mews OX29 . . . 57 A1
York Ave OX3 . . . 23 C3
York Pl OX4 . . . 21 C3
York Rd OX3 . . . 23 C4
Ypres Way OX14 . . . 48 C3

Z

Zedcor Bsns Pk OX28 . . . 55 A2

List of numbered locations

In some busy areas of the maps it is not always possible to show the name of every place.

Where not all names will fit, some smaller places are shown by a number. If you wish to find out the name associated with a number, use this listing.

The places in this list are also listed normally in the Index.

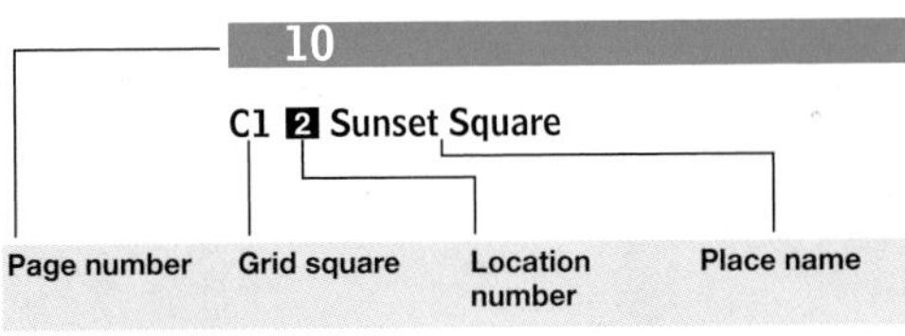

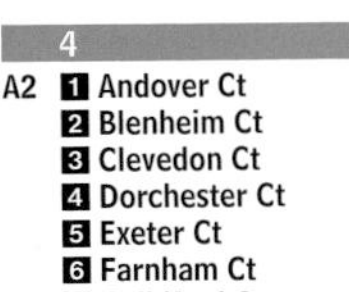

4

A2 1 Andover Ct
2 Blenheim Ct
3 Clevedon Ct
4 Dorchester Ct
5 Exeter Ct
6 Farnham Ct
7 Guildford Ct
8 Hertford Ct

9

C3 1 Miller's Acre
2 Sunnymeade Ct

21

A1 1 Buckingham St
2 Watermans Reach
3 Cloisters The
4 Burford Lodge
5 Pegasus Ct
6 Streatley Lodge
7 Goring Lodge
8 Onley Ct
C2 1 Dawson St

22

A1 1 Hawkins St
2 Monard Terr
A2 1 Jeune Hall
2 Grants Mews
3 Pembroke Ct
4 Collins St
5 South Park Ct
7 Randolph St

33

A1 1 Cranston Ct
2 Rose Ct
3 Hillsborough Cl
B2 1 Lewin Cl
2 Square The
3 Upper Barr
4 Compass Cl
5 Templars Sq

41

C3 1 Nuthatch Cl
2 Verbena Way
3 Brooklime Wlk
4 Cleavers Sq
5 Saxifrage Sq
6 Bergamont Pl
7 Foxglove Cl
8 Cranesbill Way
C4 1 Northbrook Ho
2 Whitethorn Way
3 Windale Ho

42

A3 1 Forget-me-not Way
2 Peartree Cl
4 Bluebell Ct
5 Coltsfoot Sq
6 Celandine Pl
7 Sage Wlk
8 Pochard Pl
9 Coriander Way
10 Buttercup Sq
11 Blacksmiths Mdw
12 Marigold Cl
13 Woodpecker Gn
14 Norman Smith Rd
15 Swallow Cl
16 Jack Argent Cl
17 Mole Pl
18 Campion Cl
19 Swift Cl
20 Primrose Pl
A4 1 Butterwort Pl
2 Rest Harrow
3 Periwinkle Pl
4 Starwort Path
5 Timothy Way

48

C1 1 Buckles Cl
2 Spring Terr
3 Buckland Mews
4 Juniper Ct

49

A1 1 Mayott's Rd
2 Carswell Ct
3 Crown Mews
4 Tomkin's Almshouses
5 Ock Mews
A2 3 Finmore Cl
B1 1 Banbury Ct
2 Vines The
3 Square The
4 Market Pl
5 Lombard St
6 Old Station Yd
7 Burgess Cl
8 Charter The

53

A4 1 Meadowside Ct
2 Bailie Cl
3 Musson Cl
4 Thurston Cl
5 Sympson Cl
6 Godfrey Cl
7 Draymans Wlk
B4 1 Brewers Ct
2 Winsmore La
3 Hive Mews
4 St Edmund's La
5 St Helen's Mews
6 Brick Alley
7 Mill Paddock
8 George Morland Ho
9 Neave Mews
10 Long Alley Alm-shouses
11 Maud Hale Cotts
12 St Helen's Mill

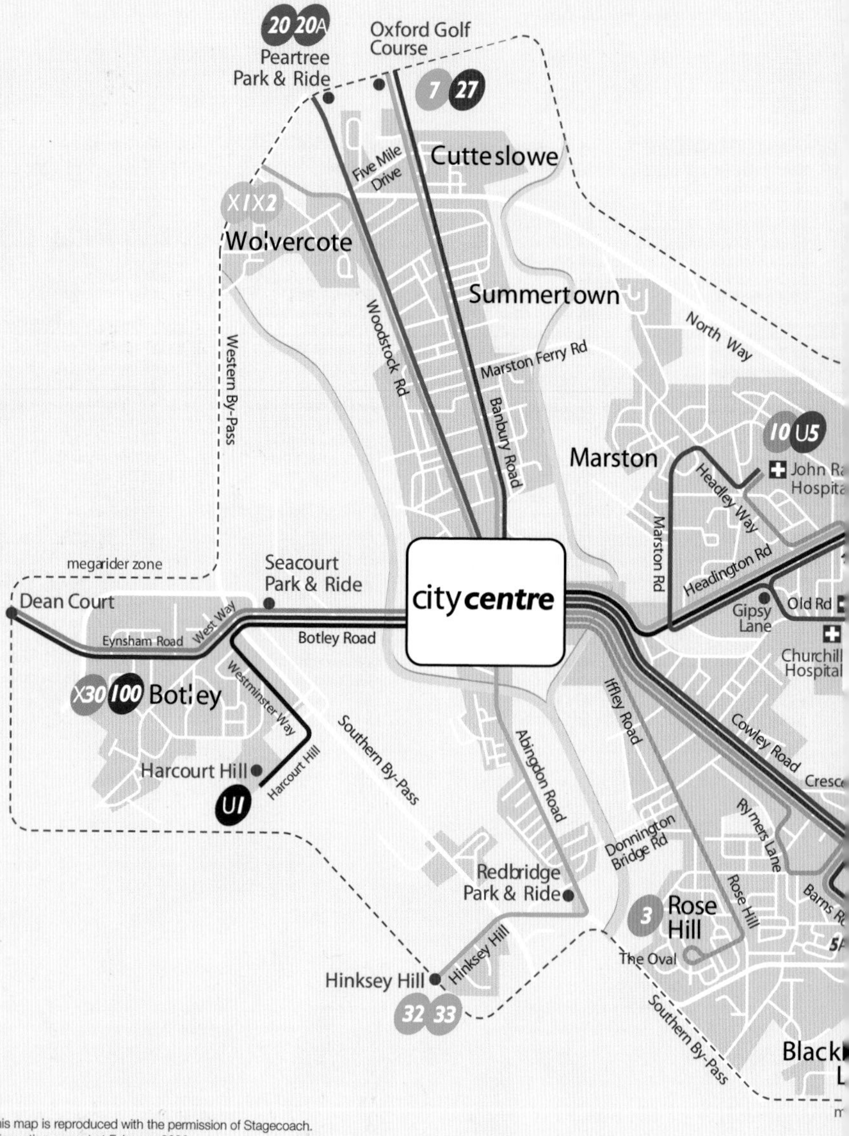

20 20A
Peartree
Park & Ride
Oxford Golf
Course
7 27
Five Mile
Drive
Cutteslowe
X1/X2
Wolvercote
Summertown
Woodstock Rd
Western By-Pass
Marston Ferry Rd
Banbury Road
North Way
10 U5
Marston
John Ra
Hospita
Headley Way
Marston Rd
Headington Rd
Gipsy
Lane
Old Rd
Churchill
Hospital
megarider zone
Seacourt
Park & Ride
city centre
Dean Court
Eynsham Road
West Way
Botley Road
X30 100 Botley
Westminster Way
Southern By-Pass
Harcourt Hill
Harcourt Hill
UI
Abingdon Road
Iffley Road
Cowley Road
Cresc
Rymers Lane
Donnington
Bridge Rd
Redbridge
Park & Ride
3 Rose
Hill
Rose Hill
Barns R
The Oval
Hinksey Hill
Hinksey Hill
32 33
Southern By-Pass
Black
L

Route	Service
Blackbird Leys - City Centre	1
Rose Hill - City Centre	3
Barton - City Centre / Kidlington - City Centre	7
JR Hospital - Headington - Cowley - City Centre	10
Greater Leys - City Centre	5A 5B
Chipping Norton - Woodstock - City Centre	20
Charlbury - Woodstock - City Centre	20A
Bicester - City Centre	27
Harcourt Hill - City Centre - Headington - Wheatley	U1
JR Hospital - Gipsy Lane - Cowley Rd - City Centre	U5
Wantage - Grove - City Centre	X30
City Centre - Abingdon - Didcot - Wantage - Abingdon - City Centre	32
City Centre - Abingdon - Wantage - Didcot - Abingdon - City Centre	33
Carterton - Witney - Eynsham - City Centre	100
Carterton - City Centre	X1
Carterton - Curbridge - Witney - City Centre	X2

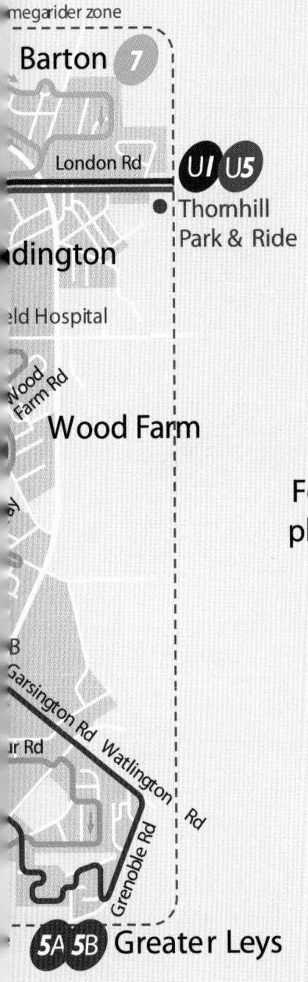

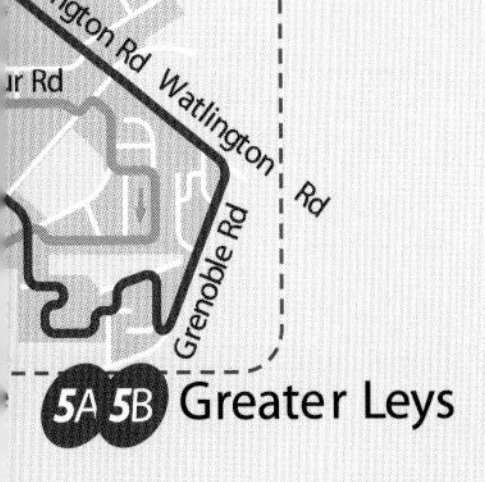

For the latest information on Stagecoach services please visit www.stagecoachbus.com/oxfordshire or call 01865 772250

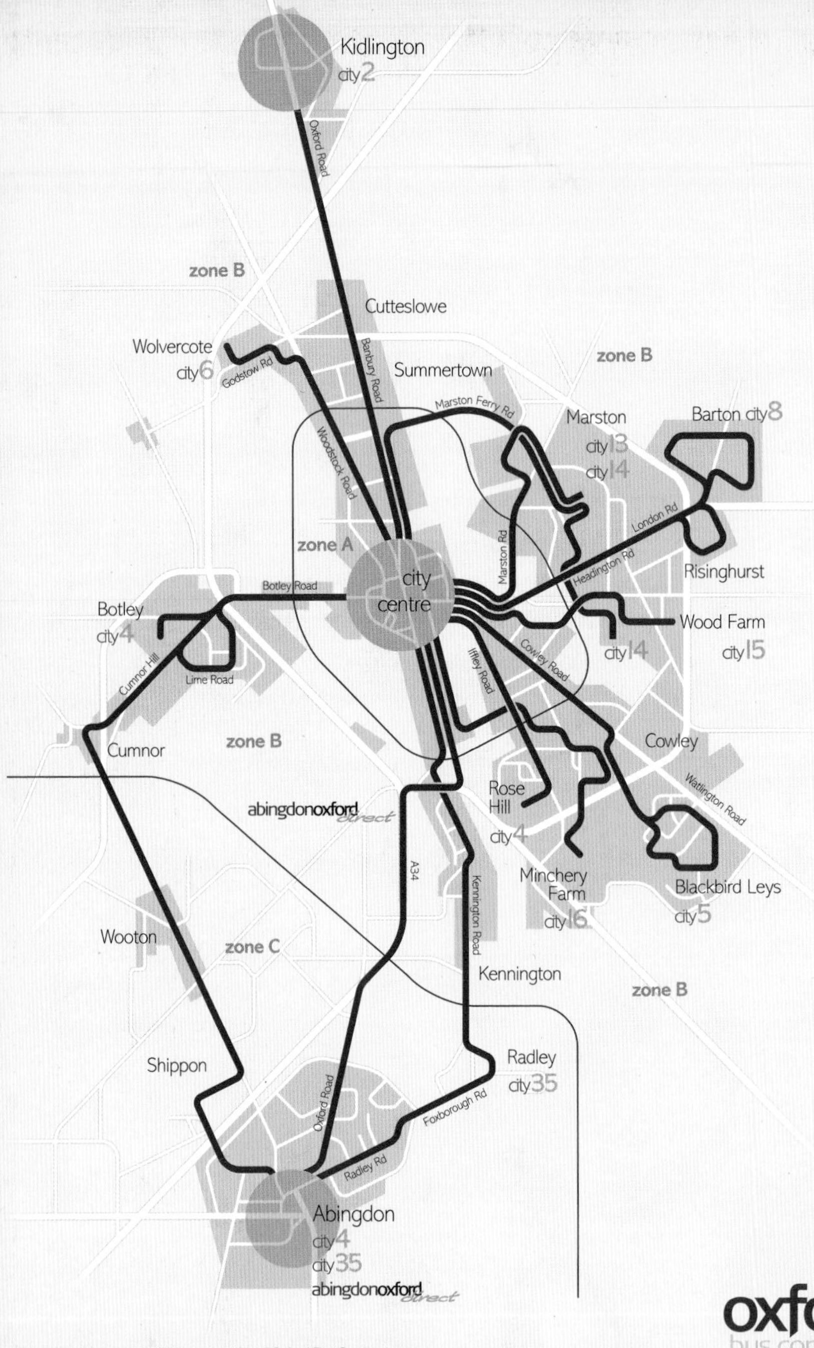

oxford bus company

Part of the Go-Ahead Group

Addresses

Name and address	Telephone	Page and grid reference